India Alive

Dedicated to the memory of Raj and Romesh Thapar

Indian Institute of Advanced Study, Shimla

Rupangi Sharma is a writer and an educationist. Her collection of poems, *A Loving Embrace*, was published in 2007. The late K.S. Duggal hailed her as 'a poet who sings to the new age'. Her focus in the field of education is on the power of technology and its transformational role in learning and teaching. She has worked with the Massachusetts Institute of Technology (MIT) Media Lab, Central Institute of Education Technology (a constituent unit of NCERT) and the Riverside School in Ahmedabad, among other leading educational institutions in India and abroad.

India Alive

Edited by

RUPANGI SHARMA

With Inputs From
MALVIKA SINGH, TEJBIR SINGH
and HARSH SETHI

ACADEMIC FOUNDATION
NEW DELHI

www.academicfoundation.com

First published in 2014
by

ACADEMIC FOUNDATION
4772-73 / 23 Bharat Ram Road, (23 Ansari Road),
Darya Ganj, New Delhi - 110 002 (India).
Phones: 23245001 / 02 / 03 / 04.
Fax: +91-11-23245005.
E-mail: books@academicfoundation.com
www.academicfoundation.com

Cataloging in Publication Data--DK
Courtesy: D.K. Agencies (P) Ltd. <docinfo@dkagencies.com>

India alive / edited by Rupangi Sharma ; with inputs from Malvika Singh, Tejbir Singh and Harsh Sethi.
p. cm.
ISBN 9789332701694

1. India--Politics and government. 2. India--Intellectual life.
I. Sharma, Rupangi.

DDC 320.954 23

Typeset by Italics India, New Delhi.

Printed and bound by The Book Mint, New Delhi.
www.thebookmint.in

CONTENTS

Section 2 | Celebrating the Birth of an Institution of Ideas

I

II

Section 3 | A Question of Issues

Introduction

MALVIKA SINGH

For a serious monthly journal to celebrate fifty-five years of uninterrupted publication, except for the few months when it was asked to submit to censorship and it refused to do so by ceasing publication because of its belief in a fundamental democratic principle of intellectual freedom, is an honour for us at *Seminar* and for its larger family of writers, readers and advertisers. I would like to salute them all for their commitment to this living idea of a lively, 'thinking India'.

India Alive is a compendium of interventions that were made by a group of extraordinary minds who collected for two days at the Indian Institute of Advanced Study in Shimla at the invitation of its then Director, Peter deSouza, to endorse and acclaim the life and times of this 'opinionated' journal. Diverse, often conflicting views are the constant ingredient within the changing themes each month and freedom of expression lies at the core of this journal. Seminar lives on and becomes stronger with every passing year because it embraces new ideas and experiments in a variety of professional fields; draws in a range of interesting people involved in unusual projects, scholars and students; and gives them all a vibrant, free-wheeling forum for energetic exchange.

My earliest memory of the birth of Seminar in 1959 in Bombay, is of my brother Valmik and I, aged seven and ten respectively, sticking stamps on the brown envelopes, helping as part of the home crew. The office was at home and working and living was one large and expansive, never ending 'happening', in my hugely secure, comfortable and happy childhood. Through the early months of the first year, my father, the Publisher, would sketch and doodle graphic typography covers for the magazine, using the many shades of colour crayons that would come in a large wooden box. He led the design and Rachel Grenfell, a close family friend who was the Circulation Manager and also an eclectic illustrator, would then fine-tune the 'creation' for the Press. My mother, Raj, was the Managing Editor, the diligent, efficient workhorse who nurtured what was her 'third child' with much love and care. She, with Romesh and Rachel as well as other friends from academia as also from the journalistic, cultural and political fraternity, would think of wide ranging themes for the monthly issues of Seminar and plan them well in advance, identifying people with different opinions on the selected subject, who would participate in the discussion, through their presentations in a 'seminar' on paper, bound within two covers. People from every conceivable discipline and with all manner of interests and passion, were ever present at the house, engaged in seamless conversations peppered with vociferous arguments and debates, interrupted by endless glasses of *nimbu paani*, coffee and ever so often, lunch and dinner. Visitors from other Indian cities, and from overseas, would add to the excitement in our rather active lives.

Then, in 1961 came the emotional wrench and the shift to New Delhi. Continuing the small is beautiful theme and secure in the privilege of being a close-knit family, Seminar settled down in Malhotra Building, an office block in Connaught Place (CP) that belonged to my maternal grandfather. Here, Raj and Romesh put down their roots and gradually, F-46, on the far end of Janpath where it connects with the inner circle of CP, became the *adda* it continues to be to date. Friends and contributors drop in for a coffee or for lunch that comes from home in a tiffin carrier. Over the years, the books in the shelves that line the walls, keep growing and ever so often Harsh Sethi, our valued colleague, packs them off to a library that can make better use of them.

Over five and a half decades, the magazine has gained the status of being a fine journal of record that tells the story of the versatile 'mind' of India, across all the disciplines that rule our lives. Because Seminar remains a 'cottage industry', an example of small, personal, worthwhile endeavour of the heart, mind and soul in this somewhat cold and forbidding new world, where commitment to an 'idea' remains steadfast and is nurtured with care, it lives and flourishes in a world where big and fat is beautiful, gloss and clutter is deemed to be aesthetic design, and where potted, quick information, easy to assimilate, is preferred fare. That easy, lazy access to information, often defined as knowledge, is the comfort level in our internet age where life is on the run, desperately competitive, and with no real time to contemplate and think. Seminar is an oasis in that space.

The 'ideas' that the magazine shares month upon month as it unpacks the many nuances of a selected theme, are for a large and diverse audience of people who are excited by contrarian positions, good wholesome analysis, debate and discussion, all of which hopefully throw up that fresh insight which takes debate to the next intellectual level. Scholars and students, thinkers and writers, professionals in diverse, varied disciplines, and people interested in the ramifications of life unfolding around them, are all potential readers/contributors of this journal. To keep pace with a world where 'digital' rules and 'paper' is fast being forgotten, we have also gone online: *www.india-seminar.com*.

Our story is a personalised one where friendship and work meet and meld, where the younger minds provide vicarious pleasure as they share their 'take' on all that is happening in our world, where failed positions are written off and new realities compel a fresh look at what was once considered obvious and right. That is the excitement, the elixir that keeps Seminar alive and going from strength to strength. On 1 September, 2014, we celebrate our fifty-fifth year of publication and to mark the anniversary India Alive gives you a glimpse and flavour of the conclave that was hosted by the Indian Institute of Advanced Study in Shimla to commemorate the fiftieth year.

My profound thanks to all the 'old faithfuls'—our corporate advertisers who supported the idea of Seminar; our contributors; our friends and well-wishers; our family, Romila, Valmik and Sanjna; all those who have worked with us over the years, bearing the brunt of a lean operation; and most importantly, Jaisal and Anjali, to whom the baton will be passed. Enjoy India Alive and keep the faith.

Acknowledgements and Thanks

When we called Rituraj and Sanu Kapila of Academic Foundation to invite them for a cup of coffee and to take a look at the compendium that we had put together, their immediate, instinctive response was heartening and positive, which is unlike most publishers who have a litany of questions laced profusely with innuendoes about what is wrong with the manuscript, its crafting and design. Our meeting was pleasantly different. They heard our 'story'. Thank you both for doing what you did.

It was Peter deSouza who had suggested over lunch at the Seminar office that the Indian Institute of Advanced Study (IIAS), of which he was the then Director, would like to host a coming together of some great Indian minds, who had also been, over the decades, men and women connected with the journal, or had written for it, or had just been hugely supportive. We at Seminar were more than delighted to partner in this unusual, mini conclave in Shimla at the iconic Viceregal Lodge in 2009. Five years later, Professor Chetan Singh, the present Director of the Institute, gave us the all clear signal to put this edition together. India Alive is symbolic of this extraordinary 'joint venture' between an Institution and Forum, both showcasing a vibrant thinking India, that celebrate the diversity of ideas, contrarian positions, multiple opinions and ongoing debates and discussions. Many thanks to IIAS for all its efforts and interventions.

It was an extraordinary group that assembled to spend three days together, in dialogue and conversation, to raise a toast to Seminar and celebrate this forum for an intellectual engagement that has represented the trajectory of Indian thinking for fifty years, ever since its inception in 1959. Nayantara Sahgal, Shyam Benegal, Gopalkrishna Gandhi, Ramachandra Guha, Sunil Khilnani, T.N. Ninan, Shivshankar Menon, Salman Khurshid, Shiv Visvanathan, Amita Baviskar, C. Rammanohar Reddy, Rudrangshu Mukherjee, Jaithirth Rao, Cyrus Guzder, Kamal Hossain (Bangladesh), Hameed Haroon (Pakistan) and Kanak Mani Dixit (Nepal), along with the in-house team of Peter deSouza of the IIAS and Harsh Sethi, Tejbir and myself of Seminar, shared many memorable hours together that weekend. I would like to thank the IIAS for permission to publish the deliberations.

Others helped from afar, from our office in Delhi, to make this event a success—N.K. Pillai who has been one of the essential discs in the vertebrae, the backbone of the magazine and its administration; Sushanto Ghorui who puts Seminar together each month under the acute, razor sharp and watchful eyes of Harsh Sethi and Tejbir Singh. Tejbir, Harsh and myself spend many hours trying to structure interesting issues and often invite scholars and other professionals to suggest special themes for issues of the magazine. That is the core intellectual stimuli and excitement that Seminar generates through the year. Thank you all for being there. The tacit, important, unquestioned and ongoing support of Indian corporate leaders, has sustained Seminar over the decades. I am grateful to all those who stood by the 'idea', for their positive response and commitment to this journal of record.

Akila Seshasayee, a young graphic designer who creates the covers for the magazine month upon month, and has been doing them for 15 years now, has designed this book with her instinctive flair for uncluttered graphic layouts and her special, unerring ability to work wonders with typefaces, creating imaginative 'images' with the 26 letters of the alphabet. Thank you for sharing your skill with us.

A special thanks to Rupangi Sharma who worked with us as an intern when she returned from Harvard and who, when presented with the raw transcripts, creatively conceived the idea of this book, its rather interesting format, its editorial design and more. She waded through the material at hand that had been diligently processed by the IIAS and by introducing additional articles and interventions from past issues, she framed a comprehensive portrait of India Alive, putting all the content in historical perspective. Many thanks for that dedicated and arduous effort that has resulted in a fascinating compendium, an album that commemorates fifty-five years of Seminar.

Malvika Singh

New Delhi - 1 July 2014

Moving Ahead

HARSH SETHI

Small journals are rarely known for their longevity. In itself this should not cause any surprise for niche, cottage industry products backed more by ideas and passion than resources or skills invariably find it difficult to negotiate the vicissitudes of the market. Mere grit and a conviction that something of value is being produced and thus worth sharing is rarely sufficient to guarantee survival.

As a reader, occasional contributor and, more recently, part of the production team, I have often wondered about the reasons behind the survival of *Seminar*. After all, not too many of the smaller ventures that came up post-independence were able to stay the course. To reach its readers without break (with the exception of the brief interregnum of the Emergency years when the journal editors chose to suspend publication rather than submit to pre-censorship) for over five decades is no mean feat. Barring the *Economic and Political Weekly* (EPW) and *Mainstream*, it is difficult to think of another small journal in the English language that has continued for as long.

It is important to point out that Seminar is not supported by a larger commercial organisation which can pump resources into it, and has to depend upon advertising support and subscription revenues, neither easy given limited circulation and zero budget for marketing. As a small venture it cannot employ staff at market salaries; nor can it pay its contributors at rates comparable to what others offer. Neither is it a news and current affairs magazine that might capitalise upon 'breaking news' and exclusives to build brand loyalty and attract a larger readership. To keep it going thus demands not just a loyal and diverse set of contributors but also a loyal and hopefully growing set of readers.

There are a few other special features of Seminar that mark it out as different from other small journals. Often single issue journals—take *Down to Earth* (environment), the *Lawyers Collective Journal* (law), *MFC Bulletin* (health), *Manushi* (women's issues) or those like *Muslim India* or *Dalit Voice* which focus on a specific social segment find it easier to build up a loyal though specialised readership. Similar is the case of magazines/journals like *Gandhi Marg, Satyagraha Mimansa, Marxism Today* and so on.

Journals like the EPW with a mix of current commentary, scholarly articles in the social sciences and book reviews have built up a loyal constituency in the academic/research world, both in the country and elsewhere in departments with an India/South Asia focus. Equally important is that the EPW transcends single disciplines and thus can cater to a wider readership.

Seminar, with a different thematic focus every month and with contributions, which while based on research and expert knowledge are addressed to the non-specialist reader, faces a peculiar challenge. It is not a popular magazine; nor is it a conventional academic one. Identifying and persuading contributors with domain knowledge and yet an ability to communicate with lay readers is never easy. Moreover readers who find one issue of interest may well be uninterested in other issues focusing on other concerns.

Much of the above is familiar to those involved with similar publication ventures. But beyond the everyday challenges of finance and personnel, soliciting contributions and expanding readership, attracting advertising support and so on is the problem of relevance. How does one judge the worthwhileness of the effort? Are we contributing to the world of ideas and discourse of policy and action? Is the mere fact that Seminar survives, when many others have not, validation enough? Not succumbing to the self-doubt that accompanies the publication of every issue remains a challenge.

While most such ventures turn into closed clubs, pushing favoured ideas, ideologies, policies and writers, Seminar has always tried hard to be open, accommodating, even welcoming of views that the editors may in their individual capacity not share. It is likely that this innate liberal quality is what attracts both contributors and readers. It also helps that Seminar, both in the days of the founding editors and subsequently has functioned as more than a journal.

Many, including those involved in similar ventures, often fail to appreciate the importance of a welcoming and inviting office where individuals drop in to share reactions, discuss ideas, offer suggestions for new themes, suggest and recommend new writers, and so on. In a manner of speaking Seminar has through its functioning style managed to create a wider, though diffused, circle of engagement, a set of individuals who look upon Seminar as also theirs. Little else explains the vast reservoir of goodwill and why over the years younger and newer individuals have continued to join in the adventure. If the journal retains some semblance of vitality and an ability to speak to newer generations, it is probably because younger scholars/writers feel confident about shaping it. But will an orientation, style and culture of functioning that has served well for well over five decades, still work in the future?

The years of the early phase of Seminar were dominated by print. This is no longer the case today. Journals and magazines, large and small, now face intense competition from both TV and the Web. The implications are not just financial —production and distribution costs, revenue models, and so on—but a fundamental change in reading and writing habits, and culture. To take just one example, we are often told that the contributions in Seminar are too dense, too long; that they no longer hold reader interest, particularly of the younger generations. Does this then imply that ventures like Seminar and the form in which they seek to participate in and to influence the world of ideas and discourse can only attract a special kind of writer/reader?

To state it more sharply, are journals like Seminar —in the issues they take up, the writing style and the form of presentation—intrinsically more attuned to the culture of an older generation? Like the editors, is the readership also ageing? And, without attracting both younger contributors and readerships, is it realistic to imagine a Seminar in the future?

There is a different set of concerns that has bothered me over my years of involvement with Seminar (and other similar efforts)—one related to the language of publication. The fear is not that English, definitionally, has in our country a restricted readership. That might be more of a worry for a publication that seeks mass readership. The greater concern is that most often those comfortable with English as a language of both thought and expression draw upon a restricted set of intellectual resources. English, in our context, while a language of communication is also a language of power and entitlement.

It is increasingly less common now to come across individuals equally comfortable with both English and other Indian languages, especially Hindi. This usually means that the ideas expressed in English, the legacy of thought and debate that they draw upon, are often untouched by ideas and debates in non-English Indian languages. Even more disturbing is the fact that what is produced in the vernacular is far too often treated by the world of English as less valuable and worthwhile—a reflection of the power imbalances in the worlds represented by different languages. Is this a continuation of the distortions created by the colonial encounter, when the knowledge produced and validated by the colonial master was classified as 'superior to' native knowledge?

In so arguing is one falling prey to a form of English bashing, a tendency most identified with the Lohia socialists? Equally, is there a danger of uncritically foregrounding and valorising the local, vernacular, native? Possibly. But without reflecting on the inherent exclusions and elitism associated with the world of English, it is likely that the ideas we produce or the concepts we deploy do not sufficiently speak to our societal condition. In some ways debates in English—be it in small journals like Seminar and the EPW, or mainstream media (print and TV)—represent a small set of individuals of similar background talking to each other. And as worrying as the limited outreach is the assumption that this discourse is superior to that in other Indian languages.

Let me end with some concerns about the future. For over five decades, Seminar has been an important participant in the world of ideas, of debates on policy and practice, helping influence the trends shaping our society and polity. This it did not by becoming a mass circulation journal, but by reaching out to thought leaders and policy-makers, teachers and students. Its design as a single theme issue, but with diverse viewpoints, drawing on experts but evolving a style accessible to a wider readership helped. Over the years, it acquired the status of a journal of record, a one-stop-site for those wanting to learn what was being debated and discussed at different points in the country's history.

But now, with a younger readership with a very different culture of accessing ideas and information, will Seminar in its current avatar survive? Or will it too, like many other equally worthwhile endeavours, be essentially relegated to the archives? Beyond the print journal, are there other ways to not just enrich debate and discourse but create and sustain a community of engaged scholars? That in many ways was a less noticed contribution of Seminar. As we look into the future, these are some issues that we need to debate.

■

Editor's Note and Acknowledgments

RUPANGI SHARMA

As one of the youngest democracies, India is often touted as a nation poised for growth. 'India rising, India shining', has been a battle cry that my generation has grown up with. At the outset, we have what it takes: a youthful population living in the world's largest democracy. Yet, there is a quivering uneasiness at upholding this mantle because as a nation we are cradled between two idiomatically opposite truths that make for a contradiction in lived reality.

We may have a youthful population, but we are also one of the oldest civilisations; and the older we get as a civilisation the greater the need to bridge memories and identities to form a foundational idea of what it means to be Indian and inculcate a sense of belonging and pride. The youth need to be summoned to build these pillars of a new India.

However, there are factors that enervate this growing youthful energy—the demographic might be changing rapidly but what of the mindset? Inherently, some of us still hold on to the adage that wisdom comes with age. Some of us—may the 'we' be organisations or individuals—are unable to truly evolve and engage with this transformation. At this critical point of transition in our nation, we need to have an infrastructure of ownership that allows youngsters to become agents of change. This, I feel, is what *Seminar* has to offer as a public institution of ideas—a forum that holds very dearly at its very root of conception, a culture of dissent and free expression—age, sex, creed, caste no bar.

Seminar's functioning goes well beyond its capacity as a journal into the creation of a safe haven where everything is up for discussion, an informal roundtable of conversations amongst thinking India. To be called into Seminar's imagination is to be ushered into a world where differing opinions are not only tolerated but are sought after with urgency. For how can we progress as a nation without a space that is hungry for the jostling of ideas and the voices of its people? Every month, for fifty-five years Seminar has served as a parliament for Indians, young and old alike, where scholars, students, journalists, politicans, social workers, among other specialists, hold their own on all matters of concern.

When I first read the transcripts of the seminar that took place at the Indian Institute of Advanced Study, Shimla, I was spellbound at the fierceness of the voices and the articulation of ideas and questions that lay restless on its pages; a chorus of dissenting opinions. At times these voices were a fusion of one another, reiterating a point, while other times they challenged each other vehemently. I have tried to make visible this *jugalbandi* of sorts in the 'Glimpses' section:

"We realised that the public discourse in South Asia needs to recognise it is not very often in the history of the building of a nation or the building of a democratic polity that something as intangible as a public institution of ideas can survive. Be it the Indian Institute of Advanced Study (IIAS) or the journal Seminar."

– Peter deSouza

"Now to speak of Seminar as a public institution is in a sense ironic...for the condition of Seminar's flourishing has been the fact that it's been a fiercely private institution."

– Sunil Khilnani

"This is just to elaborate...on the irony that vehicles of public discussion have actually been private. It has a very long lineage going back into the 19th century. I think Seminar belongs to that lineage. Ram Mohan Roy carried out his campaign against *sati* through the pages of a journal called *Sambad Kaumudi* that he virtually ran himself."

– Rudrangshu Mukherjee

As I was absorbed further into this colloquium, I recognised that this is not a seminar where one made a point and rested, this is a rare collection of ideas that has the power to spring off the text and into one's consciousness. Each question begs to be unravelled and unpacked–Nayantara Sahgal asks us to understand how we can create an idea of India that will appeal to the youth, Sunil Khilnani wonders whether online media reinforces the same ideas rather than facilitates new ideas, Amita Baviskar reminds us of Gandhi's embodied politics and how thoughts now need to be translated into action. Their electric discussions succeed in capturing Seminar's fifty years and its story of growth as played out on the stage of India's transformation through these decades.

Truly, Seminar is a historical living record of the times of India, with an arresting past in activism and politics. Its founders, Raj and Romesh Thapar, were left sympathisers who brought out Seminar when they felt that the party's politics no longer matched their own ideologies. They did not free themselves from the commitment that they had made to their country but immediately sprung into action and envisioned Seminar.

In today's world, there is a desperate thirst amongst the youth to contribute to their country. We want to make a difference, but are unsure protagonists. In an environment where technological platforms make it easier to voice our opinion, we hit on the 'like' button of Facebook pages to demonstrate solidarity to causes and sign online petitions to support others seeking the change we would want to see. But how much of this translates into 'being' the change? In this demonstration of our solidarity too, more often than not we end up servicing our biases, pre-defined and programmed by me-too media.

How does Seminar fit into this dramatically changing scenario? Seminar gives its readers a balanced view of issues, a nutritional take on matters that govern the Indian conscience. It provides its readers with a vocabulary of dissent and presents them with ideas generated from people's experiences out in the field. In reading Seminar, we are able to freely and critically analyse the churnings in our democracy. There are no hidden agendas save for the ignition of thinking minds. This is an all too precious treasure to merely stumble upon in a world that is increasingly full of profit-motivated individuals and organisations whose rule can be totalitarian in the public sphere of change.

The country is going through a transition period and so is Seminar. As in all periods like these, one must retain what works and remodel what doesn't. The way Seminar chooses to navigate this challenge will itself be a study of the vehicles which best foster this culture of dissent that is intricately tied with the publication of the journal.

I am fortunate to have opened a door in my life that led me to Seminar and the wonderful trinity of editors, Malvika Singh, Tejbir Singh and Harsh Sethi, who believe in their own voices fearlessly and create paths of dissent every month for us to travel. Mala brought me into this conversation and I feel indebted to her for her unwavering faith in my abilities. My deepest thanks to her, as well as to Tejbir and Harsh, for giving me an opportunity to participate in this seminar that has brought me so much closer to my nation's history and its present. Watching them everyday at work has been fascinating to say the least. Their largesse for the divulgence of diverging ideas will always be inspiring. I am grateful to have had the chance to become a part of this camaraderie and learn from their expertise as they often guided and nudged me in the right direction.

It has been an absolute pleasure working with Rituraj, Sanu and Sona Kapila who have been as fired up about *India Alive* as us. Their support has been crucial. A warm thanks to Akila Seshasayee who designed the dramatic and striking cover, and the layout of the book that stays true to Seminar's typographical innovations. Many thanks also to all the participants for responding promptly and giving me their time when I needed it. Through Tejbir's cinematic portraiture, the reader can participate in the unfolding of discussions and events as they happened at the IIAS; a chrysalis of cherished moments that live on.

In my family, there runs a pulsating legacy of activists, thinkers and politicians who have played critical roles in shaping the history of India. A special thanks to my grandmother, Kamala Bakshi, who has helped me understand my identity as an Indian and my parents who raised me to follow my calling as a writer.

There are perhaps more questions than answers in this volume, but these are the questions that remain unasked and will now hopefully be unmasked and explored by you, the reader. It is you, after all, that makes India come alive.

1

The Idea of Seminar

The Idea of Seminar

All These Years

Raj Thapar

Seminar by now was rooted in our minds. To me it meant far more than just another magazine. It was something to revive Romesh's confidence in himself and in the world outside, and nothing was going to deter us. The mechanics were simple. Hundreds of letters had to be written to various people explaining the aims of the magazine, frankly and without any undue glow about the outcome. We also took a decision not to expect to live by Seminar. This was important because we had seen how the business of keeping serious magazines afloat could reduce you to the marketplace. We had seen it in Patwant's case, chasing probable advertisers, dining and wining them in the hope that they would cough up an ad, spending evening after evening in hot pursuit of the same thing. This wasn't our kind of life and we were not going to let it become that. Romesh's commentaries would be the breadline and Seminar would be our fulfillment, filling the vaccum left by our former communist involvements—that wide gaping hole which was difficult to plug.

So, with the fateful 15,000 rupees in our pockets, we launched it. Once our advertising cards were printed, Romesh put a couple in his pocket and, in great trepidation and fear, made his way to the head of public relations at Burmah Shell which was then one of the largest advertisers in India. Romesh had convinced himself that his communist past, so recent as not to be a past at all, would stand in his way at every step; so when Kum Mathew, the PR concerned, listened to him with interest and signed a twelve-page contract on the spot, saying, 'Take this to the others and I am sure you will not be disappointed,' Romesh nearly fell through all the floors beneath him, all those we had accumulated in our minds through our Marxist journey. This is what communism does to one. It makes you feel terribly alone as if the whole wide world was against you, and when someone behaves with normal courtesy, you are bowled

* From *All These Years* by Raj Thapar, Seminar Publications, New Delhi, 1991. Raj Thapar was the founder editor of Seminar Magazine from 1959 to 1987.

over because it doesn't conform to the images you have fixed in your mind.

That first contract gave Romesh a rush of self-esteem and we never looked back after that. That rush almost turned into a torrent with our friend, Satyadev Mayor. He was a young chemist, had recently opened a pharmaceutical firm in Baroda, was married to the least demanding of the Sarabhai sisters, and lived in a bungalow next to the Governor's residence, overlooking Marine Drive. The evening he chanced to drop by to see us, he was confronted with a living room floor covered with thousands of envelopes for our advance mailing, and we were all sprawled on the floor, servants, children, sticking stamps on to them. Satyadev was so overcome by the sight before him, that he immediately asked me to produce the advertisement contract form. I cautioned him, 'Wait, first see what the magazine is like.' But he would have none of it. 'Bring the rate card right now,' he said. And he has remained a devoted supporter ever since, even though I almost can't remember when I last saw him.

Romesh had to swallow his share of rudeness as well. It couldn't be sunshine all the way, like when bumptious young Wally Oline of Bomas more or less showed him the door. But we collected sufficient advertising that first year to cover all our expenses. Most exciting of all was to plan the issues, to think of subjects. We had twenty-two in different stages of production before we even started, and our very first was going to be, 'The Party in Power'. Romesh was cautiously coming out of his hibernation, taking up the challenge with a ferocity which he seemed to have lost over the last couple of years.

One day he came home with a box of assorted crayons and sat down to doodle covers, strictly typographical he wanted to keep them, but since no one had so far ventured on any such advanced idea, he looked around madly for someone to execute them—and found him. Dilip Chowdhury who worked for Patwant. He was young and Bengali, and fortunately for him, born after the wash method school in Bengal had passed its peak. He was a product of Shantiniketan, Tagore's university, but by some freak chance had escaped the sentimentalism of that background, leapt out of it in a way, and we were to have a long and fruitful association with him—right until his untimely death in 1982.

Being very Anglo Saxon about time, punctual to the second, Romesh was insistent we come out on the first day of every month. Since extracting articles from faraway Delhi was not so easy, I made a trip north, trekked to Nirad Chaudhuri's house in Nicholson Road, and met this gnome-like man hopping around his room with a boundless energy which poured out of his minute frame, and his large wife waddling in the background, administering to his every whim. Yes, he would deliver in time. Then on to Sapru House where I met Sisir Gupta, another Bengali but quiet and dapper, successfully concealing raging intellectual fires within, yet preserving the face of the *Babu*. He had none of the easy arrogance of a Sachin or even a Bundle, but kept asking me what Romesh thought of this or that, not once considering that I might have an attitude as well. I had suddenly transformed into a non-person, rather like a sounding board, and found I resented it fiercely. It was one of the main differences between Delhi and Bombay so far as women were concerned—you had to assert your presence before anyone even looked at you.

Seminar had made us, in some inexplicable way, suddenly free.

I tried also to contact Indira Gandhi for an article on the Youth Congress but without success, and then made a trip to Delhi University to meet Andre Beteille whose name misled me completely—I was expecting a Frenchman. This was 1959 and our publication date was galloping towards us, we could barely wait until September—the ads were in but there had been very little response from our vast mailing list. We were printing at the same old Jai Gujarat Press, with the roof still leaking that monsoon, the place in its usual state of shambles as if a hurricane had swept through it in a rage, but also with the same expert workman, led by Ganesh Bynder whose pride in his work would never dim. At the final stage, Romesh went down with flu and I was petrified, knowing next to nothing about printing. But meticulous Ganesh Bynder would sit me down on a half-broken chair, pick up the page proofs and run his eye down the columns, taking the slightest deviation in alignment as a personal affront.

Seminar came out looking beautiful. Handling it that evening at our bang-up celebration, I knew it was there to stay, healthy from the start. We had managed every little part of the operation with the minimum of expenses from the start, and that was the secret of survival in India if you wanted to preserve the quality of what you were doing as well as your own integrity. Seminar had made us, in some inexplicable way, suddenly free. We were doing our own thing which depended on nothing but ourselves and this gave us joy which brought purpose and confidence and optimism surging back, everything falling into place, the communist nightmare having fled leaving behind the lessons we had learnt, hopefully not to be forgotten.

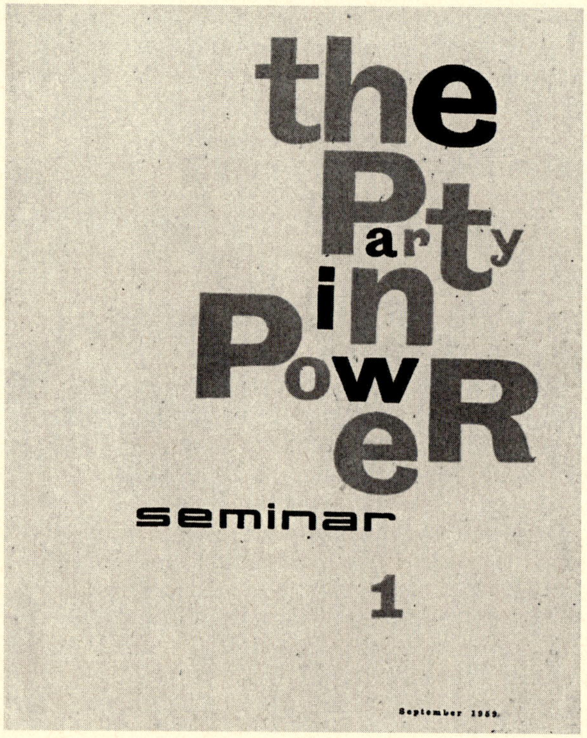

SEMINAR attempts a departure from the usual journal. It will discuss a single problem each month. The problem will be posed and certain relevant questions raised. Writers belonging to different persuasions will examine all aspects of the problem. The entire issue will be linked to the subject under discussion. There will be no editorial, no summing up. You will be free to come to your own conclusions. We hope, however, to provide you with sufficient provocative material so that you too are persuaded to join this free debate. In this way, it may be possible to answer a real need of today. There is a growing division of ideas in the country and people prefer to write where their own thought is on home ground, so to speak, safe from contradiction and attack. Here, in this journal, within the covers of a single publication, it will be possible to read opposing viewpoints, both sober and informative. This is the idea. It is a new experiment, a most difficult one and we hope it appeals to you.

seminar

the monthly symposium

EDITOR
Romesh Thapar

MANAGEMENT
Raj Thapar

CIRCULATION
Rachel Grenfell

1

The Party in Power

a symposium on the state of the Indian National Congress today

Symposium Participants

SEMINAR is published monthly from Bombay. Address : Post Bag 6155, Bombay-6 or Mayfair, Little Gibbs Road, Malabar Hill, Bombay. Telephone : 75769. Price per copy : Re. 1; 2 sh; 35 cents ($). Annual subscription : Rs. 10; £1; $3. Three years' subscription : Rs. 25; £2.10 sh; $8.

The Problem

WHAT kind of society do we want to build in India? And what do we intend to do to hasten the process? Do our plans answer fully to our needs? And are they being carried out in the way they ought to be? Why is there such a difference between the promise and performance of the ruling party? All these questions have been asked time and again during the last twelve years. But the answers have been mostly diffuse; the debate has been an excuse for polemics or rhetoric. This is the sole raison d'etre of a journal of discussion which SEMINAR proposes to be. It wants to debate all issues—political, economic, social and cultural—which concern us, in the spirit of free enquiry, so that each of them can be seen in focus.

Every month the journal will take up one problem and five or six writers will examine its different aspects from the point of view of theory as well as practice. The subject of the first issue is the Congress Party which has been in power for more than twelve years and has had enough time to give shape to its policies, on paper and in practice. Where does the party stand today? What are the problems which face it and how does it propose to meet them? Is it clear about its goals and the road it wants to take to reach these goals? Is it taking full advantage of its opportunities?

The reassessment is viewed in terms of six challenges, each of which will be dealt with by a different writer.

The ideological challenge. In the days of the struggle for freedom the Congress did not have an ideology. The struggle for political independence was not a fight for a new economic or social programme. The party sheltered men of the extreme right and also men of the extreme left. The Karachi Resolution of 1931 was at best a feeble attempt to define the economic goals of the party. When the first Congress ministries were formed in 1937 the party tried to work out an agrarian policy but the reform did not go far.

It was only after the war that the process of clarification started, first with the expulsion of the Communists from the party and then with the defection of the Socialists. The Congress became a party of the right. At Avadi, however, it voted for a vaguely socialistic pattern of society, but three years after Avadi the pattern had yet to be clearly defined. This is in effect the main ideological challenge. The Congress has yet to say in concrete terms what is the *socialistic content* of its *socialistic pattern.*

The Congress is no doubt committed to a continuous extension of the public sector with certain strategic industries reserved exclusively for the State. But it is continuously under pressure from some of its own members who are in key positions in the party and who want to check the growth of the public sector. The party is, on paper, committed to a more equitable distribution of incomes, but it has not yet taken any step to fulfil this commitment. Indeed, it is maintained that the immense growth of the private sector has led to a new anti-egalitarian trend in the distribution of incomes. Again, though the party has now decided to impose a ceiling on land holdings, it still fights shy of putting an upper limit to urban incomes, even at the level recommended by the Taxation Enquiry Commission. In fairness to itself it must define more precisely the socialistic content of its programme. Is there any other way it can meet the ideological challenge which faces it?

The political challenge. Though we have a democratic system in which the opposition parties think that their first duty is to oppose, in the new situation in which all the energies of the people have to be mobilised to build a new life, the country cannot afford the luxury of continuous party warfare. The economic and social tasks before the country, in the cities or in the villages, demand close co-operation between the different parties. For this the opposition parties do not have to wind up their business; but they have to learn to look at problems from a national, and not merely a party, point of view.

The plea of the opposition parties that it is impossible for them to co-operate in implementing programmes when they have no share in formulating or executing them is not wholly unjust. It may be difficult to form an all-party government, but it should be easy for the Congress to take the views of other parties which subscribe to its long-term economic and social objectives into consideration when framing its policies, and try to widen the area of agreement between it and others.

The political challenge which the Congress faces is primarily the need to create a wider base for all activities designed to change the pattern of economic and social life in the country. In such fields as community development, co-operative farming, food production, price control, fighting corruption and labour disputes there is immense scope for joint action.

The economic challenge. It is agreed that the primary aim of planning in our country ought to be:

i to produce enough food for our needs;

ii to build up heavy industries which will end our dependence on foreign sources of supply for our requirements in steel, machinery, oil and heavy chemicals;

iii to provide work for everyone, and

iv to raise the living standards of the people and narrow the gap between the very rich and the very poor.

How far have the two plans conformed to these aims? We have tried to increase food production, but the goal of self-sufficiency is as far as ever. We have made a start in developing heavy industry, but in machine-building we have still much headway to make. There has been some increase in national income, but there has been no perceptible rise in the standards of living of the people and there is reason to fear that the rich continue to grow richer and the poor poorer. Millions of new jobs have no doubt been created, but the backlog of unemployment in 1961 will be larger than what it was in 1956.

How can we lift the shadow that has fallen between what we set out to do and what we have been able to do so far? What are the defects in our planning? Do we need a new order of priorities? Or higher targets? Or greater national effort? Or all these things? We do not have to be experts to see that we have not made full use of our man-power yet.

The contribution of our community development projects, in which peasants are encouraged to offer their labour to dig wells, build club-houses, schools and dispensaries, has been pitifully small. There is a vast amount of work to do in the cities and in the villages, but there has been no all-out drive to mobilise the millions of idle or semi-idle people for this reconstruction work, to show them that it is in their own hands to build a better life for themselves or to give them the guidance and the leadership they need.

There is endless debate on whether the current plans are not too big for us, but few have cared to enquire whether we have made use of even our existing material resources. It is apparent that we have not done all we can to save for investment in development projects. There is no drive to collect tax on concealed income. There is no curb on conspicuous consumption. There is no attempt to create a climate of austerity in which everyone would consider it vulgar to indulge in any kind of luxury. There is no scheme to send students to the villages during their vacation to take part in community projects. There is no plan to make educated persons in the cities give one or two hours of their time every day to an adult literacy programme. Such mobilisation can do more than many a grandiose scheme costing crores of rupees. It is for the ruling party to find out what it can do to mobilise the material and human resources of the nation to rebuild its life.

The social challenge. On paper everything is fine. The ruling party is for social reform. It wants to build a new society which has no trace of communalism or casteism. It has already abolished untouchability in law and undertaken a programme for the welfare of the backward classes. But what are the real facts? The "untouchables" are still shunned by members of the higher castes. They are still too weak to assert their newly-won rights. What is the Congress doing to fight the evil wherever it exists?

The Congress is against communalism, but its leaders know that a large section of the party still thinks in terms of narrow communal advantage. The party is as ridden with casteism as ever. The social challenge before the party is one of bringing its practice into accord with its theory.

The cultural challenge. Congress leaders claim to have done much for the spread and advancement of culture. The Union Government has set up three Akadamis for the encouragement of literature and the dramatic arts. The Governments at the Centre and in the States have established prizes for authors. New museums and art galleries have been opened. This is all true. But ever so much of the cultural activity in the big cities is superficial or spurious.

The sale of books is still pitifully small. The work of translations, from foreign languages into Indian and from one Indian language into others, is still nominal. Even the quality of text books is poor. There are few professional theatres and most of the people in the small towns and in the villages are still outside the main cultural currents. The ruling party can, of course, argue that it cannot conjure up a national renaissance. But the point is whether it has done all it can to see that Government patronage of the arts is put to the best use.

The measure of the Government's own attitude to culture can be seen in the absence of adequate provision for the study of Indian culture at most of our universities. This attitude becomes all the more marked when we see the failure of the party to define its language policy with clarity and precision. The uncertainties of the language policy have indeed already done incalculable damage to the quality of education, both in schools and colleges.

The organisational challenge. Even those who are indifferent to the policies of the ruling party are painfully aware of this challenge. There is no ideological unity in the party and there is also no organisational discipline. Factions function openly in practically every State. Even party tickets at election time are distributed on the basis of factions. The leaders at the Centre cannot feel self-righteous about it, for even at the Centre there are factions.

Despite the fact that the party rules at the Centre and in all the States except one, few educated young men feel drawn to it. What is worse, the party has no effective cadres, either in towns or villages, to give effect to its programme. The organisational challenge is thus really a reflection of the ideological challenge. For it is only when the party has unity and clarity of purpose that it can discipline those who have no faith in its policies. It is only when its leaders are imbued with idealism that idealistic young men will feel drawn to the party.

In covering the challenges before the Congress, we shall be able to locate the causes of the crisis in India.

Communications

the Party in Power

Mr. Rohit Dave, M.P., suggests joint action between Congress, the P.S.P. and the Socialists on the basis of a coalition. But the diagnosis of the situation is in conflict with the remedy which he has suggested.

The first half of the article is devoted to a review of the factors which have shaped the Congress party, its present composition and apparent ideological conflict within. The writer has pointed out that to a certain extent, the left, the centre and the right are represented in Congress, which leads him to the conclusion that Congress is susceptible to outside pressure from these forces.

But what does it lead to? One would have thought that this reasoning may be a plea for creating homogenity in the Congress by radical action. But Mr. Dave does not seem to be in favour of such action. He holds up a coalition between Congress and the Socialists as a panacea. What will the country gain in terms of ideology? Even following the line of reasoning of Mr. Dave, Congress represents the three trends adequately, and is even inclined towards socialism, although he is not prepared to admit this.

In fact a coalition of this nature will be a retrograde step. Congress will loose its resistence and its pragmatic approach towards economic problems, and its independent foreign policy. I will not be overstating the case if I were to say that Congress today, taking all factors into consideration, is more socialistic than the socialists themselves.

People are apt to overlook certain salient political features while discussing Congress. It is admitted by all that Congress was a national organisation during the pre-independence era. Since then many changes have taken place and the socialists have set up a new organisation. But this loss has been made up by the foreign policy adopted by the Prime Minister and the pragmatic measures in the field of economic development. It is further strengthened by the fact that the Prime Minister symbolises in his personality the aspiration of the people for a higher standard of living and for a honest and decent political life.

The Swatantra Party started in the hope of becoming a central party because it was their logic that there was nothing to choose between Congress and the left. Actually it has turned out to be that the Swatantra Party represents the extreme right whereas on the left we have the communists; Congress is a central Party today and represents the forces of balance and integration against disruptive tendencies.

Will not the Congress lose its unique position by compromising either with the right or the left? Is it not in consonance with its policy in foreign affairs to pursue a course of non-alignment?

New Delhi, September 15, 1959 — Sadath Ali Khan, M.P.

•

There are signs here and there in India—one has still to look for them—of a certain ferment of ideas beneath the stagnant condition at the surface. SEMINAR is one of these signs. The ideological thinking still fashionable in the political arena exhausted long ago the impulse it provided to political parties, but it did have the utility of providing ballast to the latter. Today it is a perilous burden stifling the growth of new ideas.

The remedy for outdated ideological thinking is to focus attention on the concrete. Exercise of this nature revives the disused muscles

6

of the mind, dissolves the surplus fat of too much abstraction and puts the personality in condition for a better appraisal of reality. It is difficult to resist the temptation of easy generalisations, as this letter will show. But if SEMINAR constantly endeavours to return to the particular, even its generalisations will be full of value.

May I refer to two omissions in SEMINAR's discussion of the party in power? The first is the almost total disregard of personalities. Even generally this is a serious omission and in large measure explains the dry historicism and erroneous prognoses that universally distinguish so much of Marxist writing. The interest and sparkle of Marx's essays and the lifelike portrayal of the personages in them have been long replaced by the drabness which derives from the exclusive pre-occupation with mere "forces." Quite apart from this, personalities have an almost disproportionate importance in the case of the party in power today in India. Without straying into speculation about the future, a discussion of the personalities and types in the party in power would have been enlightening.

The second omission relates to the past of the party in power. In that period it regarded itself, not as a party, but as a miniature of the nation. To what extent does it consider itself a political party—one of the political parties in the country—today? You rightly refer in your posing of "the problem" to the "luxury of continuous party warfare." But parties themselves are a necessity. To what extent has the party system, as distinguished from a one-party system, taken root in India? One measure of this is the state of self-consciousness of the party in power. If the latter still regards itself as the embodiment or the nation, not only must the parties of the opposition be weak but the party system itself cannot yet have grown into a stable institution.

The party in power has a grave duty. It must resolve this question in its own mind. If a party system is to consolidate itself in India, the party in power must cut itself down to size and define its aims in such clear-cut terms as will promote the emergence of other parties on the basis of other aims. To make tall claims and confuse issues as the result of wrong identification is to undermine the party system and reverse the advance of democracy. In the opinion of its leaders, is the party in power or is the nation?

New Delhi, September 14, 1959 HECTOR ABHAYAVARDHAN

I am surprised that in a symposium on "The Party in Power," no really serious thought has been given to the formation of the Swatantra Party and its repercussions on the political hold of Congress throughout the country. Surely, the fact that the Swatantras represent conservative opinion and may soon be able to rally other similar groupings, like the Ganatantra Parishad and the Jan Sangh, should make our political pundits take note of a development which is bound to influence political life. Even now it looks as if Delhi is on the defensive. Nehru's foreign policy is under attack. The Third Plan is being revised. The credentials of the local Communist Party are being challenged. It is a fluid situation—so fluid that the resignation of an army general gets banner headlines! All this calls for deeper analysis.

Bombay, September 10, 1959. N. P.

The Thapars were attracted by Nehru's audacity in projecting democracy not only as a system suitable for India, but the only system that would keep the country together and enable it to discover its inherent genius and strength.

A New Mission

K.R. NARAYANAN

I vividly recall the spirit of the times—the latter half of the '50s—in which *Seminar* made its appearance. It was a spirit, essentially, of hope and promise, often of elation but tinged with anxiety about the fragility of that very hope and promise. Jawaharlal Nehru himself described the spirit of the time in his Maulana Azad Lecture in 1959 as follows: 'India today presents a very mixed picture of hope and anguish, of remarkable advances and, at the same time, of inertia, of a new spirit and also the dead hand of the past and of privilege, of an overall and growing unity and many disruptive tendencies. Withal there is a great vitality and a ferment in people's minds and activities.' Seminar was born out of this vitality and the ferment in the minds of men and became a mirror held up to India's political life. It was a forum for lively discussion and debate on the great issues agitating the mind of the nation.

As regards issues there was no dearth of them. It was the heyday of Indian democracy. The excitement of practising democracy in the developing society of India, with all its diversities and intricate social and economic problems in the full flood of intellectual and political freedom was a heady experience for the country. Romesh and Raj Thapar caught the mood of the country and ventured into the Seminar project with a sense of intellectual adventure and a mission of understanding, clarifying, expounding and interpreting this mood and the major issues clamouring for articulation.

The question as to whether parliamentary democracy embodied in the Constitution and propounded with intense faith and passion by Jawaharlal Nehru would be applicable to the conditions of India and be able to solve our problems was being asked by people with an underlying spirit of scepticism. The Thapars were attracted by Nehru's audacity in projecting democracy not only as a system suitable for India, but the only system that would keep the country together and enable it to discover

Reproduced from 'The Idea of Seminar', *Seminar*, September 1999.
K.R. Narayanan was the President of India from 1997 to 2002.

its inherent genius and strength. They were enchanted by the presentation of democracy as 'democratic socialism' with the distinctive content of 'socialism' in which they saw a method of transforming India peaceably into a modern nation. The originality of Nehruvian democracy was its close alliance with socialist thought and objectives together with a strong element of Gandhian principles and methods.

The novelty of this amalgam of ideas excited the Thapars as much as it did Nehru. Indeed Gandhian ideas provided Indian democracy with a moral dimension which made it join on kindly to the historical past and the philosophical heritage of India and thus acceptable to the masses immersed in poverty and ignorance, giving them the hope of being uplifted from their wretched condition without having to wade through revolutionary bloodshed and chaos.

It was the novelty and audacity of this Indian experiment that made the world sit up to the phenomenon of a new India and that possessed the Thapars with missionary zeal. In issue after issue of Seminar they discussed various aspects of this Indian experiment—social, political and economic—the process of the growth of the party system, the nature of the administrative machinery, the nature and quality of the leadership, economic planning for the country as a whole, rural development and agricultural reforms, the question of the public sector *versus* the private sector, the problems of nationalisation of industries, banking, insurance and so on, the development of science and technology for the transformation of an ancient, caste-ridden society, and above all, the Nehruvian philosophy behind all these.

The Thapars were also taken up with the integral linking of these basic domestic issues with the international questions of the day. If in regard to the domestic system Nehru asked the question, 'Why should I make a choice between the Russian and American system? Middle way or mixed economy is inevitable,' he asked with regard to the Cold War divisions of the world, 'Why should I align with one side or another because the world is moving inevitably to a one world and it is for this one world that India should work.'

The theory and the policy of non-alignment was born out of this intuitive analysis of the international situation and the destined role of India as an independent force in this emerging world order. Seminar did devote various numbers to issues of foreign policy. It is not often fully realised even by Indians that non-alignment as an approach to world affairs and as a foreign policy was evolved by Nehru in the Asian context and it was to issues like the Korean war and Indo-China crisis that the policy was first applied.

In fact it was in the crucible of Asia that non-alignment was tested as a new policy before it was adopted by Nasser, Tito and Nehru at their Brioni meeting and projected as an international movement at the first Conference of Non-aligned Nations at Belgrade. That this movement influenced the peaceful denouement of the Cold War is a fact, though not recognised by the super powers. Now that the Cold War is over, non-alignment remains relevant to the new international order and is desperately needed by the developing nations which have emerged from one kind of colonialism or another in order to maintain the essence of their independence as nations.

Indeed, if the world after the Cold War is not to slip into a new unipolar hegemonic system, it would seem that non-alignment will have to be revived and revivified as a steadying and balancing force in this pluralistic world. Seminar thus may have a new mission to perform in the world of today and tomorrow which would be in continuation with the originality of the mission it performed in the earlier period.

I can imagine how Romesh and Raj would have awakened to this new mission with their sparkling ideas and scintillating pens. Like Wordsworth in the aftermath of the French Revolution, they would not have poetically bemoaned:

> *Whither has fled the visionary gleam?*
>
> *Where is it now, the glory and the dream?*

Instead, they would have hitched their wagon to the star of a new vision and to a new dream for India and the world.

In this age of informatics, a traversing of this path from information to examination to analysis remains woefully inadequate. And that is what Seminar continues to attempt.

Memories

JASWANT SINGH

It is impossible to even begin to address this 'idea' of *Seminar* without remembering Raj and Romesh. Not simply because the idea of Seminar owes its origin to them, or on account of their establishing this journal, but because in a very real sense Seminar, in its essentials, has remained within the foundations laid by them. They built a super structure, gave Seminar an identity, but more importantly an ethos that was near unique.

Both Raj and Romesh were metropolitan-urban with left leanings and an essential, indeed irreplaceable element of the intellectual high society of Delhi. I was much younger than them, new to Delhi and its incestuous ways, entirely rural in birth as in upbringing, not at all left in opinion, and looked curiously not so much upon the social milieu of the then Delhi, or its pretension—as with all capitals that they are the country—as its intellectual engagements. That was the backdrop. In any event, well before my intrusion into Delhi, Seminar had fascinated me. Its circulation in *mofussil* India was virtually non-existent. It had a presence in some of the army reading rooms but only just. Whenever, therefore, I chanced upon this magazine of enquiry, I poured through it avidly.

Long years ago, it seems now, upon some issue or the other I wrote a letter to the Editor of Seminar. I did quite a good deal of letter writing then, being in uniform. Of course, such missives were never acknowledged and seldom published. Romesh startled me by writing a polite letter back to say that this was not ordinarily what they did, but he would, nevertheless, carry my letter in the communication section. That is really how my friendship with Raj and Romesh began. That friendship was an intellectual adventure for the three of us; Seminar was only an occasional vehicle upon which we loaded the overflow of our conversations. For that, in another sense, lay at the root of Seminar—conversation, now alas a lost art. What else, after all, is a seminar all about if not with civility, carrying a conversation through an issue.

Reproduced from 'The Idea of Seminar', *Seminar*, September 1999.
Jaswant Singh was Union Cabinet Minister, Defence, from 2001 to 2004.

The original character of Seminar established by the Raj and Romesh team was iconoclastic. It was an enquiry into the ferment of our times —remember, we are now talking of decades that seem forever away. Those were the decades that attempted a rediscovery of India—post the early euphoria of Independence. The challenge of such a venture lay both in the mode adopted, which was unique: one subject at a time, thrown open for enquiry; as in the method: comments by a wide variety of men and women published as a seminar of ideas.

That is how Seminar, in consequence, became a colloquium of ideas, not through the spoken word but rather through the discipline of the written. There was no editorial negotiation on what you thought or said. There was but one expectation, that voice be given to views through the written word, and that this examination of ideas be from diverse angles, through as wide a lens as possible.

It is truly remarkable that this journal of intellectual inquiry survived. Principally, I now know in retrospect, because of the approach that Raj and Romesh brought to the venture; also, with it, of course, the persistence with which they pursued it; the primacy of the written word in intellectual inquiry that they affirmed in the process, and, the vast array of contributors that they could invite, not so much as remote or stand-apart authors, but as participants in this exciting adventure of an inquiry into the great issues of the day. Admittedly, one of the major contributory factors was also the fact that this was well before the advent of the Indian television age. The written word continued to have great authority then, as I presume it still does, though in a considerably devalued and diminished form.

The founder editors of Seminar had their own political philosophy. But it was not fixed; it could not have been. Primarily because they were intellectually honest. They could not have been otherwise and yet make Seminar work. They observed politics, even played it on the fringes as late Indira Gandhi's friends (also one time confidants), but did not permit political participation to cripple thought. Their views evolved, with time, even I believe as Seminar evolved through the spread of topics covered in its pages, and by the intellectual churnings of the diverse contributors.

As the issues clashed, the founder editors evolved and so did Seminar. This was the measure of the founder editors' dimension, of their intellectual honesty; also their ability to grow with their authors, with the times, shaped by the experience of the issues. Seminar was not all about politics. It couldn't be. It engaged with many social and economic issues. But the dominant underpinning remained political because, just as now so then, in this stage of our evolution as a state, politics has dominated all aspects of our national endeavour.

The founder editors of Seminar had their own political philosophy. But it was not fixed; it could not have been. Primarily because they were intellectually honest.

Both Raj and Romesh left their stewardship of Seminar almost simultaneously. The challenge that confronted the second generation editors and managers lay, firstly, in not being overwhelmed by the dominating shadow of the founders, to permit Seminar to evolve as a vehicle, but still of ideas, yet much more resonant of the altered idiom of inquiry and of concerns of today's India. In this they have succeeded entirely.

The last forty years have after all seen a remarkable transformation, in the world as within our country. The velocity of change has, at times, been terrifying. Leave alone predicting or forecasting the dimensions or contents of the coming challenges, commentators have scarcely been able to keep up. From a period when the written word dominated India, we have arrived belatedly, yet not fully even now and somewhat hesitantly to the outer edges of this age of informatics. The sheer volume of information that is now available to a student or a scholar, instantaneously, is overwhelming. Also in this age of consumer electronics and the dominance of instant television news, even newspapers are late; weeklies or fortnightlies already history.

It is not a paradox that they thrive, but for one reason alone. Television informs about events: such journals (even newspapers) then tell their readers of what actually to make of these events. Filling the gap between information and education, they tell the reader what to think. This is not dissimilar to instant foods. But informed analysis and an attempt to understand the current of events (also the under-current), an examination of the unaddressed remains, at least up until now in India, has been the preserve of the written word. In this age of informatics, a traversing of this path from information to examination to analysis remains woefully inadequate. And that is what Seminar continues to attempt; Seminar and a few other journals of this genre stand apart. May they prosper and their tribe increase.

As one of the early subscribers to Seminar my great good wishes to its second generation editors, of strength to their pen, of objectivity and sharpness to their and their authors' intellect. All good luck thus to Seminar in the coming decades.

2

Celebrating the Birth of an Institution of Ideas

I

"We realised that the public discourse in South Asia needs to recognise it is not very often in the history of the building of a nation or the building of a democratic polity that something as intangible as a public institution of ideas can survive. Be it the Indian Institute of Advanced Study (IIAS) or the journal *Seminar*."

PETER deSOUZA

"Now to speak of Seminar as a public institution is in a sense ironic...for the condition of Seminar's flourishing has been the fact that it's been a fiercely private institution."

SUNIL KHILNANI

"This is just to elaborate...on the irony that vehicles of public discussion have actually been private. It has a very long lineage going back into the nineteenth century. I think Seminar belongs to that lineage. Ram Mohan Roy carried out his campaign against *sati* through the pages of a journal called *Sambad Kaumudi* that he virtually ran himself."

RUDRANGSHU MUKHERJEE

"We would still be burning widows if we were afraid of hurting sentiments. In other words, there are sentiments that it is our duty to hurt. Someone has to say so. It, therefore, becomes the responsibility of private voices to speak...private publications need to select the topics and to set the terms for what needs debating. Well, what needs discussion stretches across a huge spectrum—political, religious, economic, social, and environmental. I am sure that Seminar has dealt with this variety of issues over the years..."

NAYANTARA SAHGAL

"What are the conditions of public debate in India, today? Is there anything like a shared arena of public argument in India? What is the place within that of a journal like Seminar?"

SUNIL KHILNANI

"...I do know that the need for debate is greater than ever. It seems to me that the mind of India, if one can put it so simply, has shrunk. It has become a tiny mind."

NAYANTARA SAHGAL

"The irony is that though there is an explosion of information, there is not that quality of insight of processing information that you had in the 1950s and 1960s."

C. RAMMANOHAR REDDY

"One debate I would welcome would ask—through alignment and alliance, through the rat race and the arms race, are we not fitting into the role that others have assigned us? The cross-ventilation of ideas that this subject needs, perhaps, only Seminar can provide. Pitting arguments and opinions against each other in a no holds barred manner; in a way that the mainstream media, print or electronic, doesn't have the time or the format for and apparently doesn't think is necessary..."

NAYANTARA SAHGAL

"We had names there in print in Seminar whom we had heard of but not engaged with; in a manner that drew attention without commanding it, it did not repeat the incantations of ideological faith to propagandise them, but gave those incantations a prosaic place, as well. It did not debunk or demonise. It did not elevate or eulogise. It just said, come join us."

GOPALKRISHNA GANDHI

"Perhaps one of the things we might reflect on or cultivate today is not so much the capacity to speak or find more platforms where our own voices can be heard, but it is actually the capacity to listen, the capacity to register the range of other voices that are emerging in our democracy because that is the great change happening today."

SUNIL KHILNANI

"Lots of us are speaking and there are many forums in which we are speaking. But have we lost the ability to hear? And again there, I would like to go back to the issue of language and more than just the physical language...each language and each language tradition may be incorporating different kinds of intellectual journeys that speak to a variety of people."

HARSH SETHI

"When Seminar started, when we looked at South Asia, when we looked at our neighbours, there was always a clear idea that this will lead to action. We seem to have lost that, somehow. My question really is: how do we make India a producer of ideas? How do you see us doing it in a practical way?"

SHIVSHANKAR MENON

"In a way Seminar has been...an encyclopaedia of India's present across fifty years. That's a very important role to play, but what it means is also to be thinking about the future. What is the future for public argument and ideas in India?"

SUNIL KHILNANI

"We need to define what is India for the future...an idea that can inspire and engage the young..."

NAYANTARA SAHGAL

Kamal Hossain
B L Mungekar
Salman Khurshid

Shiv Shankar Menon

While considerable human intellectual capacity is focused on policymaking, these efforts have largely been inefficient because one of the greatest transformations in human history is taking place in the Indian subcontinent and we need new ideas for that, not just policies.

An Idea is Born

PETER DESOUZA

It is a special feeling to succeed in getting people—from all over the country, from different intellectual persuasions and professional groups—to come together at the Indian Institute of Advanced Study (IIAS) for the celebration of fifty years of *Seminar* as a public institution.

We had an intuitive sense that the IIAS should celebrate Seminar's fiftieth anniversary. We realised that the public discourse in South Asia needs to recognise it is not very often in the history of the building of a nation or the building of a democratic polity that something as intangible as a public institution of ideas can survive. Be it the IIAS or the journal Seminar.

The IIAS seemed like the natural place for celebrating fifty years of Seminar because two ideas were coming together: the idea of Seminar as a public institution and the idea of the IIAS, an institution that is committed to reflecting on the human condition.

Let's understand the great gesture of 1965 that led to the founding of this Institute in Shimla. The 1960s were described as a 'dangerous decade', with several questions being raised by international experts: will India survive? After Nehru, who? Will this country stick together?

An esteemed group of people like Zakir Husain, M.C. Chagla and S. Radhakrishnan imagined an institute committed to nothing less than reflecting on the human condition...they imagined an institute where people could not only live a life of the mind, but also reflect on the larger issues that every society must grapple with, at different periods of time. They ensured that this grand estate would be the setting for the Institute.

The Government of India has been very generous and we have built a splendid library on this estate. We have also started running schools in the summer, winter, and autumn. We see ourselves as

* Based on the welcome address delivered at the Indian Institute of Advanced Study, Shimla, in 2009.

a hermitage-plus, the plus being very important. In addition to hosting scholars for writing books, we conduct a series of seminars and workshops. In a coincidental sort of way, the archives of Seminar mirror the deliberations that have taken place in this very seminar room over the last forty-five years.

The IIAS is the ideal home for such a celebration because we are not just one institute in the universe of Indian intellectual institutions, we are a special one, much like Seminar has been and still is. The time has come for us to recognise these two institutions as intellectual spaces for forging new ideas.

While considerable human intellectual capacity is focused on policymaking, these efforts have largely been inefficient because one of the greatest transformations in human history is taking place in the Indian subcontinent and we need new ideas for that, not just policies.

The IIAS is carrying the traditional burdens, the deficits of the university system and of our research institutions. It is important to make the enormous resources of our Institute available to the country because we need to have a body of reflexive thought on this great transformation that is taking place in the subcontinent. It is time for us to nurture, support and develop this phase carefully, so that it becomes fully available to intellectual life in the subcontinent. This was the mandate that the IIAS was given in 1965 and it remains unchanged, only the language has changed with the times.

That's why we are delighted to have friends from Bangladesh, Nepal, and Pakistan with us on this occasion of Seminar's anniversary. Kanak Mani Dixit from Nepal was saying, 'South Asia is always two words with a hyphen. What if we remove the hyphen and made it one word? Will it change the way we conceptualise this space?' Those intellectual experiments need to be made now.

The Voice of India

GOPALKRISHNA GANDHI

Nayantara Sahgal and I flew in from Delhi on a special chartered aircraft, and we were duly conscious of the extraordinary intellectual equity flying on that little tube. I mentioned how appropriate it felt that Nayantara and I should be in an extreme corner of this—to be absolutely in a corner, not in the main, not in the field, but in the corner. Only to find, on landing, that there was a convoy and an ambulance waiting to bring me into Shimla. It hooted all the way and to my horror, pushed out from the road—a car carrying one of the world's greatest filmmakers, Member of Parliament and distinguished visitors from Bangladesh.

Here is somebody who tries to shrink into nothingness, aware of the fact that he is here entirely because he comes with an aide-de-camp. But now he is suddenly blown out of proportion, herding everyone aside. This just goes to show how on the fiftieth anniversary of *Seminar* the democratisation of intellectual produce that Seminar stands for can be turned on its head if a Governor is invited to join the proceedings.

I was asking myself: what is it really that propelled Raj and Romesh into what they did? They were probably just bored out of their wits to find a role for themselves in Delhi, a city effervescing with political cravenness, intellectual posturing, academic posturing, aesthetic philistinism, and everything else.

Very often, I have travelled back into my childhood memories to that part of New Delhi where the Seminar office is located. I am reminded of the fact that the massive red brick edifice of the *Statesman* office located on Barakhamba road diagonally faces the Hindustan Times House that represents the Congress Right.

Raj and Romesh literally find their niche in the same sphericity, in the geometrical impossibility of Connaught Circus. They locate themselves in a little place, to say, here are the colonial rights still trying to maintain space for itself in the Statesman

*Based on the inaugural speech delivered at the Indian Institute of Advanced Study, Shimla, in 2009.

and Ghanshyam Das Birla's *Hindustan Times*, now strongly edited by S. Mulgaonkar, but where should the voices of India find expression apart from the microphones in India? That's how it probably started. Raj and Romesh. Seminar.

Well, there are more examples of such partnerships in Sidney and Beatrice Webb, the Laskis, Kingsley Martin and Dorothy Woodman. The left had, of course, given us the examples of P.C. Joshi and Kalpana Joshi, Aruna Asif Ali and Asif Ali, Faiz Ahmad Faiz and Alys Faiz Ahmad. Couples. Couples together. Seminar.

Closer home, in office, but not in power, shaping opinion though not quite influencing decisions —Chintaman and Durgabai Deshmukh. Couples. Seminar. What did they really get about to do? They would have probably thought that India is moving out of what can be called 'the preambular stage of constitution making', where everything was said and written in Gothic font. Still not quite the foot-free Times Roman but moving out of Gothic into something which is more conversational, not convocational but conversational, not stentorian but dialogic.

Avadi[1] had happened. Everyone was talking about the socialistic pattern of society.

Bandung[2] had happened, opening new vistas. Bandung as opposed to the Commonwealth Prime Ministers' Conference happening every year in London, suddenly created a new dialogic space. Unrhymed verse, not quite free, started to replace the preambular offerings in Gothic. How was this to be fitted into public institutions? Well, if the media was an institution, it was a closely held one. We had the inevitable opposite to the Hindustan Times—the *Times of India* in Bombay and the Statesman. Believe it or not, *Blitz* and *Current* were printed from the same press, 'Sanjh Vartaman Press' in Mumbai. So, when it was not serious stuff from the right, it was a kind of a screech from Blitz.

1. Avadi Congress: This was the session of the Indian National Congress held in Avadi, Madras state, in 1955 where the socialistic pattern of society was first announced.
2. Bandung Conference: The Bandung (Indonesia) Conference, 1955, was a meeting of Asian and African states, most of which were decolonised nation states which would become pioneering members of the Non-Aligned Movement (NAM).

Extraordinary how the alternatives between semantic and sanctimonious posturing, on one hand, and streetwise smartness represented by that kind of tabloid journalism in Mumbai, left very little space for something that could be called the 'dialogues of India'.

I must say that Raj and Romesh could have opted for the classical so-called middle mode, the middle space. We are not a newspaper, we are not a tabloid—we are something else. But no, I think they did one better. An altogether new genre arose in Seminar that gave an opportunity, not in terms of the largess of a printed column, but in terms of an equality of the opportunity of expression. Soon a whole manner of conversations began to appear in print, if that is possible in the laws of physics.

An altogether new genre arose in Seminar that gave an opportunity, not in terms of the largess of a printed column, but in terms of an equality of the opportunity of expression. Soon a whole manner of conversations began to appear in print, if that is possible in the laws of physics.

We had names there in print in Seminar whom we had heard of but not engaged with; in a manner that drew attention without commanding it, it did not repeat the incantations of ideological faith to propagandise them, but gave those incantations a prosaic place, as well. It did not debunk or demonise. It did not elevate or eulogise. It just said, come join us.

I could not have entered this building without thinking of my late brother, Ramchandra Gandhi who has worked at the IIAS, and I was asking myself in a surrealistic conversation with Ramu, 'Ramu, what do you think I should say in this Seminar celebration?' And I heard him saying, 'I think you and I are fond of Hindi film songs so why don't you just say Seminar as a public institution is the media equivalent of that extraordinary song that says '*...koi do baat toh karta, koi toh kehta hello, ghar na bulata par yeh toh kehta, kuch door tak sang chalo*.' (I wish someone would chat with me, I wish someone would say hello to me, not invite me home, but at least say I'll walk along with you for a while).

That's exactly what Seminar has been doing, '*kuch door tak sang chal*' (walking along for a while). It has not gone for the *inquilabi* (revolutionary) ideologies of our times or those times, nor has it gone for the *aasmani* (celestial) loftiness of these times or those times. It has done something that small journals have tried to do. But, from a road that is neither burdened with signposts to the left or the right, nor boringly saying—not left, not right, but something in the middle.

Today, we are no different from the late 1950s in the levels of intolerance, in the levels of hollow posturing and plain philistinism, whether of the aesthetic or intellectual or the political kind. It is fairly optimistic...to believe that twenty-five years from now, in this building or another, we'll see a book...on seventy-five years of Seminar, perhaps in Murree, perhaps in Kathmandu or in Chittagong with Tejbir, Malvika and Harsh receiving bouquets from all of us, of course.

For decades after independence, India, with no military or economic clout was a leader on the world stage. Now, with both money and armed power, it is a follower. What has brought us to this pass?

The Thapars, Their Times

NAYANTARA SAHGAL

When Malvika Singh asked me to take part in this fiftieth anniversary event, I told her that I had not been in touch with *Seminar* for many years and wouldn't know what to say. Then I spoke with Peter deSouza who said, 'you can be political, personal, or anecdotal. You can say whatever you like.' I thought, well, I might have something to contribute if I can leave the more learned expositions to the powerful minds around this table, and make my talk more about the two people who made Seminar so unusual for me —Raj and Romesh Thapar. So I've made this a free ranging jumble of political, personal and anecdotal to put Seminar and the two people who created it into the context of their time.

Seminar got going in 1959 and having this discussion today, on 'Seminar as an institution of ideas in the platform for debate', reminded me that words like 'debate' and 'freedom of expression' which we now take for granted had quite different meanings in the world around us, then. What stands out about the 1950s and the next two decades is that independent thinking and analysis were in dreadful shape in two of the world's most powerful countries, the ones who were calling the shots. They were in a Cold War with each other and all debate was squashed into the battleground between the two warring sides. There was much talk of the 'free world' and 'freedom', but these words were adapted to suit whatever the two super powers thought they should mean.

In America whose gospel was the 'free circulation of ideas'—there was no sign of this—in the prevailing political climate. During the McCarthy era, those who did not toe the line were disgraced and books that were condemned as un-American were burnt or removed from library shelves. But even after that dreadful witch-hunt subsided, there was official policy with its own laid down line that was as fixed and immutable as a Soviet line. I am certain that the American think tanks were expected and funded to think within the blinkers of official policy based on the premise that communism was about to take over the world. This obsession coloured the mainstream media, the assessments of journalists, writers and others. Even the most intelligent among them, thought in terms of 'you are either with us or against us'.

India refused to take sides. Such blinkers prevented any objective or informed opinion of what was going on in India. American experts kept telling us that we were shortly going to fall apart, now I do not know whether this was conviction or wishful thinking. The fact that India kept proving them wrong did not make the slightest difference to their approach or diagnosis. There was also solid western support to the apartheid regime in South Africa, to propping up the remaining colonial regimes in Asia and South Africa. That was the climate and those were the policies in the heartlands of democracy right through the 1950s, 60s and 70s. Not to mention the coups, the assassinations and regime changes that they plotted and brought about in Asia and Africa to install pliable pro-western leaders.

From the Soviet Union, of course, we expected a laid down line but they too seemed to think that they had freedom of expression. Through the early 1950s, Nehru was being attacked in the Soviet press as a 'running dog of Imperialism' and at the same time, the Americans were calling him a 'Communist'. It would have been very funny if it had not been so pathetically ignorant on both counts.

As Nehru wanted to understand the trend of Soviet policy, he invited the Soviet Ambassador, Novikov, to dinner one night in 1949. My mother, Vijaya Lakshmi Pandit, who was the Indian Ambassador to the Soviet Union at the time, was the only other person there. Novikov was asked why the Soviet press was so hostile to India and he said, most of the Indian press was hostile to the Soviet Union and wanted India to join the capitalist camp. When he was reminded that the Indian press was not the mouthpiece of the Indian government, he said, neither was the Soviet press, it was perfectly free to criticise within the rules of Marxist analysis. This was the situation across the communist and non-communist West.

What about the East at that time or even much later? Well, I can think of no better description than Raj Thapar's, in her article called 'Our National Character', for the 1982 issue of Seminar. She's writing about a conference in Singapore of representatives from all over Southeast Asia and she says that there were five Indians among them who did not know each other. About these five, she writes, and I quote, '...they spoke their mind, criticized their government, expressed themselves passionately on every issue. All other delegates, bar none, took the positions of their governments, not out of fear alone, but out of a natural propensity to conform, not to let the side down, a part maybe of the collective ethos which so dramatically demarcates us from the rest of the East.' Well, she calls it a condition of collective conformity and she gives a hilarious account of what makes Indians nonconformist. She says, the Indian is so highly organised in terms of having to fit into caste, family and all the relationship and kinship bonds that these create so he has to escape suffocation by bursting out into individuality in whatever way he can, dress, food or worship. He cannot bear to be organised anymore. There is, what she calls, 'a fierce contradiction between the anarchic mind and restrictive social patterns.' The ways he breaks out are many and various. For example, he can entertain violently opposing beliefs together, such as being a raving revolutionary, but at the same time taking part in archaic rituals like when his son takes his first morsel of solid food. She says, '...that may be one reason why people can drift from political party to political party because they could never be sure where they belong and could easily be in two or three places at once if their physical being could be so divided...the concept of ethics has escaped us altogether because everything can be put into a relative framework. Right and wrong are for the birds'.

To deal constructively with all this rampant nonconformity, she sees rescue in individual talent, as expressed in art and crafts, in wood and metal, in cloth and paper, song and dance. Seminar channeled it into print when it invited different points of view to express themselves in a monthly symposium in its pages.

One would think that it's a routine enough exercise except that no one else had ever thought of doing it. Isn't that so? It created a space in the world of print that only Seminar, so far as I know, has occupied. It was unique too in being an individual effort, an entirely individual initiative with no institutional backing and not least, a journal like this could happen in India where a decade of independence had established free expression as a sacrosanct, as well as, a legal right. No one had to face an actual or virtual firing squad for speaking his or her mind. I mention the obvious because with the passage of time, we tend to forget the uniqueness of our position among old and new nations. We also tend to forget how much we have lost of that intellectual vigour when we compare it to the much less inspiring climate prevalent today, at least in my opinion.

Shortly thereafter, I got at home the December 1987 issue of Seminar that was dedicated to Romesh, after his death. It had a wide range of contributors. Mohit Sen of the Communist Party of India (CPI); Jaswant Singh, Member of Parliament; Charles Correa, architect; S. Gopal, Professor Emeritus at Jawaharlal Nehru University; Jehangir Bhavnagri, documentary filmmaker; Mark Tully of the BBC; and others—Indian and foreign. One of them, Eleonora Masini, describes Romesh very aptly, as a person committed to a more just and equitable future and a person in whom thought and action were connected. That issue shows how amazingly diverse his own interests were —covering politics, social problems, environment, films, theatre and none of these was an armchair interest from the sidelines. Each was an area that he was personally engaged with, including the fun of having a role in Merchant Ivory's film of *The Householder*.

I met Raj and Romesh during the 1950s, in Bombay. Bombay. That was what it was called at the time. My husband's family was connected by marriage to Romesh's family. Sometimes we would drive up together to Pune with our children, for a weekend visit, to foregather in the house of his uncle General Pran Thapar, who was then in charge of the Western Command.

Now, Raj and Romesh were very much a part of that extended Thapar clan, and yet they seemed to stand their own ideological and personal ground sometimes as amused spectators of what was going on, preserving a kind of affectionate detachment from it and remaining very much themselves. It struck me as being an unusual feat since this was a close-knit clan that packed a punch. Two of them had risen high in the Army and Romesh's father also became an art collector. His uncle, Prem was a highly regarded civil servant. Of his aunts, Premi Thapar was famous for her dedicated work among refugees after the Partition. Each and every person in this clan was a personality with a capital 'P'. Not to be swamped by the weight of all that family clout and establishment seemed to be quite an achievement.

Another curious thing was that the family didn't consider Romesh any kind of a misfit, although, he was the maverick among them. He was known in Bombay high society as a Communist, at the time. 'What on earth was he up to!' they said, '...behaving like a rank outsider, publishing a red rag called *Crossroads*.' Yet, this far out activity made no difference to his family.

I came across a note from Romesh, the other day, in reply to a condolence letter I had written to him when his father died. In the note, he says, that his father had always been accepting of his non-conformism. This may well have had something to do with the 'live and let live' realm of ideas that we took so much for granted we didn't realise how rare it was in the contemporary world. That's the background of how I got to know Raj and Romesh.

At the end of the 1960s, Romesh became a person of consequence in the corridors of power while I went the other way. I had just begun writing political commentary for the *Indian Express*. Events made me critical of the way things were going. During the next few years, I was anxious and apprehensive about the way the government was functioning and the direction it was taking. I felt emotionally scarred by the blows being dealt to the democracy Nehru had built, and I was quite unable to stop myself from spilling it all out into print.

To give you an idea of the atmosphere building up in those days: one night at a dinner party in Delhi I was accosted by a well-known lawyer whom I had never met. He told me to stop writing as I was doing. He said I was out of step with the times and I must get into line, the implication obviously was that I would otherwise face the consequences. I was furious with this man and but for my non-violent upbringing, my gold bordered

Immediately after the Emergency, what concerned us was that no such thing should happen again and the democratic institutions that had been derailed should to be restored to working order.

banarasi sari and my high heels, I would have happily dislocated his jaw. Really, it was most offensive and I did tell him that I found his remarks extremely offensive, and I would write as I please. I mention this incident to highlight the threat free expression was already facing, much before the Emergency. Maybe I was a conspicuous target, being closely related to power.

Well, far from toeing any line, I started writing at Jayaprakash Narayan's request for his paper, *Everyman's*. I went to Bihar several times to report on his Bihar movement for the Indian Express. Soon, my worst fears were realised with the declaration of the Emergency.

Those who opposed it all had their individual collisions with the new order. I was a member of the Sahitya Akademi's Advisory Board for English, along with Anita Desai and Pritish Nandy, and I asked the Akademi to condemn censorship and the imprisonment of writers and other citizens without a trial. It refused to do so and that led me to resign from the Sahitya Akademi's Advisory Board. I also resigned my position on the Authors' Guild for the same reason. One of the publishers whom I had a contract with, dumped my novel. He did this not because of its content, but because he said he could not take the risk of publishing anything by me. Another novel that was on the verge of being made into a movie was dumped for the same reason. My hard-built career was collapsing around me. I had to stop writing political commentary, of course. In June 1975, I was told to continue writing on other subjects by S. Mulgaonkar, who was then the editor of the *Hindustan Times* and also a friend. So, I set about racking my brains for subjects that would serve as metaphors for the intolerable situation that we were in. I needed to earn a living and I had to write. I found myself in good company with others who were struggling to survive. One of them was Rajmohan Gandhi with his aptly named journal *Himmat*. Seminar carried on till July 1976, surviving, I suppose as I and many others did, by confining itself to general subjects during the first year of the Emergency. From August through December 1976, Seminar stopped publishing as an act of civil disobedience.

In June 1976, I went abroad to write a book. Since I had been under surveillance in Delhi, this was the only way to avoid arrest. I also wrote about what was happening in India for the *New Republic*, the *London Times* and other papers. I saw it as an opportunity to speak for those in India whose voices had been silenced.

Immediately after the Emergency, what concerned us was that no such thing should happen again and the democratic institutions that had been derailed should to be restored to working order. One good thing the Janata government did in its brief muddled spell in power was to undo the damaging amendments to the Constitution and restore it to rights.

But years of high centralisation had shaken the federal structure and put decentralisation into mothballs. The call for a committed civil service, committed judiciary and the like, had all but destroyed our young democratic tradition, and many of us felt like we were surveying a landscape that had been mercilessly bombarded.

The problem

We resume publication, after a dislocation of six months, with the issue which could not be printed following the imposition of pre-censorship. There are some substractions and some additions to this issue in the interest of relevance. In this context we do not have to explain at very great length the urgency of the challenges which have developed in our land. The experience of the past eighteen months, particularly the brazen misuse of power and the violation of legal procedure, has helped to lift the blinkers even from those in the hateful habit of treating the less fortunate as a citizenry without rights. We are now moving into an election in six weeks. It cannot be free and fair. The press continues under restraints (SEMINAR has had to change its printers after nearly 17 years because they demanded the right to scrutinise, to censor), the jails have yet to deliver thousands of political prisoners, the opposition parties face harassment from a variety of official agencies, and the Emergency continues to throw a deep shadow over the future of this land. This issue of SEMINAR sketches the familiar path of the fearmakers and the infrastructure they build, and the role that must be played by the free spirit of men and women.

Characteristically, Romesh's practical mind concentrated not only on how to haul India out of the past traumatic decade, but also on the fundamental changes that were required for our country's future to be different. So, we got together a working group of like-minded people to identify the issues that had to be addressed. Along with six others, he came up with his *Agenda for India*. I have this 119 page document dated April 1981 and it could have been an agenda for today. It says that at the heart of the matter is the crisis of democratic and social metamorphosis. It goes into great detail about the measures to be taken. In the political and economic restructuring required, decentralisation is its overriding concern. It also covers industry, agriculture, energy, water, forests, organisation of the rural poor, wages, unionism, community health and adult education, to name some of the areas it covers and much of it is relevant today though in a changed context. The urgent need for this agenda, which no one else had thought of producing, is conveyed in its last brief paragraph that I think Romesh must have written himself. It sounds just like him, going straight for the jugular. The paragraph reads, 'India is adrift and rudderless and could be heading for the rocks. It need not. There is a beacon that offers direction, hope, and courage. There is an agenda for the 80s. If we will the future, we can make it.' For those who read it, its value was that it was not a product of any ivory tower think tank but a group of activist intellectuals who had long been involved with and committed to the subjects they were addressing. The agenda had a big opening as a public event in New Delhi. There was a lot of excitement and great expectations at its presentation. It was a time that engendered a good deal of activity to safeguard liberty in the future. Several civil liberty organisations came into being, and one of these was the People's Union for Civil Liberties. Jayaprakash Narayan had founded it and Justice Tarakunde headed it. I was associated with its public launch in Delhi when it took the decision to spread countrywide, outside urban areas, and I served as vice president for some years afterwards.

I don't remember exactly, but I think Romesh asked me for two, maybe three contributions to Seminar. One article that he commissioned was on 'dynasty'. That word has burgeoned into the plural, as dynasties have proliferated like political parties, sub-castes, backwards and even millionaires. But around the 1980s, the word 'dynasty' meant just the one and he discussed it with me at length on the phone, and I wrote the article. I remember asking him, 'Can't you pay me a bit more?' and him telling me that it was hard enough to keep the journal going.

On the December 1987 issue of Seminar, the one dedicated to Romesh, there's an undated message from him on the cover that says, 'We are still trying to break through the circulation barrier. Cottage industries like ours are always at a disadvantage but we have confidence in the quality of the product and we hope that our friends will do more in the years ahead to help us and strengthen the support for Seminar.' At the end of the message, referring to readers, contributors, and advertisers, he says, '...they've all helped to create a journal that reflects the thought and passion of a great country and a great people.' Page nine of this issue carries a notice to all book agents that reminded me of those simpler times. It announces that the Seminar annual will be out on January 1, 1988 at the price of ₹ 10.

As I said I haven't kept up with Seminar, lately, so I don't know what grounds it's been covering, but I do know that the need for debate is greater than ever. It seems to me that the mind of India, if one can put it so simply, has shrunk. It has become a tiny mind. To give an example, I was asked to take part in a panel debate on the issue of banning, a couple of years ago. The panel discussion centred on whether freedom of expression should be kept within limits so that it didn't hurt public sentiment. There had been some mob violence against works of art that especially targeted M.F. Husain. A valuable archive in Pune had been attacked because of a reference to Shivaji in a book and the film *Parzania* had been banned in Gujarat. Anyway, the man sitting beside me on the panel that day was a Member of Parliament from the Shiv Sena Party. He said he wanted to make it quite clear that he didn't believe in banning. He asked, 'Why should we ban books when we can get hold of some of the books and burn them?' So that was one way of objecting to banning. Now the bizarre aspect of this is that such statements have acquired respectability. They are represented in parliament. There has been no public voice, media programme or mainstream publication taking them head on. No public voice has said that if sentiments are hurt, let them be hurt. There would be have been no Hindu Code Bill, if sentiments were not to be hurt. We would still be burning widows, if we were afraid of hurting sentiments. In other words, there are sentiments that it is our duty to hurt. Someone has to say so. It, therefore, becomes the responsibility of private voices to speak—as I did on that occasion. Private publications need to select the topics and to set the terms for what needs debating.

Well, what needs discussion stretches across a huge spectrum—political, religious, economic, social and environmental. I am sure that Seminar has dealt with this variety of issues over the years, in their contemporary settings. But, as with Romesh's Agenda for India, their relevance continues in changed conditions and settings. To give you an illustration, Mahatma Gandhi's commandment that 'no human being should carry another's filth' started a social revolution. But today, a national agenda that aspires to super power status has no solution for garbage disposal, filthy roadsides, rivers and hillsides across the land.

One post-modern Indian condition is the zeal for conformity. The craze for banning is one aspect of it, the majoritarian agenda to bottle and pickle Indian into a monoculture based on one religion is another, and the monotonous refrain that socialism prevented progress is yet another. Then there is the conformity imposed on us from outside, through some aspects of globalisation.

One debate I would welcome would ask—through alignment and alliance, through the rat race and the arms race, are we not fitting into the role that others have assigned us? The cross-ventilation of ideas that this subject needs, perhaps only Seminar can provide, pitting arguments and opinions against each other in a no-holds-barred manner; in a way that the mainstream media, print or electronic, doesn't have the time or the format for and apparently doesn't think is necessary—dealing as it does with what is topical, what is in the news, and not with fundamentals.

For decades after independence, India, with no military or economic clout was a leader on the world stage. Now, with both money and armed power, it is a follower. What has brought us to this pass? This is the kind of question that Seminar could ask. Otherwise too, there is no dearth of subjects in desperate need of debate. I can think of two. The elitism of justice that lets wealthy murderers and rapists walk free, and a hard look at the grim reality in our face, of Indians at war with India.

I have a suggestion to make. Seminar is fifty years old and appearance does alter with age. Maybe it's time to abandon its somewhat sober format and come out in a startling new incarnation of colour to attract a new generation of readers. Its wider reach is important for the future—for the thinker, the writer and the reader who will not be driven into line.

Public and Private, Debate and Ideas

SUNIL KHILNANI

Seminar was born at the end of a decade—the 1950s that saw great busyness in the creation of public institutions. Indeed, in many ways, it was probably the most active moment of public institution-building in our history. Many of these institutions have since failed, dissolved into the dust of files and the murk of dim lightbulbs. Some of them have been unglamorously routinised and have become the very pillars, taken for granted, that sustain India today. Few of them have kept any of the auras of their initial creation.

Now to speak of Seminar as a public institution is in a sense ironic, or at least there is a double entendre in the title of this section. For the condition of Seminar's flourishing has been the fact that it's been a fiercely private institution. A tiny, one must say, almost an exclusive club, bearing very much the individual impress of its founder's preoccupations with his own resources. It carried on in many ways with a kind of blithe unconcern for the passing moods and fashions of public life. It maintained close relations with political elites and with the wielders of state power but it was never beholden to them.

It was like all significant intellectual ventures: individual, private and idiosyncratic. Idiosyncratic to the point of its handcrafted style, its handcrafted feel, its very austere production values, the *khadi* paper it used, its proto-Punk typography, which was in advance of the face of the 1980s, those of you who remember the *Punk* magazine in Britain. Also, the kind of ads that it carried which were public service ads; they were not interesting photographs, it was sort of austere—this refusal of commercial imperatives, in a way. Yet, of course, it was precisely this autonomy that endowed it with a public voice and authority.

Seminar was born at a moment and in a context when there was great public busyness and rather little private initiative. Today, of course, it's a complete reversal of that situation. It's a moment of great private busyness in our public life, but a stasis in the invention of public institutions. There

Seminar was born at a moment and in a context when there was great public busyness and rather little private initiative. Today, of course, it's a complete reversal of that situation. It's a moment of great private busyness in our public life, but a stasis in the invention of public institutions.

is a kind of collapse in our ability to imagine a public institution, now. So, the conditions of its birth are precisely the opposite today in terms of the broader context of public and private initiative.

What are the conditions of public debate in India, today? Is there anything like a shared arena of public argument in India? What is the place within that of a journal like Seminar? Is public discussion simply too fragmented to speak of a common domain or arena or a public sphere as academics like to talk about?

There are several developments that have made it much more difficult to sustain the idea of a common arena of conversation or debate or argument today. The existing linguistic multiplicity of our nation means that there are so many different spheres of argument and debate in different languages occurring at any given time in India. We have also seen a huge proliferation of various forms of media, both electronic and print, and this is something that will continue with the gradual expansion of the Internet.

The question for us is: is this proliferation ultimately going to be integrated or is it going to be divisive? Is it going to be something that actually does start to create connections across these different domains of discussion? Or is it actually going to be simply the proliferation of private conversations happening in different bubbles across our country? That's something that a journal like Seminar has to face as a condition of its survival. But it's also a condition of the survival of any kind of a common project that we might have as a nation. This question of whether these processes and trends are ultimately going to be more integrative or more divisive is something worth asking.

Adding to this fragmentation, we are also seeing a sharp generational change. Nayantara Sahgal noted this change, in terms, of how one might rethink the look of a magazine like Seminar. But, it's not just the look of Seminar, it's also about its content. When one hears the potential leader of the largest party or one hears India's best-selling author in English saying essentially, 'Who needs history? Why do we care about history? Why am I interested in the past? I am only interested in the future.' One has to register this thought. This is a real reaction that is happening in the next generation. One can bemoan it, and one can lament it but the fact is that it is happening. It poses a real challenge to thinking about 'now' in a broader context. How are we going to be able to maintain that capacity for perspective? I think that was one of the great things that the intellectuals who shaped our lives in the 20th century had. They were very engaged with the 'now', with the present, with the immediacy of things. But, they always saw beyond it and behind it. It was that capacity for perspective—it was not a scholastic capacity, it was not born of a profound love for the smell of archives, but it was just an imaginative capacity. How does one generate, inculcate and diffuse that? How does one call people into that kind of imagination? I think that is something any political project will have to face, let alone an intellectual project.

There is also the question of: how do we, as a group of thinkers, make sense of these unprecedented epochal changes? I do not mean how do we have an opinion about this, but whether there is an empirical basis on which we're talking about what is going on. All too often, I find this to be rather thin.

One of the things that I find troubling is the collapse of hard Indian social science...the fact that the numbers of people who went out into the fields in the '50s and '60s and actually saw what was happening, was much more than is the case today. It's much easier to write your PhD on cultural studies than it is to actually go out, live or work in remote conditions that are the reality of our country today. The weakness, the thinness of the knowledge base on which we are opinionated today is a great concern. Let me connect it to the question of thinking about an Indian journal of ideas in the context of the wider world.

Perhaps one of the things we might reflect on or cultivate today is not so much the capacity to speak or find more platforms where our own voices can be heard, but actually the capacity to listen, the capacity to register the range of other voices that are emerging in our democracy because that is the great change that is happening, today. When we begin to listen to these range of voices they are so strange to us that we don't think they have any validity or reason behind them; to create the space for those voices and bring them into a conversation we can still be a part of is going to be one of the great challenges.

Now, I'd like to talk about Seminar in the context of the wider world and the scope of its preoccupations. The fact is that many of the great journals that began in the 1950s and the subsequent decades have been very much focused on our own Indian preoccupations. Seems to make complete sense. But there has been an essential parochialism about them. From time to time when there has been an interest in, turning to or coverage of international topics, it's very much conceived in our own terms, for our own purposes. The converse is that the little of what has been said in the Indian intellectual life over the last fifty or sixty years within India has really been of enormous interest to the rest of the world. It's been of interest to the people in other parts of the world who have been interested in India. But the idea that the set of Indian arguments and ideas generated within India have made the world sit up and take notice is not that true today. It was true in the middle of the last century. It was true in the century before that.

The last such mind was probably Nehru's and the world was interested in hearing what was being said. The absence of that is something we should think about. Even as we rightly congratulate ourselves on the role we play in our own internal debate...if we are this great, vigorous, vibrant, intellectual democracy—isn't it time that we are aware not just about the rest of the world, but that the rest of the world is interested in what we have to say beyond India or India's relationships? One of the questions we might ask of our vigorous press is that why has it not really become a regular part of the international world of debate?

In 1975, one of the great periodical reviews of modern times called *Les Temps modernes* was launched. It was a French journal started by Jean-Paul Sartre. His colleague, the philosopher Maurice Merleau-Ponty, wrote a presentation for its inauguration and he used a phrase saying that he hoped Les Temps modernes would become an 'encyclopedia of the present'. In a way Seminar has been that. It has been an encyclopedia of India's present across fifty years. That's an important role to play, but what it means is also to be thinking about the future.

What is the future for public argument and ideas in India? What are the languages of thought, not just the natural languages, but the intellectual languages of thought we can hope for? Where will the ideas come from? Where and how will they be discussed? The last question is related to the impact we might hope to have on the wider world, as we move away from a kind of oppositional stance to the world order, as we move away from an idea of resistance or refusal.

How are we going to be producers of ideas? Not just consumers of ideas, not just diffusers of ideas, but if we really wish to be a knowledge society—what's going to be the horizon of our efforts to be producers of ideas and knowledge in the world? That doesn't mean aspiring to become some cosmopolitan Esperanto. It doesn't mean not talking about what we know best. It doesn't mean cutting oneself off from the detail of the local. On the contrary, it means having the confidence to see what is universal in the local, to be able to take on the very particular corruption in our society and the systematic injustice in our society. To see the many different features of our society which drive us around the bend or enthuse us and from a fine grained analysis of that particularity, of that minutiae, to generate universal insights. I think that's the task of a self-confident intellectual enterprise. I think we do have the richest material, today. We have the richest resources. It's really a question of turning that into thoughts, arguments, ideas and persuasions.

Discussion

Point, Counterpoint

RUDRANGSHU MUKHERJEE

This is just to elaborate a point that Sunil briefly touched upon, on the irony that vehicles of public discussion have actually been private. It has a very long lineage going back into the 19th century. I think *Seminar* belongs to that lineage. Ram Mohan Roy carried out his campaign against *sati* through the pages of a journal called *Sambad Kaumudi* that he virtually ran himself. I am deliberately taking examples from Bengal because I am most familiar with it. Ishwar Chandra Vidyasagar took up the issue of widow remarriage on the pages of a journal called *Som Prakash* that he ran single-handedly. The major turning point in the development of Indian literature was a journal called *Bangadarshan* owned by Bankim Chandra Chatterjee. We have many such examples, *Modern Review*, Ramananda Chatterjee and *Economic Weekly*, Sachin Chowdhury.

I think we need to look into this irony. Perhaps this irony is inevitable, that public discussion should be privately owned and privately channeled.

KAMAL HOSSAIN

As a Bengali, one feels that this tendency on our part to want change rather than to accept the status quo and be passive is a thread that runs through our history. We had an excellent introduction on the preambular and the Gothic. Now, we have moved from the preambular to the beginning of a transition. We are celebrating fifty years of Seminar, some years ago it was the sixtieth year of independence and the fortieth or fiftieth anniversary of the Universal Declaration of Human Rights (UDHR). In a way, we are all caught up in a process of change.

This great subcontinent is a huge human world chain, this project of change, of changing reality.

The UDHR, one would have said was a Bengali document: optimistic, in the face of reality. Look around you, colonialism was there everywhere, apartheid was there, the holocaust had just taken place. So it defied reality and I feel that is a Bengali characteristic which I would like to share with the whole of India.

The UDHR, in a way, inspired India to say no—to say no to injustice, to say no to intolerance, to say no to arrogance, intellectual or otherwise and instead, to say that every human being is entitled to respect, equal in rights and dignity. I think I'm very impressed by what our other fellow Bengali, Amartya Sen, had to say about this...he says, they are not merely words but they are words that ignite consciences. It makes people say no to injustice, no to intolerance, no to discrimination, no to exclusion and therefore, generates energy for change. At this point, I just want to say this—we, from Bangladesh, fought for independence the second time, because we said no to the reality that was confronting us for twenty-four years after we had first voted for independence. That's characteristic of us; that however impotent we might be, however powerless we might be, however disempowered the surrounding circumstances may make us, there is something called human conscience. And this human conscience has to, in a way, ignite and generate energy so that knowledge is not enough, it's knowledge for a purpose and that purpose is to change the status quo...whether it is in terms of economic and social rights, political rights, freedom of thinking or freedom of expression. We have already got such a preamble in both of our constitutions.

These are shared values and shared aspirations, not in a hypocritical sense, but in a genuine sense. One might argue that these ideas are coming from incestuous, urban intellectual, cosmopolitan people. My instinctive response to that is to say, let's test this. Let's go to every village in India, Pakistan, Bangladesh, and ask a person, 'Do you value human security? Do you want your child to come back safe from school?' Every member of the human family would respond in the same way. I am not prepared to accept a view that says this is all urban, intellectual, cosmopolitan luxury. Let's hear the voices. Yes, of course, we must hear the voices of the Dalits, of the excluded. But let us relate to them as members of the human family, first. I see no reason why a Dalit would want his child to be vulnerable to danger, vulnerable to physical assault any more than the richest person's son or daughter. It's not intellectually arrogant to say—let us all reflect a human consensus.

An aspiring symbol for us should be Sisyphus (from Greek mythology), someone who is always rolling the boulder up the hill. As I said, the Bengali motto is 'never say die'. We have pushed the boulder up, it rolls down to point zero and we start rolling it up again. We have done it throughout our history and we would like to share with all the fellow members of our human family, from Kabul right down to Myanmar, that we are pushing the same boulders. Some are a little further up, some have it rolled down and are rolling it up again. But there is no escape from that. That's why I feel the 'human condition' that is the focus of the Indian Institute of Advanced Study is the correct framework, because the human condition requires a commitment to change; it will be this commitment that will ignite the human conscience and generate the energy to start pushing the boulder up.

C. RAMMANOHAR REDDY

Nayantara Sahgal spoke about the cottage industry. That's something that worries me. A publication that is a cottage industry has verve, a certain élan, a certain fizz, and yet being a cottage industry means there's a struggle for survival. What worries me is that once we become professional, once we become stable, we may lose that fizz. The most frightening thought, then, is that two journals which provide so much excitement, in terms of thinking and debate—do they have a certain life of their own before they become dull and respectable? I am not talking only about Seminar. Fifty years in that sense is a short time. I am also talking about the *Economic & Political Weekly* (EPW). This is a question that worries us that as we become more organised, we may become duller.

The second point is about what Nayantara mentioned, the question of intolerance and how as publishers we may, day by day, bit by bit, begin to cut our clothes to suit the fashions of the day without even knowing it. We are pushed on a daily basis, on a monthly basis...so when we think about our survival, then we do things without worrying about our larger mission. I'm not sure how many of us are conscious about this happening.

On Sunil Khilnani's point, which Rudrangshu also brought up, about public institutions getting strength because they are private—in a sense, all media institutions, have to be private to retain their power. It's also a question of the degree of how private they are. I don't think a media institution that is a collective will work.

I agree that, without letting our authors down, the quality of hard social science has deteriorated. The irony is that though there is an explosion of information, there is not that quality of insight of processing information that you had in the 1950s and 1960s.

Something I am concerned about is what I call the 'relocation of thinking on India' as part of the larger process. The latest Seminar has ten contributions from scholars and thinkers who are living and working in India, and eight are from those outside India. They may be students, they may be Indians working on India, they may be scholars of Indian origin working on India...is there something to be worried about there? This is something that I see happening in the EPW, as well. Articles that qualify for publication seem to be coming from Indians working abroad and one can say, what's wrong with that? Nothing wrong, but then why is the EPW published from Mumbai? It might as well be published from London. Why should Seminar be published from Delhi and not Washington? That, perhaps, is reflective of certain larger changes that are taking place and maybe there's something to think about there.

HAMEED HAROON

I am very struck by Sunil's points about how people generally do not look to India or to a personality or personalities in India for ideas on mainstream interests around the world. Generally, people tend to look to thinkers in India or the subcontinent for views limited to India and the subcontinent. I think that's an important matter that needs to be thought of in great detail. I think our preoccupation with ourselves essentially comes from a sense of nationalism. Our lack of security with respect to our knowledge about matters of concern outside this region is best addressed when people who originated in this region, go and live outside this region. This may have something to do with the quality of our universities, media and information databases. I feel if one turns around and looks at a country like India, one will see how poorly informed it is about Pakistan. There is much more knowledge about India in the public domain of Pakistan than vice versa. When we are so unable to come to definitive ideas with respect to our neighbours, there is some room to wonder if we are able to achieve and nurture an international level of quality of thinking without sending our people outside. I think it may be a reflection or a link to the point you raised, but whether or not I am able to make that linkage, I feel that the point that you cited is certainly critical.

HARSH SETHI

I am keen to understand the distinction between the many distinct enterprises we end up calling a public institution. Is it a journal, is it a university...why not a museum? Why not something that is not even structured like that?

In South Asia, for example, one can think of the *katha vachaks* (story tellers) and the ways in which they influence how people think of substantial issues to do with the human condition. This is very different from the kind of discourse and the kind of lack of knowledge we talk about when referring to policies.

I completely agree when Hameed says that our understanding of our neighbours, given the kind of immense obsession that the Indians have with Pakistan, our abysmal state of understanding even regarding the most basic things about the neighbour is something that ought to be bothering people, but it doesn't. And it's not only because of practical things...how many Indians can we think of who might have done field work in Pakistan? Or are the Indian experts in Pakistan only those that are located abroad and happen to have an Indian name, or people from the Foreign Service or journalists posted there and members of the RAW (Research and Analysis Wing)? Is that the only kind of expertise that we have? Because we don't seem to have any understanding...that's one kind of problem that we have. We may need to diversify the forms of how things get heard and talked about.

The second point, a significant one that Sunil made, is that we seem to have lost the ability to hear. Lots of us are speaking and there are many forums in which we are speaking. But have we lost the ability to hear? And again there, I would like to go back to the issue of language and more than just the physical language...each language and each language tradition may be incorporating different kinds of intellectual journeys that speak to a variety of people. A lot of our theorising about public institutions, public debate, public reason, and a lack of it, is to do with this peculiar world of English in our environments. I suspect that our understanding of other worlds and how they debate and what they debate is flawed, and may have implications in terms of how we pose questions.

KANAK MANI DIXIT I would like to get back to the issue of language. Before that, the point about how Indians know very little about Pakistan could be taken further, perhaps even to say, how little Indians in the English language discourse know about the other parts of India, as well, besides other parts of South Asia. This also brings up this issue of who's producing the knowledge and who is ingesting it. To think that we have here today, the EPW and Seminar, two organisations that are providing the knowledge base for a country of a billion plus. Then we need to look at the larger South Asia that is a fifth of humanity and ask, what is their knowledge base? India itself is most of South Asia.

Talking about discourse in the English language—it is very important, but how far can it reach? There was an attempt to bring out a journal, an academic journal in the English language that died, another attempt in Nepali that died. There is nothing in that space, right now.

The academic generation of knowledge and more importantly, its presentation: how much of that is happening? Are we locked into English...with all the importance that it has for the further spread of knowledge—is that even happening? Is what is being generated in English moving into other languages? Frankly, it's not. So then, what are we losing? The other side of this—is there a lot happening in the other languages academically, perhaps in a different stream? Is that being transferred into the English language stream given that the English language rules South Asia?

T.N. NINAN Journals of ideas are always small to medium scale. They can't be mass produced by their very nature in the same way that publishing works best as a cottage industry. But the question I have is about this: the EPW is published in Mumbai and Seminar started from there and came to Delhi, could it be published today from any other city in India? In today's context, can you imagine any other city in India producing a journal like Seminar? And what is the role that Delhi has now? In a piece by the late publisher, Ravi Dayal, he talks about publishing being based in Delhi. We have some of the better universities, think tanks, libraries, and funding, here in Delhi. Where are we headed in terms of how much Delhi plays a role in this kind of thinking?

SHIVSHANKAR MENON Both Nayantara Sahgal and Sunil Khilnani showed some kind of regret that India is no longer a source of ideas for the rest of the world, at least not quite in the way it was in the 1950s. That might partly be explained by the fact that there was a Cold War. A Cold War in a sense empowered those who chose not to take sides. It empowered the middle ground. If you had other ideas, the world listened to you. You are not in that situation anymore. In fact what Sunil mentioned about the parochialism of much of our intellectual discourses; it has actually happened everywhere else in the world. It's quite frightening to walk into an American bookstore and see that there's very little that interests you, unless you are interested in America. So it's not a phenomenon peculiar to us. I say this not in order to justify what's happening. There's no question that we need to think of ourselves as producers of ideas for the world, we need to break out of parochialism, and we need to discuss how we can do that.

The other point I wanted to make was that we keep grumbling about how little we understand each other's neighbours. In Pakistan, there have been very few PhDs on India. The figures for India are only slightly better. I often wonder, we have this idea that we need to have the perfect knowledge of each other, of ourselves. Did we have perfect knowledge, is that how we ended up in 1947? I actually think we have better knowledge of each other today, than we did then. We have better knowledge of ourselves, speaking to Kanak's point, we actually know more about ourselves and our own societies as a result of what Seminar has done through the years. The problem is really that we are looking for an ideal and it stops us from doing things that we could do among ourselves.

When Seminar started, when we looked at South Asia, when we looked at our neighbours, there was always a clear idea that this will lead to action. We seem to have lost that, somehow. My question really is: how do we make India a producer of ideas? How do you see us doing it in a practical way?

SUNIL KHILNANI

Let me start with a question that Rudrangshu and Harsh came back to, about the public and its relationship to the private. Of course, private sources for ideas in society are necessary and vital. All the interesting ideas do come from the private domain and that's exactly the point I wanted to celebrate about Seminar. I though will make a distinction between a public sector and a public sphere. We tend to think of 'public' as the 'public sector', part of the state. But that's not the way the term 'public' emerged as an important one in Western history and ideas. The public was something that sat somewhere undefined, between the state and society. It was neither subject to the workings of the market, nor was it subject to the depredations of power of the state. It was somewhere in between. It belonged to no one in particular. It's that sphere with which we have been struggling as intellectuals, writers, journalists, researchers: to try and demarcate in our society, somewhere that is free both from the imperatives of profit, but also from the oppressions of power. In the definition of that space and indeed, in the maintenance of that space, the private is crucial.

To discuss the point about parochialism that came up in a number of remarks, I do think it is connected to nationalism. We are still shaped by nationalism. It's an important thing. It's going to be a part of politics over the next decades, if not least within Asia. But, we will have to take a measure of that and see where it's constricting us intellectually. While it is an important political instinct, it's not the best way one thinks about something. That's a distinction we might become more aware of.

I think this question of a knowledge base, both of our own society and also those of our neighbours...yes, I feel we do know much more than we did, fifty or sixty years ago. But still, we have to ask whether that is enough, given the kind of enormous shifts that are happening and their rapidity, and not just in our own society. This is something that is moving faster than the eye can blink. That kind of scale and speed needs some continuous analysis and narrative. A narrative gives a journal the capacity to be not just the encyclopaedia of the present, but the story of the present as it unfolds.

I think we didn't talk about our largest neighbour, China, which of course, Shivshankar Menon knows more about than any of the other participant. I may be wrong about this, but I think we had more people working on China in the 1960s than we have today. We have probably had more experts, outside of government, who spoke the language in the 1960s. That's not a viable situation and we need to address it.

The other very important point that T.N. Ninan raised is about the centralisation of ideas. After a long time, it's made Delhi, quite an interesting place to be in, if you're interested in ideas. But I'm not sure that it's good for the health of the larger society. What initiatives are underway in other cities? If the current objective is to create a think tank, let's all try that, see the mistakes of it and find better institutions that do the job better. Every city wants its think tanks. That's a good initial stage to go through. I think we need to diffuse sources, not least because they become listening posts. We can then hear a broader range of voices.

The question of language, yes, of course, that's a natural condition of our discussions and it always will be. There are great limitations to English. But I also think that partly, the initiatives should be coming from other languages to want to translate...because they feel that there are interesting enough ideas that speak to them, that they want to hear and debate about in their own language. We do see this happening in some of our regional cultures. It's not just a question of push, there has to be pull as well. There has to be demand for it.

The point that Shivshankar made about the Cold War being a condition of Indian audibility is a very important one. But at the same time, this historical explanation can't be an excuse for the inability of producing ideas, today. After all, we are in a situation where there are a whole series of global matters whose outcomes are influenced by us.

It's a very difficult question: how can we be a source of ideas for those other than ourselves? But, I think it is a combination of analysis and rhetoric. It is a combination of being able to produce the hard knowledge and being able to convey it, in a way that has some force and that engages with the interests of other people. It is true there has been parochialisation of intellectual debate across the world, but in a sense that is an opportunity.

NAYANTARA SAHGAL

Writers are not talkers. Sunil has said everything that needed to be said in response to the questions raised. But, starting with you, Shivshankar, I am surprised that one should think in terms of the Cold War. There are choices to be made in every generation, in the context of the times. In our case, extremely important choices in the context of globalisation, the way we are going...do we want to go that way? How far do we wish to join the rat race or the arms race or whatever race is going on? I personally don't find the intellectual vitality here dealing with these questions. I don't know why that should be accepted. Perhaps, we have gone very far in the realm of technology, information technology and in those areas we have in fact specialised so much that we have lost history, geography, culture and art. There are choices to be made. We need to define what is India for the future. That idea of India was Nehru's India and now, we need—perhaps a larger, slightly different idea of India—that can inspire and engage the young, who are most of India.

About Pakistan, we have such close understanding. What could be closer than the bonds we have over music, art and films. Now there is a growing understanding of Pakistan through this sort of overflow of wonderful fiction that is coming out of their country. These are the ways in which people understand each other. Not through data collected, questionnaires produced and answered. These are the ways we have to engage. We should engage more and more. That will produce a bond between people, which is already there. It doesn't have to be created—it has to be built on more and more.

Speaking to the point on the public-private controversy, I should imagine that in a well-working democracy, with a well-working public sector, there should be no adversarial situation between public and private. The public sector produces the organisation or the service, and the user is a private person, between them they either produce a successful product or a bad one. The government provides a bus, if we go in and spit on the floor and urinate in a corner, it's not going to be a good service but if we treat it well and demand good service, it will be a very good service. There has to be complete cooperation between the idea of public and the idea of private.

II

"Newspapers are said to be the rough first draft of history, and history, of course, is encapsulated into books. So where does Seminar fit in?"

T.N. NINAN

"Seminar comes closest to one of the great ideals of the philosophy of science in the twentieth century, the idea of cognitive justice. Now this is not the standard developmental mush about participation, this is not the standard sentimentality about listening. Cognitive justice is an actual supplement to the democratic imagination where every form of knowledge, as a way of life, as a lifestyle and as a life cycle, has a right to survive."

SHIV VISVANATHAN

"...this notion of cognitive justice is powerful but potentially dangerous, because, the idea that all these 'different ways of life' should be included is correct, but there are judgments to be made between them...cognitive justice does not simply mean recognising every single way of life as equivalent."

SUNIL KHILNANI

INDIAN INSTITUTE
OF

"It [Seminar] is an archive of debates and arguments about our democracy….Seminar is an archive of all kinds of themes, arguments, topics, and ideologies relevant to the faith and future of our Indian polity."

RAMACHANDRA GUHA

"To call Seminar an archive is a misnomer because Seminar is actually an archive embedded in the glorious oral tradition. Seminar is gossip personified. Voyeuristic, tender, wonderful to listen to, utterly sympathetic, thoroughly contemptuous, and yet out of that it created a listening pool. A way of listening that could then be converted into a way of writing…Seminar has a brilliant oral imagination: it's this style that in a way embodies the medium of democracy, because democracy in India needs to be simultaneously oral and textual. Anyone who has spent five hours of gossip in Seminar sees the transition between orality and print…"

SHIV VISVANATHAN

"What's striking about Seminar and the EPW is that this a special place for the young and obscure…not the distinguished, the entitled, also the young and obscure from all parts of India who contribute to both journals…another thing they have in common is that they are published in English…we don't need to be apologetic about it."

RAMACHANDRA GUHA

"The point I was suggesting was never to be defensive about using the English language, not at all. How do you communicate across India and South Asia, other than in English?"

KANAK MANI DIXIT

"It's fantastic to be a cottage industry, but it brings the question of survival with it. You have to start looking at numbers, there

are long spells where the publication would be a labour of love, born of self-denial, and ruthless cost cutting, which Seminar has done and so has the EPW. But how long do we go on? There's also the issue of philanthropy. In recent years, if it weren't for two large grants by two Trusts, we would be in real trouble at the EPW."

C. RAMMANOHAR REDDY

"...the point is very important because if we look at the Bengali journals of reformers, none had the longevity, none lasted half a century. We need to seriously think about this: how do we survive as a cottage industry?"

RUDRANGSHU MUKHERJEE

"I think that my instinct as a publisher working with a rather diverse group, is that philanthropy is not the answer because to have to ask, at a certain level, is to lose...I also think it needs to go on the web. There needs to be a distribution of workloads. There has to be of retention of titles, in a collective sense. You need to create a larger programming structure in which you survive, within which it becomes feasible for advertisers, rather than philanthropists, to think of you as a viable unit...you need to change technology, remove this aversion to numbers, shed the reluctance to exclusivise the printed word as the main communication domain..."

HAMEED HAROON

"I am surprised that so much time was spent on publishing and so little on the idea that editing Seminar was a great act of fun. The beauty of watching three of them work for 10 years...see the creativity at play and the tolerance of how the group worked. It was a miracle. You can't think of three more egotistic people. The synergy was superb. You can't turn it into a technological solution."

SHIV VISVANATHAN

"On the issue of numbers and the reach of journals like Seminar or the EPW: I think you do need to reach out just for the efficacy of the ideas, especially, since these are journals of politics and ideas, of the present, and not literary journals."

SUNIL KHILNANI

"There are two key issues of quality and reach. Clearly the EPW and Seminar are providing something much more reflective and insightful. I hope that Seminar continues to be read by people who are influential...Seminar as an intellectual ghost of the political class, I think, is a fascinating insight."

RAMACHANDRA GUHA

"I wonder what would it mean for a historical researcher in 2059 to be looking at Seminar. Right now, that person will be very excited and I hope that continues..."

JAITHIRTH RAO

I think one of the things that we miss in India is what Americans call 'long form journalism': the space to explore issues and ideas at length, so that you are left with an understanding of what they are all about.

Intellectual Archive

T.N. NINAN

Newspapers are said to be the rough first draft of history, and history, of course, is encapsulated into books. So where does *Seminar* fit in? It fits somewhere in the middle. I think one of the things that we miss in India is what Americans call 'long form journalism': the space to explore issues and ideas at length, so that you are left with an understanding of what they are all about. Long form journalism can be of two types. One is comment itself, which is what Seminar mostly does, and the other is reportage, which we don't have in Seminar. But it fits one of these two categories and, therefore, it serves the purpose of being an intellectual archive. A lot of this becomes clear in flipping through the book, *Indian Persuasions*.[1] The volume carries a selection of articles published in Seminar, over the decades.

Being an economic journalist, I was particularly interested in which articles were included in the 'Economy' section. The section starts off with two of the best names in the business, Amartya Sen and Jagdish Bhagwati. These were written in 1959 and 1960, and from the perspective of the latter 2000s it is interesting to look back and ask: whose ideas have stood the test of time? Who had the better ideas half a century ago?

Other than one journalistic piece, the financial writing stops in 1975 with Montek Singh Ahluwalia's essay, which encapsulates a whole range of issues one would need to focus on in the coming years. It's intriguing that in the most interesting period of India's economic reformers, there don't seem to be that many fresh ideas coming through on the pages of Seminar. What does this say about the state of Indian economists rather than the state of the Indian economy?

1. *Indian Persuasions: 50 Years of Seminar* edited by Rudrangshu Mukherjee, Roli Books, New Delhi, 2009.

What's striking about Seminar and the EPW is that this is a special place for the young and obscure.

Seminar, the Seminal Archive

RAMACHANDRA GUHA

I am going to open by offering my respectful homage to Comrade Balchandra Triyambak Ranadive, without whom there may have been no *Seminar* at all. This is not simply a joke or a facetious comment.

It takes us back to the intellectual history of India, in particular to the year 1948, to a conference held in Kolkata. Six weeks after Mahatma Gandhi's assassination, the Communist Party of India, in an act it should still be repenting, replaced Comrade Puran Chand Joshi as General Secretary of the party with Comrade Balchandra Triyambak Ranadive. One was austere and humorous, and the other was charming and playful. One believed in what Nayantara Sahgal reminded us about, earlier, 'you have the right to freely criticise everything except what the party tells you not to criticise', and the other was the more cosmopolitan, liberal-minded intellectual and especially a deep patron of the arts, of culture and of photography.

With P.C. Joshi at the helm of the Communist movement, there was a chance that the Communists and the Congress Party members could collaborate creatively; the Congress Right that Gopalkrishna Gandhi talked about could be marginalised, and there was also an opening for progressive and idealistic young intellectuals, filmmakers, writers, thinkers to be fellow travellers, in the original sense of the term. All this was extinguished after Ranadive took over the party, and I think Raj and Romesh Thapar took a long time in recovering from it, which is why in 1959, Seminar was started.

Now we are talking about Seminar as a historic archive, an intellectual archive. So I thought I would give you a sampling of the issues, the topics covered in each issue in two select years (I have the titles of issues taken up by Seminar in four years but that will take up too much time, so I will limit it to two years)...it's a totally random selection. In 1961, which were the twilight years of Jawaharlal Nehru in a sense, these were the topics covered in the monthly issues of Seminar: Socialism Today; The Census; Our Foreign Policy; Waste; The Writer at Bay; Administration; North and South; Communalism; Philosophy; Science; Advertising; Music. Move forward to the year

Seminar is more than an intellectual archive. Seminar is an archive of all kinds of themes, arguments, topics and ideologies relevant to the fate and future of our Indian polity.

1974: a year of political rivalry and crisis in India. Think of the topics covered in 1974, and I'm just giving you the bare title, but you can get a sense of the themes, arguments and controversies that would have been covered. Indian Muslims; Population Threat; The Students Speak (because the Jayaprakash movement was about the youth); The Untouchables; Marxism in India; The Multinationals; The Architect in India; The Indian Ocean; The Energy Crisis; Growing Food; The Cinema Situation.

Extraordinary, how contemporary the themes are and, of course, these themes would have been covered from a very wide spectrum: intellectual, ideological, disciplinary, and geographical. In all the issues, may it be the Indian Muslims or Population Threat or The Untouchables or Indian Ocean—you would find a great diversity of opinion—stylistically, politically and disciplinary.

This is just to give you a sense of what Seminar is as an archive. I think intellectual archive is a wrong word. It is an archive of debates and arguments about our democracy. Examples of intellectual archives would include, *Contributions to Indian Sociology*, which is an outstanding Indian journal, an archive of sociological thinking, and *Indian Economic and Social History Review* which started around the same time as Seminar, in the early 1960s and is an archive of historical scholarship. But, Seminar is more than an intellectual archive. Seminar is an archive of all kinds of themes, arguments, topics and ideologies relevant to the fate and future of our Indian polity.

Now, how does Seminar compare to other journals in India? There's one obvious comparison with the *Economic and Political Weekly* (EPW). Ashok Mitra, well known economist and former finance minister of West Bengal, is maybe the only Indian left today who knew both the journals since their inception and had a close connection with both. In an article published in *The Telegraph*, he talked about the two journals on the occasion of the EPW being in its sixtieth year and Seminar in its fiftieth year...it's an interesting contrast.

The first aspect of the contrast is, Mumbai *versus* Delhi. It's wonderful that the EPW is in Mumbai and Seminar is in Delhi. If they had both been in Delhi, there would have been a great collective loss in the range and richness of the intellectual discourse in the country. It's a bipolar thing. Eclectic *versus* thematic. Weekly *versus* monthly. Left *versus* liberal. I hope Ram [editor of the EPW] doesn't misunderstand what I am saying but I feel that ideologically the EPW sees itself as a left liberal journal. In that sense, Seminar may have a broader spectrum of contributors. Seminar is liberal and, therefore, more inclusive in the kind of range of themes and writers it can call upon.

There are similarities, too. Both of them are genuinely pan-India. The contributors and readers are from all over India. What's striking about Seminar and the EPW is that this is a special place for the young and obscure. I speak partly out of personal experience. I owe a great deal to the EPW, because its former editor, late Krishna Raj, asked me to write for the journal in early 1981. I also wrote to Romesh Thapar. I didn't say, that incidentally I am the first, second or third cousin of your close friend, Dharma Kumar [a noted economic historian]. That probably would have sent my letter to the waste paper basket. I just wrote to him saying that, I have an article to write for you, Sir, will you consider it? So, it's not the distinguished, the entitled and the ennobled, but also the young and obscure from all parts of India who contribute to both journals. I think that's something very special that both these journals share.

When you think of Seminar and the EPW, another thing they have in common is that they are published in English. I wasn't going to talk about this, but there has been some anguish and anxiety on the role and relevance of English language journals, in the earlier section. Are we really capturing the pulse of the people? Are we ignoring voices heard in other languages not just in India, but also, in a country like Nepal? I don't think we need to be apologetic at all.

If you look at the history of comparable journals in India, if you look at Bengal, which Rudrangshu talked about...there were journals in Bengali, but then there were journals in English. Ramananda Chatterjee published *Prabasi* for the Bengali outside of Kolkata or outside of Bengal. Then he started *Modern Review* because he wanted to reach others, as well. Why did Tagore write *Nationalism* in English and not in Bengali? Same with *Indian Social Reformer* published by K. Natarajan in Mumbai. The two relevant journals then, were Modern Review in Kolkata and Indian Social Reformer in Mumbai. Both were pan-India, both embraced a wide range of issues vital to the intellectual and democratic life of the nation, and both were published in English. So you can be sensitive to other voices, but I don't think you need to be apologetic or feel elitist in any way about publishing in English because we have very honorable predecessors.

Of course, you can compare Seminar to the EPW. You can compare Seminar and the EPW to the Indian Social Reformer and Modern Review, in the past, or you can do a comparison across countries to other such journals. In terms of contemporary journals, one can think of *Prospect* or the *Weekly Standard* in the UK, the *New Republic* and *Public Interest* in the USA. We have discussed these journals as cottage industries, and we have discussed the fact that they have small circulation. Again, there's no need to be apologetic about the small circulation. I think it's vital to quality. As writer Arthur Koestler used to say, 'I would gladly exchange a hundred readers today for ten readers in ten years' time and one reader in a hundred years' time.' I think that's a sentiment we can appreciate. In terms of Seminar or the EPW, you'd rather reach one reader who can influence many others.

50 years of Seminar, 600 issues, 7,000 articles. What you need to do, now, is to create a permanent archive for our democracy, for our intellectual life—get specialist editors for a volume maybe on communism, a volume on *adivasis*, a volume on music, a volume on architecture, and ask the editors to be ruthless about excising articles that don't fit.

Many articles that I have read in Seminar have influenced me, but I would especially like to mention an article written by General K.S. Thimayya in the July 1962 issue of Seminar. It's probably the only one he may have ever written. He wrote the piece after he had retired, and it spoke about our relations with China, options *vis-à-vis* China. He says the political class has two options: to conclude a definitive border treaty with China or get arms from the West, otherwise we would be overrun by the Chinese army. It's an archival idea that throws up things that are still highly relevant.

The last personal point I would like to mention, I met Raj and Romesh Thapar much before I met their daughter, Malvika. They probably didn't notice me. I was a college boy and in those days, I used to hang around the house of my cousin and teacher, Dharma Kumar, and they used to be there. I was deeply struck by their vitality and their bonding, their deep ties. I began writing a novel (gladly never completed it) whose first scene featured Raj and Romesh Thapar. The idea came while hearing Dharma Kumar and others talk about the legendary New Year's parties which the Thapars famously hosted at their Kautilya Marg residence. The novel had Romesh Thapar organising the setting in the lawn. It's dark and he trips, the music system goes off and blows a fuse, and Raj Thapar comes and bails him out, restores the power and rescues the party. This was the kind of impression that the couple could make on someone who was a silent eavesdropper.

Seminar is a place where you are asked to be witty and be treated like a halfwit. Seminar is a place where you are ridiculed because it celebrates the ridiculous.

Constructing Seminar

SHIV VISVANATHAN

There's a *Seminar* for every person and each one constructs his own Seminar. The Seminar that I am going to construct is of a different order. The topic of Seminar has been exhausted, except for predictions of its future. Seminar is a seductive thing. It always invites the storyteller and the anecdote. By the time they've exhausted the story and the anecdote, there's little left to analyse.

The question I asked myself while sitting here is: how does one talk of a Seminar without anecdotes? Imagine Seminar had disappeared. No Raj, no Romesh. None of the trinity of the present editors: Malvika Singh, Tejbir Singh and Harsh Sethi. Then I want to ask, how do I reconstruct the magic of those three rooms and the hospitality of those three people? What made Seminar an exceptional archive? Here was a club, a snooty little club that became an intellectual commons. Here was something almost feudal in style that encouraged radical and dissenting moods. Here was something that mastered skepticism, and yet encouraged every new idea and innovation in the '80s and '90s. How did Seminar manage this collection of contradictions? I think, in a deep and fundamental way, this is the only thing understated about Seminar—its methodology. It depersonalised the three editors. Seminar was the first magazine to use illiteracy as a master technique of editing. Illiteracy as a heuristic of contempt for the expert and those in power by saying, if you don't clarify, you don't entertain. There's a powerful democratic methodology.

The second point is that Seminar has a way of softening attitudes, where the cynic could become the skeptic, and the skeptic could become a source of hope, for all kinds of moments and all kinds of autobiographies, because Seminar provided that kind of home where politicians in power could come in cover for a short while, complain, and then go back to their moth eaten careers.

Thirdly, it turned the art of table manners into a civics of dissent where the eccentric, the idiosyncratic, the radical, the dissenting and the marginal, could all come together to create a civics of dissent, because, to a certain extent, the intolerance of the mainstream can only be managed by the intolerance of dissent. Seminar was one place where the dissenting imaginations could tolerate each other. Three personalities evoked three impersonal styles to create something that was not an archive. To call Seminar an archive is a misnomer because Seminar is actually an archive embedded in a glorious oral tradition. Seminar is gossip personified. Voyeuristic, tender, wonderful to listen to, utterly sympathetic, thoroughly contemptuous and yet out of that, it created a listening pool. A way of listening that could then be converted into a way of writing, and to talk of Seminar as only something in print, I think, is unrealistic and unfair. Seminar has a brilliant oral imagination: it's this style that in a way embodies the medium of democracy, because democracy in India needs to be simultaneously oral and textual. Anyone who has spent five hours of gossip in Seminar sees the transition between orality and print, and even a few fatal entries into the digital space.

That's one place where you will never see Seminar confident–in the digital domain. Yet, that is really what redeems Seminar, its ability to make interesting mistakes.

Seminar began as an ethics of politics. Forget Seminar, forget Raj and Romesh–Seminar is a collection of all the dissenting parties, all the negotiations, all the coalitions, and if you remove the word Congress and put Seminar in, you get the issue. In fact to a certain extent, it takes over the traditions of the Congress by turning it into an intellectual heuristic.

The second thing it does beautifully is that it moves from the ethics of power to the ethics of knowledge. It's the one place where varieties of opinion are presented, and it adds to the imagination of democracy by saying, there is no official definition of democracy. Each man defines his citizenship, each man defines his democracy, and each man has to become a series of contestations, sites of memory. What makes it really endearing to me is that Seminar comes closest to one of the great ideals of the philosophy of science in the 20th century, the idea of cognitive justice. Now, this is not the standard developmental mush about participation, this is not the standard sentimentality about listening. Cognitive justice is an actual supplement to the democratic imagination where every form of knowledge, as a way of life, as a lifestyle and as a life cycle, has a right to survive. The tribal, the nomad, and the marginal become theories of knowledge. He's a 'way of life' and till democracy recognises these marginals as ways of life and as theories of science, it will always be subject to the developmental onslaught. It is as an ethics of power, as an ethics of memory and as an ethics of knowledge that Seminar adds to the democratic imagination.

It's playful, but I think it's a play that transcends general seriousness. It demands entertainment. In fact, I was putting together a series of quotations that people told me, about their general attitude to Seminar. Seminar is a place where you are asked to be witty and be treated like a halfwit. Seminar is a place where you are ridiculed because it celebrates the ridiculous. Seminar, as someone else told me, is the only place where they call a spade, a shovel, so we can dig deeper. It's that style of created content, the style of the three editors with three separate kinds of archival imaginations, three separate kinds of archival classification, and three forms of memory and listening. By combining the oral and the print, Seminar miniaturises the democratic imagination.

The last story, the only personal one, is that I showed Seminar copies to my three daughters, and each one responded in a very interesting way, in terms of an indication to the future. The first, who is an archaeologist, said it's brilliant but what I really like is the way it relates word to world. Seminar creates the Hobson-Jobson and the Hanklyn-Janklin of modern democracy. Its ability to generate a whole kind of vocabularies on dialects of power is really what makes it interesting. It's not the formal politics, it's not the formal affirmation of democracy, but it is the ability to create dialects of power debating with each other. So, even policy becomes the set of dialects that contest and debate the nature of the state. My second daughter loves the word chill out. She said Seminar is something beautiful because it chills out on politics. Democracy becomes a form of entertainment and power gives you the possibility of dreaming in different ways. My third daughter, who is still in school, is much more matter of fact. She said, it's very useful for my social science projects, it speeds things up. And then two of the younger ones looked at me fondly and said, it must be a nice place, and I said I had never thought of that. They said: if they could let you write so often, it must be nice.

It's the one place where varieties of opinion are presented, and it adds to the imagination of democracy by saying, there is no official definition of democracy. Each man defines his citizenship, each man defines his democracy, and each man has to become a series of contestations, sites of memory.

Discussion

Point, Counterpoint

RUDRANGSHU MUKHERJEE

Ram [Ramachandra Guha], could we have the other two years of *Seminar* issues, especially if they are in the 1990s, when the new generation of editors looks after Seminar?

RAMACHANDRA GUHA

In 1993: Towards 2000 AD; The North-East; Politics of the State; Health for All?; Nuclear Power; Cricket Culture; Our Urban Future; Socialism in Crisis; Communal Divides; Reserved Futures; The Eighth Plan. In 2004, the year of a major election: Beyond the Verdict; Changing Chennai; Are We Learning?; India Shining; The Diaspora; A Mandate for Change; Celebrating Women; New Priorities; Working Conservation; Amchem Goem; Elusive Justice.

RUDRANGSHU MUKHERJEE

There is continuity, despite the generational break. That is the point I wanted to make.

KANAK MANI DIXIT

The point I was suggesting was never to be defensive about using the English language, not at all. How do you communicate across India and South Asia, other than in English? My concern is: how do you take the knowledge, presented in a magazine like Seminar, to the vernacular intelligentsia? So that it oils the larger politics. As far as I can make out right now, it happens through Seminar's material being picked up by academia and by media such as it is and transferring it into the English language discourse, and some of it filters into the vernacular discourse. But, is there a more direct way to make material available to the vernacular intelligentsia?

JAITHIRTH RAO

I'd like to talk about the issue of Seminar as an archive...and Ram's references to *Modern Review*, I think, that is the key to understanding the last fifty years. The way, today, Harsh, Tejbir and Malvika decide on whom to invite and for what, has kept it unusual for a magazine and lively...I find it fascinating.

Ram [Ramachandra Guha], you mentioned the fact that unusual talent, talent without prior track record gets recognition. I do hope that will continue and I think how you successfully continue doing that is going to be key to making Seminar just like the Modern Review was, for that time period—the seminal magazine that we all go back to if we want to understand that period.

I wonder what would it mean for a historical researcher in 2059 to be looking at Seminar. Right now, that person will be very excited, and I hope that just continues...in terms of the way you have your contributions going.

C. RAMMANOHAR REDDY

Two sets of comments, basically on what Ram [Ramachandra Guha] talked about and a continuation of what was said earlier...about the language issue, I don't think any of us is apologetic about publishing in English. It is really two sets of related issues. One is of filtering material that is published in the vernacular, into the English medium. We know that the vernacular media is now extremely vibrant, but we have no clue of what they are discussing or what they are speaking about and therefore, of their politics and their art...and so what we are putting out is very much the production of those who are familiar with English, or forced to be conversant with English. The other side, again, what Kanak was saying about translating...we've thought about it at the *Economic & Political Weekly* (EPW), even tried it, but it's not easy. I think it's very important to translate some of the material we put out into regional languages. Somebody asked me, 'Why don't you translate economic issues in Hindi? Do you know what students read when they want to understand these issues? They read *Yojana*.' Yojana is a Government of India publication...this brings me to the other pressures of being a cottage industry.

It's fantastic to be a cottage industry, but it brings the question of survival with it. You have to start looking at numbers, there are long spells where the publication would be a labour of love, born of self-denial, and ruthless cost cutting, which Seminar has done and so has the EPW. But how long do we go on? There's also the issue of philanthropy. In recent years, if it weren't for two large grants by two Trusts, we would be in real trouble at the EPW. You have to think of how philanthropy can support our publications. We are always tethering towards collapse...and therefore, we can't take initiatives such as the one being discussed about language.

MALVIKA SINGH

I think we need to collectively get the corporate sector, particularly, at this juncture in our life as a nation, to accept the fact that they have to advertise and take seriously, journals and magazines such as ours...we need people like Guzders, Raos and the 'Ninans' of the world to actually push that agenda for us. Because even they need...all our disciplines, all our professions need something that triggers new ideas in different realms. The two generations are actually meeting now, and we've got a lot of young people...we need to evolve further with the corporate sector involved, to support ventures like ours. That way we will not die a natural death or have to take grants which we do not want to take because they come with agendas... our cottage industry journals represent a kind of exchange where you come, meet people and exchange ideas—that's the luxury for us and that's what we treasure.

RUDRANGSHU MUKHERJEE

A quick rider to what Ram and Malvika said...I think the point is very important because if we look at the Bengali journals of reformers, none had the longevity, none lasted half a century. We need to seriously think about this: how do we survive as a cottage industry? How does the EPW or Seminar continue as a cottage industry? Remaining as it is, improving its standard of quality, but not going to sources of funding which have an agenda or conditions attached to it, as Malvika mentioned.

SUNIL KHILNANI

I think this idea of Seminar being, in a way, the intellectual ghost of the political class seems to be a very correct one. I think that is what it has been: this haunting of ideas that have gone behind the political class.

However, the notion of cognitive justice is powerful but potentially dangerous, because, the idea that all these 'different ways of life' should be included is correct, but there are judgements to be made between them...cognitive justice does not simply mean recognising every single way of life as equivalent. I think we do need to evaluate them...and that business—of judging, evaluating, assessing, and to call things by what they are—that is what journals of ideas and politics must do.

On the issue of numbers and the reach of journals like Seminar or the EPW: I think you do need to reach out just for the efficacy of the ideas, especially, since these are journals of politics and ideas of the present, and not literary journals. Linked to that, yes, these journals should have a higher profile, a larger role. The question is: how is that done?

The crisis of funding this kind of work is not only within India, it's worldwide. It's already hit many of the newspapers and journals, across the world. Philanthropy is one way, but it is at the end of the day a generosity and may I say, the whim of the giver. It's not accountable. It's not necessarily continuous. There has to be some way of institutionalising this.

About anthologies and generating more out of Seminar, that's a good idea...but one of the things I think is totally lacking is any account of the history of our intellectual life over the last sixty years. I think a very interesting volume would be one on the history of small journals over the last sixty years, beyond 1947; to do a study of the *Himmat* or the EPW, and see the conditions of success and failure and reach and so on.

HAMEED HAROON

I think that my instinct as a publisher working with a rather diverse group, is that philanthropy is not the answer because to have to ask, at a certain level, is to lose. I have watched what has been happening in the Indian print media over the last twenty years, with a particular amount of horror. I have seen newspapers with a lot of integrity, absolutely subordinated to commercial interest. I once wrote a piece in Seminar as to how the print media is beginning to subordinate itself, rather than insulating itself from commercial interests.

We have to accept an esoteric definition of what constitutes 'style' in a particular high quality periodical, some of the inessentials will have to be changed, and there has to be a more vigorous market process. I don't mean Adam Smith's invisible hand. But, there has to be some new way of conceding how the survival of such quality periodicals and journals can continue, and it's a South Asian phenomenon, not just an Indian phenomenon.

Some entail higher cost and some don't, but actually the problem is not of cost. The shoestring budget must be relative to what you produce. Also, tying quality journals irretrievably to the printed word is a bad idea. The problem lies in the printed word: the obstacles to it being accepted and being allowed to move across borders.

For example, in the case of India's quality journals, if an amalgamation was possible across borders, then we are speaking of larger numbers, and numbers are not irrelevant. You can define your reach in terms of the quality of people or the spread of people you want to reach, but you can't be against a quality journal serving larger numbers, simply because larger numbers are interested in it. Larger numbers would probably fulfill the purpose for which you established yourself and that is not to be an esoteric index of ideas only, but also to be an index of ideas that can cause a change and a transformation in larger thinking attitudes. This is possible if you think of a marketplace of ideas that is South Asian in nature rather than just specific to India.

I also think it needs to go on the web. There needs to be a distribution of workloads. There has to be of retention of titles, in a collective sense. You need to create a larger programming structure in which you survive, within which it becomes feasible for advertisers, rather than philanthropists, to think of you as a viable unit.

You need to change technology, remove this aversion to numbers, and shed the reluctance to exclusivise the printed word as the main communication domain, and to confront the visual image in the printed form; for example, a visual video diary done of Shyam Benegal, just his personal feelings or his personal impressions, three or four times a year, there would be a tremendous response...all this opens the way for new methods of response without directly compromising your ideology.

But more important, there are other sub-methods contained. Why not subsume the blogging method? Like you are blogging right now, in one sense. If all of us are sitting here and tolerating it, we must find it interesting. Surely more like us, would find it interesting. A revision of the technology and the economics of quality journals without compromising the essential posture, but indeed by extending their reach and allowing the collective umbrella to collect advertising could lead to the kind of reform that you are talking about.

AMITA BAVISKAR

A small suggestion about Ram's idea of thematic anthologies with the other one of Ram's comments, about the need and the thirst for social science material in other languages: I wonder whether that could be a moneymaking idea. Given that there is a need for books that discuss communalism or climate change, and environmental issues, perhaps those selected articles from past issues of Seminar could be translated and sold as regular books and as readers for students.

HARSH SETHI

I'm a little intrigued. Of course, things can be better marketed, there can be better ways to raise money, but we need to get back to some of the core questions. What makes something valuable? Why does it have resonance? Since we are a club of a certain kind, do we see the limits of the kind of resonance that our intellectual products create? If one wants to link the production of ideas, in any concrete setting, to the kind of democracy that Shiv was talking about, then it's important to be able to transcend the limited exercises that we do...it's within that context, that the issue of language was raised.

The issue of language was being used as a metaphor, in terms of the number of different worlds that we are able to successfully interact with or appreciate, and much was made about the fact that there is a lot of speaking and writing, but there is inadequate hearing; and unless there is sufficient hearing, you are not going to get the resonance that you need, either for sustainability or for change. The demand on something like the EPW or Seminar, again to use them as metaphors, is more than being able to capture the angst of the time and rather to be able to speak of the time. We were talking about the creation of public institutions, contributing to cultures of public reasoning and public debate...is it that products of this kind contribute to the creation of that public culture?

SHIV VISVANATHAN

A group of tribals from Gujarat sought us out to develop of a new idea for them, in the Constitution. It was a demand for a wider theatre of judgement, because many of these tribes and nomads disappear before they can make that judgement. There is both a theory of knowledge and a theory of power in it. I think it does demand judgement, but the plurality of judgements involved, and the nature of contestation makes knowledge a very simple part of it. That's why they asked that the idea of cognitive justice be built into the directive principles of the Constitution. Some of the tribal leaders make the most fascinating statements on the Constitution.

Secondly, I'm surprised that so much time was spent on publishing and so little on the idea that editing Seminar was a great act of fun. The beauty of watching three of them work for ten years was to see the creativity of play and the tolerance of how the group worked. It was a miracle. You can't think of three more egotistic people. The synergy was superb. You can't turn it into a technological solution.

MALVIKA SINGH

There was no methodology. We just learnt to respect each other. We were responsible to bring Seminar out. Nobody said, you back off, I back off, it just happened. I was a complete novice at this, I just happened to be an inheritor. But, we built it. We managed to carry it. We learnt on the job. I think that you can have a lot of money, but the whole thing will die a natural death if you didn't have the passion.

RAMACHANDRA GUHA

There are two key issues of quality and reach. Clearly the EPW and Seminar are providing something much more reflective and insightful. I hope that Seminar continues to be read by people who are influential. Like when Ninan reads it and the ideas are communicated to his reporters, his editors, through his newspaper...

Yes, you also have to reach across languages. My thesis is that the Indian intellectual culture was genuinely bilingual and now it is becoming monolingual. Bangladesh and Nepal were exceptions. We have a separation of discourses and we face a genuine problem.

Seminar as an intellectual ghost of the political class, I think, is a fascinating insight. There is a long tradition of thinker-activists in India...the people who made history in India in the last 200 years, also wrote most interestingly about it. That tradition seems to have died. It is true that democracies are founded by visionaries and run mid-career by mediocrities. But, if we think about it, Seminar stepped in when that tradition died and in that sense, it is the intellectual ghost of the political class.

III

"...perhaps Nepal's experience also relates to the experiences of smaller regions of India: in times of incredible turmoil and times of change, there has been nobody to hold up a mirror to it all. Some level of analysis is required. A point that I thought I should make is that the absence of a publication like *Seminar* in the national realm of Nepal, impacts our evolution. We are out here writing a Constitution, we have a very wide and elected Constituent Assembly that represents all the ethnicities and regions, but the depth certainly is lacking."

KANAK MANI DIXIT

"...there's something about the printed word that encourages a certain kind of reflection and thought whereas television and the audio-visual world speak to the senses in a different way. These different modes of appeal are also complicated by the political economy of the media: the insertion of advertising—'we'll come back to this after the break'—breeds a lack of depth and reduces attention spans."

AMITA BAVISKAR

"It's interesting to go to Al Gore's book *Assault on Reason* and its chapter on 'The Politics of Wealth'. Most of the writing on corruption we have is almost overshadowed by what he's said on how wealth in a way has controlled media, controlled the information available, and diminished people's capacity to reason and make judgements...this is what should be a source of worry."

KAMAL HOSSAIN

"What was interesting through this entire journey was that you saw India in its totality, all Indians saw India in its totality. But in the last fifteen years, this has suddenly changed and it has changed in such a dramatic way that today, there is no rural India in cinema. You can't see village India, particularly in Hindi cinema, which determines the kind of films being made in all other languages. I cannot understand how we can afford suddenly to forget that there is a rural India and make it just fall off the map."

SHYAM BENEGAL

"...a lot of film content is actually being driven by an imagined NRI (Non-Resident Indian) community. As far as rural India is concerned, I am a little less worried because *Sholay*, for instance, presented a very romanticised rural India. *Jab We Met* has a little bit of rural India, extremely romanticised, artificial and unreal. The problem I have with Hindi movies is they always show the trader as an evil person who is exploiting the Indian poor. Kind of creating an anti-market sentiment in keeping with the prevalent ideological fashions of the 50s and the 60s. The trouble is that in the 1990s, in moving towards the defence of regular free markets, we seem to have jumped to crony capitalism."

JAITHIRTH RAO

"The middle class is concerned much more with itself —protecting its privileges and aspiring for more. Economic liberalisation has not only empowered this class but created a sense of entitlement: we are here by virtue of our merit, we deserve to be here; other people who have failed to climb the social ladder are morally or psychically inadequate."

AMITA BAVISKAR

"Four acronyms that you need to look at when you talk of changing the public sphere. The RTI or Right to Information Act is a major development. It's changing the face of democracy. The second is the PRI or Panchayati Raj Institutions, what with funding going straight to PRIs and women getting reservations. The third is the PIL or public interest litigation...fourth is CSR or corporate social responsibility. That's the emerging area."

SALMAN KHURSHID

"...since the 1990s, the judiciary has not just become simply indifferent, but actively antagonistic to the concerns of the urban poor. We have a Judge of the High Court who ignores the state's

utter mismanagement of urban land, and its failure to facilitate the construction of low income housing, who proclaims that resettling an evicted squatter at government expense is like rewarding a pickpocket. Penalising the poor for a predicament forced upon them by the state is a travesty of the original impetus behind Public Interest Litigation: to expand the scope of justice to include the poorest and most vulnerable citizens to whom justice had been denied. Yet, ironically, the judiciary does not seem to be aware of this profound shift in its orientation."

AMITA BAVISKAR

"What Amita said about middle class attitudes and media attitudes towards slum-dwellers and path-dwellers is striking and disturbing...one of the examples of this is the environmental movement in India. Amita and I became scholars because of the journalistic influence on us. Every newspaper had an environment correspondent. Have they been re-designated as stock market correspondents?"

RAMACHANDRA GUHA

"...when martial law was the most severe in Pakistan, that was when the press was the most read and most powerful. That was the time people read between the lines and expressed opinions. Democracy has seemed to create a kind of apolitical callousness among the media as a watchdog...unfortunately, there's a strange paradoxical result that increasing democracy offers even less protection to the media from intervention, from corporate interests and arbitrary government action."

HAMEED HAROON

"Looking back at more than sixty years of independence ...electoral democracy, no military interventions, you can congratulate yourself on that...India has gone way ahead in political and economic change but it is the redistributive part, the social justice part, which needs serious questioning. And serious questioning itself is a maturing of democracy.
So, I will ask the Indian Institute of Advanced Study and Seminar—tell us how the democratic processes can be made to deliver. It's the critical intellect, the critical engagement with reality that Seminar has provided a forum for: a forum to get people who are intellectually sophisticated to relate to the reality that calls for change."

KAMAL HOSSAIN

I feel Seminar has South Asia as a sensibility. It may be a publication out of Delhi, but in sensibility, if you were to understand South Asia as a positive term, then I think Seminar is a South Asian publication.

South Asian Publication

KANAK MANI DIXIT

Let me speak firstly as a Nepali and then as a 'South Asian'. I'd like to address the issue of where *Seminar* would have been in a country like Nepal or in the larger region of South Asia. Simply put, Nepal has gone through a telescoped experience, in the last twelve years. Look at the rise of the Maoists, the mass murder in the royal palace in 2001, the rise of state brutality in response to Maoist brutality, the kind of ethnic identity politics, and the kind of plains *versus* hills politics; these issues have come to a head in Nepal, but, without a magazine such as Seminar to put some meaning to it. The fact is that in the vernacular, in Nepali language or any of the languages in Nepal, or even in English, there is an inability to contextualise for the intelligentsia and then, to reach out to the larger realm.

I believe that, although, I am speaking of Nepal as a microcosm, it is a small country that can be related to a state like Assam, Balochistan or Sindh. India as a whole is a subcontinent and it's hardly even a country because there are so many variables.

I think, perhaps Nepal's experience also relates to the experiences of smaller regions of India: in times of incredible turmoil and times of change, there has been nobody to hold up a mirror to it all. Some level of analysis is required. A point that I thought I should make is that the absence of a publication like Seminar in the national realm of Nepal, impacts our evolution. We are out here writing a Constitution, we have a very wide and elected Constituent Assembly that represents all the ethnicities and regions, but the depth certainly is lacking. Even the very members of the Constituent Assembly would agree. Why is it lacking? I go back to the point that there has been an absence of a medium. There are various reasons for this, historical and otherwise. But, this is a fact.

Talking about South Asia, and I feel we need to think of South Asia as more than a region of eight countries, as defined by South Asian Association for Regional Cooperation (SAARC), and perhaps add Burma and Tibet to it; if you look at the penumbra of this region you will not get a proper sense of what 'South Asia' means.

South Asia would be, in my definition, more of a sensibility, so there is no 'ultra' of anything in it, especially 'ultra nationalism', and when you are not ultra-nationalistic and centralised, then you look more to the regions and the local.
So, in an incongruous way, what South Asia means while trying to be regional is actually trying to be more localised, whether it is the federal or local government. I feel Seminar has South Asia as a sensibility. It may be a publication out of Delhi, but in sensibility, if you were to understand South Asia as a positive term, then I think Seminar is a South Asian publication.

Now let's move away from Seminar the magazine into the society, which is where Seminar as a publication functions and hopes to function. What are the changes that have overtaken society? What changes do we see up ahead for a publication like Seminar to try to cover?

When a corporate entity makes a film, it is not really interested in what you wish to make, but in what those films should look like, something like a material aspiration of young people in the country. This material aspiration of young people determines everything, and the process of a globalisation acts as a catalyst.

Cinemascope

SHYAM BENEGAL

My connection with *Seminar* is rather slim and tenuous. Romesh Thapar wrote me a letter, asking if I would like to write an article on the changing trends in cinema in the '70s. It was then that I also happened to subscribe to the magazine and read it for perhaps a year or two, before my subscription ended.

I know a lot about Malvika. She's been a wonderful host and runs a great salon. When she invited my wife and myself to this seminar, I expected a kind of salon and in some ways, it has been. Well, let me cut all this short and go to my real concern. I'd like to put forth my own concerns about what is happening in the world of cinema and television, today.

My real concern is Indian cinema, now over a hundred years old, and I'd like to discuss it in terms of the dominant discourse in the Hindi language because it influences the cinemas of the country in all the other languages. One of the major problems is that a great deal of diversity and plurality in our films is fast disappearing. Hindi cinema got caught up in the nationalist movement when it started, even before India became independent, and what was interesting about that time was that nationalism played some part, symbolically or otherwise, in our films. Since India was largely seen as an agrarian country, rural India was always central to our narrative concerns.

After independence, our cinema has evolved into a certain kind of form. South Asian cinema, generally, has a very specific form that is very different from the cinemas of the rest of the world. This means that it's not easy to create genres of our cinema because our films need to have a kind of entertainment that gets everybody into the theaters. It has to cater to a general taste and that has made our films the way they became—a narrative with songs and dances. But, this style is part of a long tradition of entertainment in our country that goes back to classical and folk performing arts traditions, according to which your aesthetics and satisfaction are supposed to come from the blend of nine essences of emotions or *Navras*. Navras is a very crucial part of our entertainment. Cinema just automatically took that form and developed it...but it has become very easily formulaic and we carried this as a baggage of our films, until India became independent.

There was a school of thought, particularly during the early years of Indian Independence, that said we have to think about the poor state of affairs of the Indian cinema, and the usual refrain was that the 'kind of films they make don't seem to have any connection with reality'. All that culminated in a committee being formed under the chairmanship of S.K. Patil. They looked into all aspects of films, even financing...don't forget that cinema was not considered an industry until 2001.

Even when we became the largest film industry in the world, we couldn't raise finances from legitimate financial institutions like banks. It had to be through moneylenders, financing at all kinds of rates of interests. This caused a boom and bust situation, constantly. So, when the Patil report came, the Government of India thought of having a Film Finance Corporation funded by it. The Corporation was meant to be an autonomous entity. Some films were produced by the Corporation, but that was not enough. Obviously, when you are producing something like around 900 films a year, if you are going to support 5 or 10 films, it is not going to make any kind of a lasting impact.

Then, concerns were raised on how Indian films are not professionally made, and you need to have people who are properly trained in the art and science of filmmaking. It was, therefore, decided to have a film institute. So the National Film Institute was formed in 1960-61. There was a Children's Film Society, too.

There was also a statist view that cinema should be an instrument of social change. This remains the statist view today, as well. It means that everybody recognises that films are very important for the society. There is a place for cinema in society because it is very influential and so, something has to be done about it.

In the 1950s when Satyajit Ray made *Pather Panchali*, it was suddenly recognised that this is what cinema should be like. When Indira Gandhi became the Information and Broadcasting Minister, she felt it necessary to keep stating that this was the kind of cinema that India should be producing. Suddenly, Ray was seen as the person who would show a new direction to Indian cinema, even though, his films were in Bengali, and hardly shown anywhere else in India, except at film festivals. Only after he died were all his films shown on Indian television. For the first time, all of India saw Satyajit Ray's films. For all those many years that he made films, he was known but never seen, except in Bengal—so people only knew him as a name.

By the early 1970s, when the first graduates came out of the film institute, they wanted to break away from the kind of cinema that was being produced. I wasn't trained at the Film Institute, but I was also one of those people who thought of making different films. You cannot be caught in this kind of filmmaking that is like a procrustean bed; if you thought about making a film in Hindi, you had to design your subject and narrative in a particular format and setup. One had to breakaway from it. So, the 70s became a decade when suddenly something called the 'New Cinema' or 'Parallel Cinema' movement started. It was a rather silly way of saying that this was 'commercial' cinema and that was 'parallel'. One could never understand what it meant because all films are meant to be commercial anyway, one needs to cover the costs of making it.

What was interesting through this entire journey was that you saw India in its totality, all Indians saw India in its totality. But in the last fifteen years, this has suddenly changed and it has changed in such a dramatic way that today, there is no rural India in cinema. You can't see village India, particularly in Hindi cinema, which determines the kind of films being made in all other languages. I cannot understand how we can afford suddenly to forget that there is a rural India and make it just fall off the map.

This has happened in television, too. You will still be able to see rural India only in the very local channels. What are the reasons for this? Who is determining this? Is it the filmmaker or television channel producers who are determining this? Is it the market determining this?

After independence, our cinema has evolved into a certain kind of form. South Asian cinema, generally, has a very specific form that is very different from the cinemas of the rest of the world. This means that it's not easy to create genres of our cinema because our films need to have a kind of entertainment that gets everybody into the theaters.

Ultimately, this is being determined by the market place, by the consumer industries, by people who are sponsoring and who are advertising. In television, certainly, it is the people who are advertising and who are sponsoring. Everything is determined by Target Rating Points (TRPs), and they are determining the kind of programmes you are going to create, whether you like it or not. It is one of those terrible problems that television is trapped with.

Well, you cannot just sit there and say that the government should help. How is the government going to help in a situation like this? Television business is enormous and it has to be funded. It's being funded privately, which is a brilliant thing. But who is financing all that? It's the sponsor. And sponsorship means you have people who have things to sell, who wish to advertise, who take up your programmes and determine how your programmes should be made on the basis of who's watching them, where it's being watched and so on. The focus is on having your films or television programmes being seen by people who have a disposable income.

The other thing is that the content itself derives from creating characters that are a part of this scheme. Firstly, any Hindi film you look at, today, you will find that they are setting fashions for metropolitan cities, for the 'A' class towns. Secondly, the kind of cars that they travel in...ten years ago when you talked about a car, you didn't worry about which model of the car. Today, if I'm making a film there is a pressure on me to show my hero traveling in a BMW or a Ferrari. These are the people who are supporting the film.

This whole thing has turned everything on its head so that village India has gone. People who cannot buy products and services are gone. They are not your concern anymore. Your world is of a particular kind that prevents you from looking outside of that. This, I fear, is what has overtaken us. This is the problem that we are going to face.

I decided a couple of years ago, that it was important even for me to revisit a village. I had to work out a whole lot of strategies in order to reintroduce our Indian village to our audiences. I made a film called *Welcome to Sajjanpur*, but I had to do it essentially as a comedy. How else am I going to gain the attention of an urban audience? Who is this urban audience I am talking about? I am talking about people who go to multiplexes because that's where the money is: one person seeing your film pays you ₹ 250 per ticket. That's the manner in which the film business has turned, ever since we became an industry and the financing went into the hands of corporates. Today, there are about six or seven corporate entities that finance most of the films. When a corporate entity makes a film, it is not really interested in what you wish to make, but in what those films should look like, something like a material aspiration of young people in the country. This material aspiration of young people determines everything, and the process of a globalisation acts as a catalyst.

I don't wish to see this only as a matter of criticism because it has also helped a lot of young filmmakers to come into the business. They would have never been able to do this, twenty years ago. In fact, from the time we started making films in the 1970s, there were generations of filmmakers who lost out altogether because they had no such opportunities. This is the plus side, and these are the forces that are at play all the time. Maybe there can be some more discussion on the issue.

Perhaps in the aspirations of people in small towns, in the aspirations of young people in rural areas, we might see the emergence of new practices and, hence, new kinds of public spheres.

Shrinking Public Sphere

AMITA BAVISKAR

We have been discussing the importance of ideas and intellectual debate in shaping public life and transforming the world, and have noted how there has been a qualitative decline in this sphere. Ideas that stretch the limits of our social imagination, ideas that challenge and stimulate, ideas discussed vigorously yet respectfully by ever-larger circles of participants—such ideas and debates seem to be scarce now. Sunil Khilnani pointed out that, unlike during the period of nationalist struggle, the world now no longer looks to India for inspiration when it comes to ideas that can radically revise their sense of justice or how to secure it. Ram Guha spoke about the importance of tracing the history of ideas through biographies of intellectual figures and lamented how Indian scholarship suffers from a major lack in this area. It is appropriate that we are having this conversation at the fiftieth anniversary of *Seminar*, a journal that, together with the *Economic and Political Weekly* (EPW), is the closest thing we have to a living archive of ideas and debates about social issues in post-independent India. Like other forms of print capitalism, to use Benedict Anderson's phrase, a journal like Seminar has created 'an imagined community' of readers, who through the debates on its pages are able to see themselves anew as part of a thinking and acting collectivity. Not only does this community constitute a public sphere by itself, but also, by bringing in debates within more specialised circles of people involved in different aspects of public life, it reflects a wider public sphere that exists beyond this immediate readership.

We have mainly been talking about ideas as texts, as words on paper to be read and reflected upon, to be inspired by. However, in South Asia, the world of ideas has an existence beyond and even apart from the written word. The biggest political ideas that touched the largest number of people and transformed their lives in unimaginable ways were large, precisely because they were not limited to literate audiences. Of course, the greatest example of that is Mahatma Gandhi, for whom writing was a constant accompaniment to action, to ideas conveyed directly through a different set of practices:

There's a difference between the era when Seminar started and the times we live in now. It's the way in which the idea of a bourgeois public sphere—indisputably elite, English-speaking, upper-caste, male-dominated—nevertheless contained a commitment to a more inclusive notion of public interest, however imperfectly realised or fitfully pursued.

spinning *khadi*, making salt, cleaning latrines, going to jail, or *Satyagraha*. These were practices that knit together communities, not through words but through practices that were culturally resonant, yet politically transformative. Gandhi's embodied politics reminds us that social change does not simply flow from great ideas, but depends on how they are translated into actions, and that actions that ignite the world can do so without needing the written word to give them legitimacy. It is, therefore, important to celebrate Seminar as a significant element, but, nonetheless, only one element within a public sphere that is much wider than the world of words and extends beyond, into the realm of embodied practices. The issue before us, then, is larger than the decline in a public sphere of rational discussion and intellectual debate; it is about the decline in an embodied public sphere of ideas in action, ideas like democracy, freedom and justice.

In my research on environmental politics in urban India, I have been following how the idea of the public sphere as embodied in a set of spatial practices has been narrowed down since the 1990s when economic liberalisation began. This is reflected in the attitude of the upper courts that in the late 1970s and 1980s, employed the concept of public interest to address the concerns of a number of social groups who were excluded from the public sphere. The *Olga Tellis* judgement, protecting the right of pavement dwellers in Mumbai to live close to their places of livelihood, is a leading example of such judicial activism on behalf of the poor. However, since the 1990s, the judiciary has not just become simply indifferent, but actively antagonistic to the concerns of the urban poor. We have a Judge of the High Court who ignores the state's utter mismanagement of urban land, and its failure to facilitate the construction of low income housing, who proclaims that resettling an evicted squatter at government expense is like rewarding a pickpocket. Penalising the poor for a predicament forced upon them by the state is a travesty of the original impetus behind Public Interest Litigation: to expand the scope of justice to include the poorest and most vulnerable citizens to whom justice had been denied.

Yet, ironically, the judiciary does not seem to be aware of this profound shift in its orientation. It continues to regard its orders and decisions as defending the public interest—for instance, by enforcing anti-pollution laws—despite compelling evidence that the burden of such orders falls disproportionately on the poor, even though they are not responsible for creating the problem being addressed. The project of making Delhi 'clean and green' by forcing hundreds of thousands of people out of work and by demolishing the homes of more than a quarter million people is based on a narrowed conception of the 'public' being served. Clearly, those losing their homes and livelihoods have been squeezed out of the judicial conception of the public.

The shrinking of the public sphere is visible on the streets of Indian cities. The roads in our metros and towns have come to be ruled by cars and other private motorised vehicles. The interests of private vehicle owners—the richer, more powerful section of society—predominantly drive the direction of street planning, at the expense of public transit users, cyclists and pedestrians. In Delhi, for instance, forty-two flyovers were built across major intersections in time for the Commonwealth Games in 2010. Flyovers allow motorised vehicles to zoom ahead but are useless for bicyclists and rickshaws, and they force bus commuters to walk long distances to change buses. Pavements have been narrowed to create more road and parking space, so pedestrians have a tougher time. The parallel lanes that were originally designed for bicycles—for instance, all along the Ring Road—have now been taken over by motorised traffic. 'If the roads are crowded, build more roads.' This simple supply-side solution has overwhelmingly prevailed over the more sustainable strategy of regulating private vehicles and investing in road-based mass transit systems.

This privileging of private motor vehicles in the traffic of public flow reflects our urban planners' elitist priorities and their conviction that the vibrant spaces of Indian cities where diverse peoples and activities are accommodated—pedestrians, vendors, rickshaws—have no place in a 'world class' city. The presence of the poor is now not to be tolerated, not only on city streets but in the city itself. The apartheid style evictions from the city and segregated settlements on its outskirts testify to this spatial reconfiguration. It is telling that the media coverage of these kinds of issues has also decreased dramatically. The demolition of working class settlements in Delhi over the last eight years has affected thirty to forty lakh people, yet there has been a near total media silence on the issue. This reflects a sea change in the role of the media in constituting a public sphere: if there was a sense of responsibility earlier about representing the newly independent nation's citizens, the primary task now seems to be to deliver potential customers to advertisers, a transaction where the poor don't figure at all.

There's a difference between the era when Seminar started and the times we live in now. It's the way in which the idea of a bourgeois public sphere—indisputably elite, English-speaking, upper-caste, male-dominated—nevertheless contained a commitment to a more inclusive notion of public interest, however imperfectly realised or fitfully pursued. On the pages of newspapers, on university campuses, even in upper middle class drawing rooms, conversations extended beyond the direct concerns of those participating to include the subject of *Dalits*, women being burnt for dowry, undertrials who had been held for years without ever appearing before a magistrate and so on. There was a discernible Left liberal culture that prescribed that the intelligentsia care about these things and take a stand.

We now have a paradoxical situation in that the bourgeois public sphere has expanded to include new upwardly mobile entrants from non-metropolitan, Hindi, Tamil or Gujarati-speaking, OBC (Other Backward Classes) caste backgrounds and yet, despite its increased size and social diversification, the middle class's conception of the public sphere has shrunk. The middle class is concerned much more with itself—protecting its privileges and aspiring for more. Economic liberalisation has not only empowered this class but created a sense of entitlement: we are here by virtue of our merit, we deserve to be here; other people who have failed to climb the social ladder are morally or psychically inadequate. Thus, even when the middle class expresses public concern, as it has in the last couple of years about corruption and crime, its preoccupation is with how it affects 'people like us'. By a self-serving sleight of hand, the *aam aadmi* (everyman) has been conjured up in middle-class garb. His chief concerns are *bijli, sadak* and *paani* (electricity, roads and water supply), not *roti, kapda aur makaan* (food, clothing and shelter)—the essentials for bare subsistence that millions of Indians still struggle to get. The activism of the post-liberalisation middle class rarely extends beyond its own concerns. Of course, its pursuit of those concerns may also benefit society at large, but that is not a specific goal of such activism. And since middle-class political demands take attention away from the desperate needs of the poor, and are even hostile to them, such mobilisations of the public sphere tend to be exclusionary and oppressive.
There is, therefore, a shrinking of the political imagination: the social world is becoming larger, but the ways to understand that world and to be concerned about it, have shrunk.

This change is partly related to economic liberalisation and the mindset it creates, and the kind of changes in consciousness it promotes. But it is also technological—there's something about the printed word that encourages a certain kind of reflection and thought whereas television and the audio-visual world speak to the senses in a different way. These different modes of appeal are also complicated by the political economy of the media: the insertion of advertising—'we'll come back to this after the break'—breeds a lack of depth and reduces attention spans. The peculiar public sphere that news television spawns is something that analysts like Sevanti Ninan have written insightfully about; the rest of us need to think much more about it, also in terms of how to transform it.

The hope for India lies in the fact that there are multiple public spheres jostling against each other: bourgeois, communal, casteist, patriarchal, and hyper nationalist groups do not have hegemonic power and they must contend with considerable opposition from those they seek to marginalise and exploit. There is so much happening across the country, be it the fight against displacement by large industrial projects, the campaign for the Right to Food, Dalit assertion, Maoist war. All of these, in different ways, direct our attention to the larger question of democracy and justice, forcing the bourgeois public sphere to respond.

The shrinking of the public sphere is visible on the streets of Indian cities. The roads in our metros and towns have come to be ruled by cars and other private motorised vehicles. The interests of private vehicle owners—the richer, more powerful section of society —predominantly drive the direction of street planning, at the expense of public transit users, cyclists and pedestrians.

Change is also often the outcome of unexpected conjunctures. For instance, the corporate world's interest in rural India is motivated by tapping the buying power of people in small towns and villages: the fortune at the bottom of the pyramid. The new modes of consumption that they encourage have redefined social identities and social practices: using sanitary napkins can enable girls to go out of the house, owning a mobile phone can equalise access to communication.

So perhaps in the aspirations of people in small towns, in the aspirations of young people in rural areas, we might see the emergence of new practices and, hence, new kinds of public spheres. They might not always be public spheres that meet our notions of what is progressive and proper. They might be deeply offensive, and they might directly attack the values that we hold dear. But the fact that there is that vibrancy, and that there is that possibility, creates an excitement as well as hope for the future that I think and hope Seminar will be a part of.

Discussion

Point, Counterpoint

NAYANTARA SAHGAL

I want Shyam to share his experience about a film that he had to abandon because of corporate influence.

SHYAM BENEGAL

It's a story about a young woman Noor Inayat Khan, who became a British spy in the Second World War. Inspired by the book, *Spy Princess: The Life of Noor Inayat Khan* written by Shrabani Basu, Lord Meghnad Desai and his wife went about writing the script. Of course, I was a part of the process because I was very keen to make the film. I wanted the story to be centred on Noor's world which was essentially both Indian and European. The Indian sensibility of it attracted me to the story. Here was someone who was a pacifist, who was born in a Sufi family, became a British spy for the S.O.E (Special Operations Executive), which was a very cynical organisation designed to find out how the Gestapo operated, and they sent these people without them realising that they would be caught within a matter of a couple of weeks and killed. The longest any person lasted before going into France was seven weeks. But Noor eventually lasted more than a year, before she was caught and killed.

I couldn't raise the money in India, largely because they felt that it wouldn't make enough money. The British Production Company decided to make this film, but the most important thing for them was that it had to become a regular British wartime spy story; not the extraordinary story of Noor's father, Inayat Khan, being the first Indian musician who goes out of India in 1909, as a *dhrupad* singer and a *sitar* player and finds that the only way he can make a career is as a court musician for Czar Nicholas II. The Russian Revolution happens and he leaves his family and comes back to his little village in Agra. And Noor, his daughter, is imbibing all these values...it was an extraordinary story.

JAITHIRTH RAO

David Dhawan, who is a commercial film director, was telling me that earlier the Bollywood directors would look for the first two weeks of box office. Now they look at London and New Jersey box office collections, just as much. Therefore, a whole set of scripts are being romanticised, almost falsified to fit a non-resident Indian's (NRI's) imagined sensibility of India, and a lot of film content is actually being driven by an imagined NRI community. As far as rural India is concerned, I am a little less worried because *Sholay*, for instance, presented a very romanticised rural India. *Jab We Met* has a little bit of rural India, extremely romanticised, artificial and unreal. The problem I have with Hindi movies is they always show the trader as an evil person who is exploiting the Indian poor. Kind of creating an anti-market sentiment in keeping with the prevalent ideological fashions of the '50s and the '60s. The trouble is that in the 1990s, in moving towards the defence of regular free markets, we seem to have jumped to crony capitalism.

SHYAM BENEGAL

The perfect example for what you are saying is a film called *Guru*. What does Guru do? What is the moral stance in that film? As long as you can get away with murder, you are okay. As long as you can get away with any kind of scam, you are fine. That is again the other aspect of what is happening. On the one hand, it is becoming urban centric, on the other hand there is a total disappearance of any social consciousness or morality. It is this disappearance that worries me, because the largest audience in this country, ninety per cent, is under thirty-five years of age. We are the youngest country in the world. All of us who are making films—what are we doing? What are we telling them? We know that cinema has a great amount of influence. I am not saying we should sit here moralising, though this was the attitude at one time. There is also a tradition in the Indian performing arts, it goes back to Sanskrit drama, even if you have a tragedy, it's not like the Greek tragedy: you are never left without hope. There's always a sense of hope somewhere, but the disappearance of that is worrisome.

RAMACHANDRA GUHA

What Amita said about middle class attitudes and media attitudes towards slum-dwellers and path-dwellers is striking and disturbing...one of the examples of this is the environmental movement in India. Amita and I became scholars because of the journalistic influence on us. Every newspaper had an environment correspondent. Have they been re-designated as stock market correspondents? Certainly, environment reportage has stopped.

There is a larger issue about the mainstream media abdicating its role...hence, Seminar and the *Economic and Political Weekly* (EPW) become that much more important. However, I have one minor disagreement with Amita. You are talking about environmental issues, livelihood, and housing issues...I think television is marginally better than the print media. Television houses are individually controlled, anchors have large stakes and there's a visual aspect to showing environmental degradation which is more vivid. The other point is that we have not discussed the Internet, the emerging public sphere. Are these issues being discussed in cyber space?

AMITA BAVISKAR

I agree with your point of view, but the news channels that have proliferated in the last few years have caused problems in terms of content, they are repeating themselves. I often tell young reporters about the stories they can do, various ways of covering them in interesting ways. There is a lot of creative energy among young journalists. These are potentials.

The Internet I did not touch upon because it always gets hyped—the issues of access are still seriously daunting. Within that limited sphere, journals like Seminar could become more interactive. For example, I don't think that at the moment people can post comments, can they?

C. RAMMANOHAR REDDY

We thought blogs are the new form of interaction, so we opened up articles on the Internet for comments. In eighteen months, we got around fifteen comments. Our readers are not the kind who would comment, or maybe it's also how we put it across. It's not an easy thing to say, let's open it up, get some discussion going. So much so, we pulled it out. Now we are rethinking it.

PETER deSOUZA

There's a comparative dimension to our discussion and I'd like to bring in viewpoints about Bangladesh, as an outside observer, with all the risks and limitations involved. There is an increasing vibrancy in the public sphere in that country. You have, for example, an increasing presence of women in the public sphere, there's also a very active youth movement in Bangladesh. The Book Fair is a celebration and huge photographs appear in newspapers of crowds pouring in. Language Day, February 21, is such a major event that every university makes it a point to celebrate it. The growth of this public sphere is actually beginning to act as a bulwark against extremists and fundamentalists.

AMITA BAVISKAR

I would like to clarify that I don't mean to suggest I see the public sphere in India as moving in a different direction than Bangladesh. I would stress that there are multiple public spheres, many of which seem to be expanding and might yield unexpected outcomes. I was basically talking about the bourgeois public sphere and the role of print journalism and print commentary...where do we see a shift?

PETER deSOUZA

Two of the biggest newspapers in Bangladesh are huge, in terms of circulation. Secondly, even the phenomenon of the 'talk show' on television has become a very popular dimension of the print and the electronic. There is an energising of the public sphere in that country in the last 15 years.

HAMEED HAROON

The topic is a complex one...when martial law was the most severe in Pakistan, that was when the press was the most read and most powerful. That was the time people read between the lines and expressed opinions. Democracy has seemed to create a kind of apolitical callousness among the media as a watchdog. Women journalists were born during the Zia-ul-Haq years. They all had very short lifespans, though, but the kind of reporting they did was remarkable. It seems that when autocracy or totalitarianism exists, a kind of counter-model or image is created where society assumes a certain responsibility to refute and fight back.

In Pakistan, there has been a huge growth in television, but the laws of television and press are not equal. The word 'press' is interpreted as print media, and thus, the laws are with respect to the print media. Electronic media journalists are not so well protected.

In some respects, under democracy, the movement towards television and the economic pressures of recession have created a very strange environment where democracy is seen as creating a lower response threshold to illegalities by executives or public institutions, thereby weakening the public sphere, with no one prepared to take up the moral safeguards. Corporations tend to feel that dictatorship and totalitarianism are unstable for the conduct of business or growth, and they feel safer in democracies. Unfortunately, there's a strange paradoxical result that increasing democracy offers even less protection to the media from intervention, from corporate interests and arbitrary government action.

SUNIL KHILNANI

On the potentiality of the Internet for public sphere, the question of access is very important. In India, a very small number of people have the access. But in the long term, everything suggests that the Internet is best for reinforcing the views of people that are already held by them, but it doesn't generate debate or exchange of ideas. It simply creates chat rooms for people...enforcing each other's beliefs. That seems to be the general purpose, far from creating a common public sphere for the exchange of argument and persuasion. Internet in that sense perhaps only helps in closed societies where you don't have other domains.

GOPALKRISHNA GANDHI

The mention about the Book Fair in Bangladesh reminded me of Nirad Chaudhari. In his *Autobiography of an Unknown Indian*, he describes the episode of an earthquake, not the 1934 earthquake that brought everything down in the East, but another earthquake. He describes how he sees the building collapse and loses consciousness. Two days later, he returns to the place. Why? Because he wants to retrieve a book that he had been reading when the earthquake struck, and because it was a library book that he had to return. So, there was this extraordinary book culture in that part of the world. And it still exists in all the towns of West Bengal as in Bangladesh.

I want to refer to another dimension of changing public spheres. There's an extraordinary link between people and the world of business. The fact that dowry deaths are very common was brought back very sharply to me in Kolkata, where there was a self-immolation by a bride who had been placed in that circumstance by references to her complexion. Around the same time, there was a great burst in the advertising of complexion creams. I wrote to a company which was making these and said, 'Look, I am not really concerned about your manufacturing line but there is a social aspect to it. You cannot possibly increase the tensions in the world of dowry demands by what you are doing...this is getting translated into a social problem.'

He wrote to me, 'Gopal *bhai*, Fair and Lovely *nahi karta*, Fair and Handsome *kari chey*.' (Brother Gopal, we can sell 'Fair and Handsome' to men, instead of 'Fair and Lovely' to women.) I wrote back saying that I don't think it makes much of a difference. We are not so foolish to think that advertising a particular bleaching action will only affect men.

Now, Seminar started in 1959, and we prided ourselves in our stand on everything that had to do with South Africa. Advertisements that had to do anything even remotely with South Africa were banned. Consumption of anything from South Africa was unthinkable, so that it was not just a case of government action, but it was a consensus in society. Today, though we are so strongly entrenched in the same world of diplomatic alignments and affiliations, I cannot believe that the inheritors of the same society and political bequests can live with this day in and day out—an advertisement which sells a brand that is meant to elevate a certain form of appearance.

KAMAL HOSSAIN

I'm glad that Peter has shared his impressions of Bangladesh. It is very encouraging to hear something like this, because I don't think it's reported in the media here or anywhere. In fact there are these positive elements of change taking place...with time, things have happened which are a source of inspiration. You talked about South Africa, but what about 1971, which was one of the finest hours in India when you hosted one crore people from Bangladesh and supported our cause for liberation. I still keep meeting people in the interior—ordinary people who relate to you. By people I mean, urban, educated people who are reading newspapers.

In India there are so many counts on which you find that the Indian democracy is working. Criticism is very impressive because it shows that you have developed a capacity for it—finding the shortcomings, deficiencies and the weaknesses in the working of democracy.

The problem is with the upper middle class that feels we are ungrateful because of subsequent changes in the Bangladesh government, peculiar action at the government level.

Looking back at more than sixty years of independence...electoral democracy, no military interventions, you can congratulate yourself on that. Compare our experience. We started on the same journey in 1947 and where has it taken us? India has gone way ahead in political and economic change but it is the redistributive part, the social justice part, which needs serious questioning. And serious questioning itself is a maturing of democracy.

So, I will ask the Indian Institute of Advanced Study and Seminar—tell us how the democratic processes can be made to deliver. It's the critical intellect, the critical engagement with reality that Seminar has provided a forum for: a forum to get people who are intellectually sophisticated to relate to the reality that calls for change.

It's interesting to go to Al Gore's book *Assault on Reason* and the chapter on 'The Politics of Wealth'. Most of the writing on corruption we have is almost overshadowed by what he's said on how wealth in a way has controlled media, controlled the information available, and diminished people's capacity to reason and make judgements...this is what should be a source of worry.

Why is it that after six decades of democracy, there are still obstacles and barriers in moving towards redistributive change—a sense of fairness, and a sense of justice? I am reminded of Nehru's remarks in an interview that he gave just months before his demise. He was asked about the biggest difficulty he faced and he replied, 'Creating a just society by just means.' He then paused and said, 'Creating a secular society where religion has no meaning for the people.' These words are still an agenda for us, now.

We all know that we have outstanding political leaders in our midst. We have not talked about politics in the whole discussion, we have talked about democracy...democracy would deliver if the politics were not the politics of wealth. This is time, sixty years on, to have real analysis and reflection, to which end I hope that a journal like Seminar enables creative engagement between academia, research centres and all the people here who are awaiting a change which is the promise that independence made to them.

On the idea of different public spheres: I think we need to have a shared, common public sphere and not just in the same nation state.

SALMAN KHURSHID

Four acronyms that you need to look at when you talk of changing the public sphere. The RTI or Right to Information Act is a major development. It's changing the face of democracy. The second is the PRI or Panchayati Raj Institutions, what with funding going straight to PRIs and women getting reservations. The third is the PIL, public interest litigation. Most of it is good. Fourth is CSR or corporate social responsibility. That's the emerging area. Somewhere there is this whole idea of possibly moving away from the moribund reservation thesis to affirmative action, in the true sense, with corporates joining hands with the government in more affirmative action than reservations has given us, since jobs are mainly in the private sector rather than the public sector.

IV

"The most important single characteristic of Indian society for ages has been the inbuilt discrimination in the system. Democracy, to some extent, has corrected this and we cherish democracy because in the known history it is the best form of government that has evolved so far. But what kind of power remains in the hands of the people once they elect their representative for five years? Which institutions are there to check the mandate? Which institutions are there to compensate for this lack of capacity to monitor the elected representatives?"

BHALCHANDRA MUNGEKAR

"The more honest political arrangement would be if you had a proportional representation system, and then there would be a sense that you are participating in governance, no matter where you vote. Whereas today, if your candidate loses, you feel alienated, and you feel that you are no longer a part of the political government system."

SALMAN KHURSHID

"I am surprised to hear the call for proportional representation as a way of dealing with the question of identity because in fact

all the evidence suggests that proportional representation is precisely the system that freezes identities."

SUNIL KHILNANI

"The origin of corruption is regulation."

JAITHIRTH RAO

"...the American banking experience will tell you that non-regulation doesn't necessarily take away corruption. This is something that you could devote a whole Seminar issue to."

SALMAN KHURSHID

"...privatisation comes automatically with regulation because markets need regulations, and this is the problem that arose in Russia...that the very process of privatisation along with a new set of regulations created businessmen who, to varying degrees, controlled the political process. And the combination of businessmen controlling politics, of course, leads to oligarchy."

T.N. NINAN

"The other question is about whether the ghost of ideas can inhabit the body politic again? There is a certain kind of conventional view, of our politicians having been great thinkers, in the past. It was all about ideas and not about interests. Today, it's all about interests and not about ideas. That's a caricature both about the past and about how it is today. The question then is: what sorts of ideas are politicians today looking for? What kinds of interests do they have in ideas? Where do they look for ideas?"

SUNIL KHILNANI

"What about ideas which are not popular and which don't have electoral payoffs? I am talking about the ideas that are the right ones to be implemented, but require an immense amount of persuasion to be put across. Is there anyway that even unpopular ideas can become part of policy?"

AMITA BAVISKAR

"We don't even know whether the agreement with Americans on the 123 (nuclear deal) was a popular or unpopular idea and I

think this is the fundamental question...many of our supporters during that parliamentary debate were opposing us when we were actually getting into the election, saying that they were sorry that they supported the Congress government, at that time. So how does the poor Indian decide when we create this kind of confusion? How does he decide what is right, what is good?"

SALMAN KHURSHID

"...our ability to hear has gone down. There is just too much sensation, too much shouting. Talk shows? It's so loud and raucous. Are we just being self-flagellatory? I refuse to believe that in a country that is growing, where there are lots of young people who are experimenting with lots of stuff, that they are not talking, that they are not producing things, they are not exchanging ideas. Our discussion often gets stuck and that has partly been the problem with journals like *Seminar* or the *Economic & Political Weekly* (EPW). If we want to look at these really big ideas, do we have a new theory of justice? Do we have different kinds of ideas about equality or representation or freedom of choice?"

HARSH SETHI

"We will have another generation, under forty-five, sitting around this table, and we should be the observers because only then will we begin to understand about how overpowering we have been on a whole new excited, energetic and vibrant generation that we have kept out of the largest space."

MALVIKA SINGH

Social Commitment

BHALCHANDRA MUNGEKAR

I understand that running *Seminar* is a matter of social commitment. That is the thing that needs to be cherished, besides what they have done regarding the world of ideas. I consider myself a concerned citizen and from that point of view, I would like to express some issues I think are very important at this juncture of the Indian nation state. The question is of the capacity of the Indian nation state to effectively deal with certain social, economic and cultural problems, with a sense of urgency. The most important single characteristic of Indian society for ages has been the inbuilt discrimination in the system. Democracy, to some extent, has corrected this and we cherish democracy because in the known history it is the best form of government that has evolved so far.

But what kind of power remains in the hands of the people once they elect their representative for five years? Which institutions are there to check the mandate? Which institutions are there to compensate for this lack of capacity to monitor the elected representatives?

Let me give a simple illustration. Every alternate day, we discuss the corruption of *babus*. Now, babu is a term used in a derogatory sense for the IAS (Indian Administrative Service) and the IPS (Indian Police Service) officials. But, I feel it is the political class in this country for one reason or the other that has injected systematic corruption and the babus are made the scapegoat. Though it maybe true that these babus are partly responsible for this financial corruption, but I feel they are not its main source.

An important leader of one of the major political parties in the last Lok Sabha election gave the promise that if we are elected, we shall bring back black money from the Swiss banks. The question is: who put the money in the Swiss banks in the first place? This element of corruption exists from top to bottom, even at the lowest level.

I shall give you another instance of the Forest Rights Bill. I was privileged to be Chairman of the committee and I drafted that Bill. For fourteen months it was languishing because people cared

An important leader of one of the major political parties in the last Lok Sabha election gave the promise that if we are elected, we shall bring back black money from the Swiss banks. The question is: who put the money in the Swiss banks in the first place? This element of corruption exists from top to bottom, even at the lowest level.

more about tigers. One fine day, I had to tell the Prime Minister that without underestimating the importance of tigers, 8.5 crore tribals are definitely more important. The entire discourse was that forest tribals are responsible for deforestation. Throughout the world, forests exist just because of tribals. So, how is it that we think tribals will finish the forest?

Going back to discrimination in the Indian society, I feel, caste is not prominently discussed in the Indian social discourse. Dr. B.R. Ambedkar was the last person to raise the question about caste. Despite all affirmative actions and provisions of the Constitution, nineteen crore Scheduled Castes are virtually living as second grade citizens. Other Backward Class (OBC) people give advertisements in the 'Matrimonial' section of the newspaper that inter-caste marriage is preferred, but in brackets they write that, 'SC/ST should excuse us'. To quote Ambedkar, 'morality is caste-bound', even ethics is caste-bound, your respect is caste-bound, and loyalty is caste-bound. In fact, the Indian people's first loyalty is to his or her own caste. Nation comes later, if not last.

8.5 crore tribals and around 13.5 crore Muslims makes nearly 41 crore people, including SCs, STs, and minorities and I don't use the term 'minorities' in general; I specifically mean Muslims because post-independence, Indian politics is largely intermingled with the state of the Hindu-Muslim relationship. Minority is too general a term. I'd like to take this opportunity to ask a question and this question needs to be raised not only in terms of socioeconomic and cultural variables, tangible or non-tangible, but also in terms of individuals and groups of people. The question that needs to be raised in the public discourse is that: if all non-Muslim Indians, who form eighty-five per cent of the country, get scared of the Muslim community, how will the Muslims feel safe in India? I want to bring to attention, specifically, the Hindu-Muslim relationship and the space that the Muslims occupy in the Indian political, social and cultural discourse. From 6 am, in the morning, to 10.30 pm, at night, you see hundreds of television channels, all kinds of cultural programmes and discourses. Have you heard the word 'prophet' being uttered at any time? Despite the secular characteristic of the Indian state mentioned and initiated in the Indian Constitution, what are the undercurrents of the Indian state, in terms of culture?

The second point is about disparity and destitution. According to the Planning Commision, an estimated 250 districts in this country are affected by Naxal violence. The Naxal violence problem is not a law and order problem. It's a problem of exclusive economic development and the utter failure, for various reasons, to share the legitimate fruits of economic development with the marginalised groups, tribals in particular.

The last issue is about the kind of intellectual discourse in the country. Intellectuals generally differentiate themselves from common politicians and politicians are considered as unwanted. By and large, if all sections of society, other than politicians condemn politicians, then why do people in general prefer politicians over intellectuals or academicians? Is there any disconnect between them? Is it that the intellectuals also belong to the ruling classes and take sides?

These are the important questions that I ask as a concerned citizen. Perhaps, there will be a legitimate equation between the common people, the intellectuals and the academics —when intellectuals everywhere in the world show enough courage to go against the interests of the classes to which they belong.

I have wondered whether corruption doesn't begin with the efforts to get yourself elected and whether we would have been better off if we had followed Nelson Mandela's model and taken to proportional representation, instead of first-past-the-post.

Intellectual Ghosts of the Political Class

SALMAN KHURSHID

A phrase was used, earlier, of *Seminar* producing the intellectual ghosts of the political class. I am delighted to be back amongst the ghosts again. It's interesting that there was mention of this lack of sync, lack of communication between the intellectual class and politicians. I think this is a very sad state of affairs. One does feel alienated. Talking about films, there was the phase where films like *Aaj ka MLA* came out, and politicians became the objects of hate amongst ordinary Indians. More recently, a different kind of political culture has been portrayed, closely associated with the underworld, the kind the film *Sarkar* and others have portrayed. Public figures and politicians certainly do agonise about this and some of them are happy to continue with that profile while others are extremely worried about it.

The problematic thing, of course, is how do we put it right? There have been attempts made in electoral reform in trying to put it right. We are put into a tough disciplinary mode when elections are announced. You can't even do anything useful once elections are announced. You just have to stop. Since elections take place all the time, you have to be careful. But the problem is that beyond the election period, suddenly there is nobody who can control politicians and coalition politics also makes it worse.

I want you to think of any other country in which elections means constant interviews with the chief election commissioner on television. The American election takes place, the British election takes place but you don't even know who the chief election commissioner is there. Here, people might know the chief election commissioner more than they know the likely Prime Minister. But that's the kind of system we have developed here. This is part of an old structure where the District Magistrate is very important and the others really have to fall in line to get little things done by him.

The problem, really, is of the role of the Indian politician, the representative of the public. The electors expect him to be a magician and perform tricks that will solve all their problems. He is

I want you to think of any other country in which elections means constant interviews with the chief election commissioner on television. The American election takes place, the British election takes place but you don't even know who the chief election commissioner is there.

unable to do so, more so now that with devolution of power money is going directly to panchayati raj institutions (PRIs), which is a good thing. He or she has really nothing to offer except reach out to caste or communal identities and that's what is troublesome about the Indian political system.

I have wondered whether corruption doesn't begin with the efforts to get yourself elected and whether we would have been better off if we had followed Nelson Mandela's model and taken to proportional representation, instead of first-past-the-post. Because first-past-the-post puts a premium on one's identity as an individual belonging to a particular caste, community or to a particular religion. This is something that we are very scared to talk about, presumably because my party used to roll with two-thirds majority, getting forty per cent of the vote. Today, the major parties in the country struggle to get even twenty-eight per cent of votes. They have to deal with others who have got five per cent, three per cent and six per cent, with a huge number of seats.

The more honest political arrangement would be if you had a proportional representation system, and then there would be a sense that you are participating in governance, no matter where you vote. Whereas today, if your candidate loses, you feel alienated, and you feel that you are no longer a part of the political government system.

Discussion

Point, Counterpoint

JAITHIRTH RAO

The origin of corruption is regulation. Today, we don't have a 'licence raj' (licencing system), so we don't have to pay anyone to get a licence or prevent a competitor from getting the licence. This is what we were doing, previously. So why don't we go head-on and consider private sector education. Currently, most engineering colleges and medical colleges in states like Maharashtra, Karnataka and Tamil Nadu are owned by politicians, technically these are not-for-profit institutions where basically cash is taken under the table for giving admissions. They are for profit, but they are for the private profit of the trustees rather than the profit of the institution. Corruption happens from regulation.

There are two classes in this country: English-speaking and non-English speaking. Why doesn't the state simply give vouchers and let people go to the private English schools? It's like in the old days when only Brahmins could read Sanskrit and the rest were not allowed to. We are redoing that with English.

SUNIL KHILNANI

I am surprised to hear the call for proportional representation as a way of dealing with the question of identity because in fact all the evidence suggests that proportional representation is precisely the system that freezes identities. People tend to vote in blocks for their particular parties because they know that they will get a certain percentage. It's become much harder to have fluidity of political identities, wherever the proportional phase has been used. No electoral system is obviously perfect. There are always approximations, but for the specific question of keeping identities fluid, the first-past-the-post system is actually quite an effective way and part of the volatility of the Indian system is a result of it. So, certain groups will one day vote for one party, the next time for another and so forth—that's an empirical question.

The other question is about whether the ghost of ideas can inhabit the body politic again? There is a certain kind of conventional view, of our politicians having been great thinkers, in the past. It was all about ideas and not about interests. Today, it's all about interests and not about ideas. That's a caricature both about the past and about how it is today. The question then is: what sorts of ideas are politicians today looking for? What kinds of interests do they have in ideas? Where do they look for ideas? What is the market for ideas amongst your colleagues? Ideas are driving a lot of what's happening today. It would be interesting to hear from you, Salman: why do some of these ideas get through and others don't? What are the filters? Why is it that some come to be valued and other's don't.

T.N. NINAN

How many democracies have found a solution to the problem of funding the political process in an honest manner? Very few. You take Japan or the U.S. There was a time when you thought Britain had found an answer because the Labour Party was funded by the trade unions and the Conservatives had more money. But now we know that is not the case. You look at Italy. How many democracies have found a solution to the problem of political funding? That's my question.

The comment I have is that privatisation comes automatically with regulation because markets need regulations, and this is the problem that arose in Russia...that the very process of privatisation along with a new set of regulations created businessmen who, to varying degrees, controlled the political process. And the combination of businessmen controlling politics, of course, leads to oligarchy.

AMITA BAVISKAR

About ideas that make their way from the public sphere to political action... my first response would be that if there is an electoral payoff, then certainly it does happen, like the National Rural Employment Guarantee Act (NREGA). But what about ideas which are not popular and which don't have electoral payoffs? I am talking about the ideas that are the right ones to be implemented, but require an immense amount of persuasion to be put across. Is there anyway that even unpopular ideas can become part of policy?

RUDRANGSHU MUKHERJEE

This is to Sunil and I'd like to have a wider discussion on this—if you are thinking of the history of the political ideas of modern India—would we be looking at politicians as a source of how these ideas work or are received? I think we would be looking at other kinds of sources, what we are calling the 'public sphere'. We would be looking at intellectuals and thinkers who have actually articulated ideas that have become political through a process and politicians may not have been involved in that process. There have been very few politicians who have also been thinkers. I am just putting forth these points as questions.

HARSH SETHI

It's not that we are not producing ideas. It could be that we have been unable to construct a common public space or a, common public sphere so that there is receptivity to ideas, but there is very little travelling of these ideas from one particular kind of bounded domain into another. Intellectuals of a certain persuasion talk to each other and whether the kind of ideas they discuss have resonance elsewhere in the world, that's the kind of question that has always bothered me.

We have always liked to believe the glorified description of our national movement, that we had people who managed to speak across classes, across languages and across regions. Therefore, a small act of Mahatma Gandhi in Dandi meant a huge thing to people down in Kerala. So today, when we look at it, we seem to be living in not just divided and multiple worlds but worlds with boundaries that appear to be relatively impermeable which is why Peter is able to sense the vast amount of excitement when he goes to Bangladesh.

Our ability to hear has gone down. There is just too much sensation, too much shouting. Talk shows? It's so loud and raucous.

Are we just being self-flagellatory? I refuse to believe that in a country that is growing, where there are lots of young people who are experimenting with lots of stuff, that they are not talking, that they are not producing things, they are not exchanging ideas. Our discussion often gets stuck and that has partly been the problem with journals like *Seminar* or the EPW. If we want to look at these really big ideas, do we have a new theory of justice? Do we have different kinds of ideas about equality or representation or freedom of choice? We seem to have very little grounded, empirical work.

If our public sphere is so deeply divided, what is it that becomes the mandate, the responsibility, and the challenge towards the forums that seek to contribute to the making of ideas in the public sphere? To see that they actually have resonance...that's the challenge that we face.

MALVIKA SINGH

I think that we are raising all these questions without any of those representatives around this table. I'm now completely convinced that in the next Seminar issues, we will arrange and take all these points that have been raised by many of us around this table. We will have another generation, under forty-five, sitting around this table, and we should be the observers because only then will we begin to understand about how overpowering we have been on a whole new excited, energetic and vibrant generation that we have kept out of the largest space.

SALMAN KHURSHID

I think it is important to flag two things. One was the market of ideas amongst my colleagues. I think this is a worrying thing. We now seem to run governments without any major input from people like you. Newspapers are read, but I am not quite sure that many of my colleagues read Seminar before they decide what to do. They would certainly read it if someone brought it to their notice, but I don't think much of that happens. Things have changed in government largely because the impetus comes from the bureaucracy. Political masters have accepted this and move forward.

Amita talked about what does one do if you have an unpopular idea? We don't even know whether the agreement with Americans on the 123 (nuclear deal) was a popular or unpopular idea, and I think this is the fundamental question. There are a lot of middle class people who thought it was a wonderful idea. There are a lot of people who thought it was a disastrous idea and they vigorously debated and questioned it, and we all know it was touch-and-go in Parliament. But was Parliament responding to what people thought, or was it responding to something that they were calculating themselves? I think this is a very big question.

I don't even know how much we needed of the 123 in the election campaign that came afterwards. Many of our supporters during that parliamentary debate were opposing us when we were actually getting into the election, saying that they were sorry that they supported the Congress government, at that time. So how does the poor Indian decide when we create this kind of confusion? How does he decide what is right, what is good? But as far as consensus building is concerned, didn't Mahatma Gandhi try consensus building on the issue of Partition —to get away from Partition and he didn't succeed. He was deeply hurt and disappointed because he couldn't prevent it from taking place.

There are unpopular causes that some politicians have gone down fighting for, but generally, most politicians today just leave an unpopular cause alone, and this is a sad thing for us to reflect on.

This issue of honest funding of election is a very major thing. I don't think we have enough information available on this. But corruption and regulation, the American banking experience will tell you that non-regulation doesn't necessarily take away corruption. This is something that you could devote a whole Seminar issue to.

Much of the corruption we saw in the last twenty years, in this country, took place in privatisation processes. When private sector gets involved with government, there is corruption, or at least gleams of corruption. I think we need to talk much more about that. Maybe like the *Panchayat Raj*, the first generation misuses it, the second generation begins to assert itself, and by the third generation you have a full-blown, comfortable democracy.

On Sunil's point about empirical evidence on proportional representation, this is something that certainly needs much greater discussion. In the last twenty years, caste parties, particularly in my state of Uttar Pradesh, have emerged simply because of first-past-the-post. Nobody votes for a good politician, nobody votes for a person who works in his constituency. It's a combination of communities: sometimes a stable combination, sometimes unstable. It's an area on which empirical evidence would lead to further discussion.

I think this short discussion leaves open avenues for many more issues of Seminar to come out.

The grand estate

Top left: (L to R) Kanak Mani Dixit, Ramachandra Guha and Tejbir Singh
Top right: Vimala Ramachandran and Manek Guzder
Middle left: Peter deSouza and Mohini Menon
Middle right: Romesh Chopra, Neera Benegal, Louise Khurshid, Malvika Singh and Hameed Haroon
Bottom: Malvika Singh and Hameed Haroon

Top left: Amita Baviskar and Tara Gandhi

Top right: Kamal Hossain and Shivshankar Menon, Ligia Noronha (extreme right)

Middle left: Shivshankar Menon and Gopalkrishna Gandhi, Ramachandra Guha (extreme right)

Middle right: Hameed Haroon and Abha Narain Lambah

Bottom: (L to R) Cyrus Guzder, T.N. Ninan and Jaithirth Rao

Peter deSouza at the inauguration ceremony of the IIAS bookstore

Top right: Nayantara Sahgal cuts the ribbon
Right: Perusing the collection

INDUS
BOOKS
birth...threshold
A FIELD OF ONE'S OWN
Vikram Seth
Amitav Ghosh
INDIA
ANCIENT
VARANASI
Vidula Jayaswal

Left: Shyam Benegal
Right: Abha Narain Lambah

Entering the Indian Institute of Advanced Study, Shimla

From left to right: Kamal Hossain, Salman Khurshid, Harsh Sethi, Shivshankar Menon,
Nayantara Sahgal, Vimala Ramachandran, Kanak Mani Dixit, Shiv Visvanathan and Mohini Menon

Malvika and Tejbir Singh

Salman and Louise Khurshid

Abha Narain Lambah and Shivshankar Menon

Top left: Indian Institute of Advanced Study, Shimla
Top right: (L to R) Rudrangshu Mukherjee, Salman Khurshid, Louise Khurshid and Malvika Singh
Middle left: Gopalkrishna Gandhi and Sunil Khilnani
Middle right: Sunil Khilnani, Gopalkrishna Gandhi and Harsh Sethi
Bottom: Inside the Indian Institute of Advanced Study

Top left: (L to R) Peter deSouza, Salman Khurshid, Amita Baviskar, Nayantara Sahgal and Tara Gandhi

Top right: In conversation: Malvika Singh with Shyam Benegal, and Sunil Khilnani (on the right)

Middle left: (L to R) T.N. Ninan, Romesh Chopra, Rudrangshu Mukherjee, Sevanti Ninan and Vimala Ramachandran

Middle right: Malvika Singh and Peter deSouza

Bottom: T.N. Ninan, Romesh Chopra, Rudrangshu Mukherjee and Sevanti Ninan

Profiles

AMITA BAVISKAR is a sociologist whose research focuses on the cultural politics of environment and development. She is the author of *In the Belly of the River: Tribal Conflicts over Development in the Narmada Valley* (OUP, 1995) and has co-edited *Elite and Everyman: The Cultural Politics of the Indian Middle Classes* (Routledge, 2011). Currently an Associate Professor at the Institute of Economic Growth, Delhi, she has held visiting positions at Yale, Stanford, Berkeley, the London School of Economics, and Cornell and Sciences Po. She has received numerous awards, including the 2010 Infosys Prize, 2008 VKRV Rao Prize for Social Science Research, and the 2005 Malcolm Adiseshiah Award for distinguished contributions to development studies. She serves on the boards of several academic journals and non-governmental organisations working on environmental and social justice issues.

BHALCHANDRA MUNGEKAR is an economist and a Rajya Sabha member. He specialises in agricultural economics and is an expert on Dr B.R. Ambedkar's work. He has been Vice Chancellor of the University of Mumbai and has served in the Planning Commission and the Agricultural Price Commission of India. He was the Chairman and President of the Indian Institute of Advanced Study, Shimla.

C. RAMMANOHAR REDDY holds a PhD in Economics and has been a journalist since 1988. He was Associate Editor of *The Hindu* before becoming Editor of the *Economic & Political Weekly*, Mumbai, in 2004.

GOPALKRISHNA GANDHI worked in the Indian Administrative Service from its Tamil Nadu cadre from 1968 to 1978. He was Secretary to the Vice President of India (R. Venkataraman) and Secretary to the President of India (K.R. Narayanan). He was the first Director of The Nehru Centre, London (1992-1996), India's High Commissioner in South Africa and Lesotho (1996-97), Sri Lanka (2000-2002), Ambassador to Norway and Iceland (2002-2004), and Governor of West Bengal (2004-2009). He was the Chairman of the Indian Institute of Advanced Study, Shimla (2011-2014) and The Kalakshetra Foundation, Chennai (2011-2014).

HAMEED HAROON is the Chief Executive Officer of the Dawn Group of Newspapers. He has a Master's in East Asia Regional Studies from Harvard University and has received his Master's in Political Economy and a Master's in Economics from Boston University. He was instrumental in setting up Dawn News, Pakistan's first English language television news channel. Currently, he is the Chief Executive Officer, Pakistan Herald Publications. He has been awarded the *Sitara-e-Imtiaz*, Pakistan's highest civil award in recognition for his role in the promotion of art and culture. He has also been awarded the Italian Order of Merit by the President of Italy (2006).

HARSH SETHI is the Consulting Editor at *Seminar* since 1996. Previously, he was the Acquisitions Editor at Sage publications and Editor of *Lokayan Bulletin*. In his role as Fellow at the Centre for Studies in Developing Societies, he was the lead editor of the CSDS-Lokniti Study, *State of Democracy in South Asia*, 2006. He was Deputy Director, Indian Council of Social Science Research, New Delhi. He co-edited *Foul Play: Chronicles of Corruption 1947-97* (Banyan Books, 1998) and *Social Change Through Voluntary Action* (Sage, 1998). His research work has spanned a vast variety of civic and social issues.

JAITHIRTH RAO has been a banker and an I.T. entrepreneur. He now runs a start-up in the affordable housing space and is mentoring a budget housing finance company. Additionally, he is an investor in various start-ups and is mentoring companies in the domains of women's empowerment, skills development, management education, publishing software and legal outsourcing. He is Chairman of NASSCOM Foundation, Chairman of the India Foundation for the Arts and a Trustee of the Sujaya Foundation and the Mathematical Sciences Foundation. He regularly writes columns for the *Indian Express* and the *Economic Times* and occasional pieces for *Seminar*. He has published a book of poetry, *Gemini II* (Penguin, 1994), and a book of essays, *Notes from an Indian Conservative* (Rupa, 2009). Rao is a graduate of Loyola College, Chennai and has advanced degrees from IIM Ahmedabad and the University of Chicago.

KAMAL HOSSAIN did his BA (Honours in Jurisprudence), MA, BCL, DPhil (International Law), 1964 from the University of Oxford. He has been a Barrister at Lincoln's Inn (1959), has been a Research Fellow (1977-1979) at Nuffield College, Oxford and a Visiting Fellow (1976-1977) at All Souls College, Oxford. He is a Senior Advocate in the Supreme Court of Bangladesh. He was the Chair of the Constitution Drafting Committee, 1972, and has also held several positions in the government as a Member of Parliament, Minister of Petroleum and Minerals (1973-1975), and Minister of Foreign Affairs (1973-1975). He is a member of the international arbitral tribunals (ICC, ICSID and UNCITRAL) and was the Judge ad hoc for *Malaysia, ITLOS Tribunal, Malaysia v Singapore* (2003); *UNCLOS Annex VII Tribunal, Guyana v Suriname* (2005-2007).

KANAK MANI DIXIT is the Editor of *Himal Southasian* magazine and the Publisher of *Himal Khabarpatrika*, both based in Kathmandu. Highly respected as a journalist in the South Asian region, Kanak's related interests include archiving, public transport, heritage conservation, translations and writing for children. He is author of *Peace Politics of Nepal* (Himal Books, 2011) and *Dekheko Muluk* (Jagadamba Prakashan, 2009). He is active in civil rights work with a special focus on accountability. He is also Chair of the Film Southasia, the premiere documentary film festivals of South Asia. He holds an LLB degree from Delhi University and a Master's degree in International Affairs and a Master of Science in Journalism, both from Columbia University.

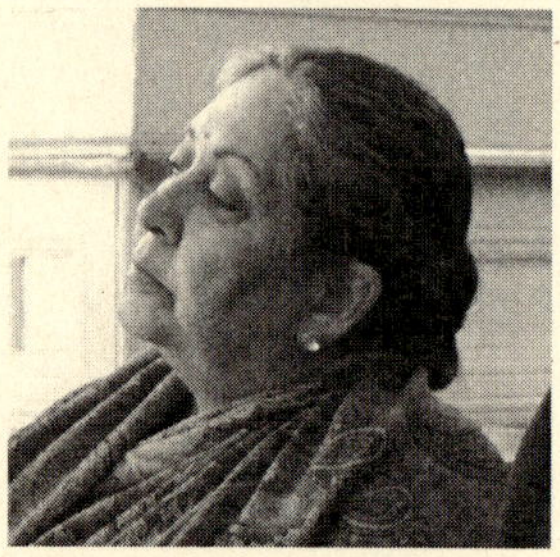

MALVIKA SINGH is the daughter of the late Raj and Romesh Thapar and publisher of *Seminar*. She has authored several books: *Perpetual City: A Short Biography of Delhi; Bhutan: Through the Lens of the King; New Delhi: Making of a Capital; Delhi: India in One City; and Snowdon's India*. She has edited *Delhi: The First City; Chennai: A City of Change; Hyderabad: A City of Hope; Kolkata: A Soul City; Lucknow: A City Between Cultures; Mumbai: A City of Dreams* and *Freeing the Spirit: Iconic Women of India*. She has also worked in theatre and films, and was decorated as a Dame in the civil merit honours list of the King of Spain in 2009. She was a founder member and served as Vice Chairperson, Indian National Trust for Art and Cultural Heritage (INTACH).

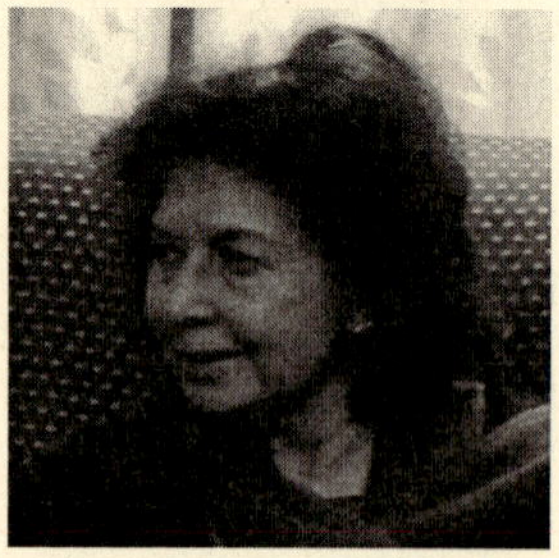

NAYANTARA SAHGAL has written nine novels and eight works of non-fiction. She is a recipient of the Sinclair Prize for fiction, the Sahitya Akademi award and the Commonwealth Writers' Prize. A member of the Sahitya Akademi's Advisory Board for English till she resigned during the Emergency, Sahgal served on the jury of the Commonwealth Writers' Prize in 1990 and 1991. She has held fellowships in the United States at the Bunting Institute, the Woodrow Wilson International Center for Scholars and the National Humanities Center. She is a member of the American Academy of Arts and Sciences and was awarded an honorary doctorate in literature by the University of Leeds in 1997. She is associated with the founding of the People's Union for Civil Liberties and served as its vice president during the 1980s.

PETER deSOUZA was former Director of the Indian Institute of Advanced Study, Shimla, from 2007 to 2013. Prior to this, he was Senior Fellow at the Centre for the Study of Developing Societies. In addition to numerous articles, he has co-edited two books, *India's Political Parties* (Sage, 2006) and *Speaking of Gandhi's Death* (Orient Blackswan, 2010), and authored *Contemporary India: Transitions* (Sage, 2000). He was one of three principal investigators of a five-nation study, *State of Democracy in South Asia* (OUP, 2006).

RAMACHANDRA GUHA is a historian and biographer. He has taught at the universities of Yale and Stanford, held the Arné Naess Chair at the University of Oslo, and been the Indo-American Community Visiting Professor at the University of California, Berkeley. In 2011-12, he held the Philippe Roman Chair of History and International Relations at the London School of Economics and Political Science. His books include: *The Unquiet Woods* (University of California Press, 1989), *A Corner of a Foreign Field* (Picador, 2002), *India After Gandhi* (Macmillan/Ecco Press, 2007), *Gandhi Before India* (Penguin India/Random House, 2013) and, as editor, *Makers of Modern India* (Penguin India, 2010).

RUDRANGSHU MUKHERJEE is a historian and currently Editor, editorial pages, *The Telegraph* and the Vice Chancellor of Ashoka University, Sonepat. He is the author of four books on the revolt of 1857 and editor among others of *The Penguin Gandhi Reader* (Penguin, 1995) and *Indian Persuasions: Essays from Seminar* (Roli Books, 2009).

SALMAN KHURSHID till recently was Union Minister of External Affairs. A lawyer and writer, he has held several ministerial positions in the Government of India. His acclaimed play, *Sons of Babur*, has been translated into several languages and performed across the country, as well as in the UK. He has also authored *At Home in India* (Vikas, 1987) and *If Winter Comes* (Vikas, 1994).

SHIV VISVANATHAN is Professor at O.P. Jindal Global University, Sonepat. He was Professor, Dhirubhai Ambani Institute of Information and Communication Technology (DA-IICT), Gandhinagar, India, and has held the position of Senior Fellow at the Centre for the Study of Developing Societies (CSDS) in Delhi. He has also taught at the Delhi School of Economics. He has held visiting professorships at Smith College, Stanford, Goldsmiths, Arizona State University and Maastricht University. He is the author of *Organizing for Science* (OUP, 1985), *A Carnival for Science* (OUP, 1997) and co-edited *Foulplay: Chronicles of Corruption 1947-1997* (Banyan Books, 1999).

SHIVSHANKAR MENON was National Security Advisor to the Prime Minister of India from 2010-2014. He served as Foreign Secretary of India from October 2006 to August 2009. He has served as Ambassador and High Commissioner of India to Israel (1995-1997), Sri Lanka (1997-2000), China (2000-2003) and Pakistan (2003-2006). He has been a member of the Atomic Energy Commission since 2008. A career diplomat, he served in China (thrice), Japan and Austria. He has an MA in Ancient History from Delhi University.

SHYAM BENEGAL is a prolific director and screenwriter, who with his first four feature films, *Ankur* (1973), *Nishant* (1975), *Manthan* (1976) and *Bhumika* (1977), created a new genre which he prefers to call 'New' or 'Alternate' cinema. He won the highest award in Indian cinema for lifetime achievement, the Dadasaheb Phalke Award (2005). He was also awarded the Padma Bhushan in 1991. He has authored three books based on his own films, *The Churning* with Vijay Tendulkar (1984), *Satyajit Ray* (1988), and *The Marketplace* (1989). His mini series for Rajya Sabha TV is titled *Samvidhaan—The Making of the Constitution of India*. The University of Calcutta and Jamia Millia Islamia have honoured him with an honorary DLitt.

SUNIL KHILNANI is Avantha Professor and Director, King's India Institute, King's College London. He was educated at Trinity Hall, Cambridge, where he earned a first class honours degree in Social and Political Sciences and at King's College, Cambridge, where he received his PhD in Social and Political Sciences. Prior to becoming Director of the King's India Institute, he was, from 2002 to 2011, the Starr Foundation Professor at Johns Hopkins University's School of Advanced International Studies (SAIS) in Washington D.C., and Director of South Asia Studies at SAIS, a programme that he established in 2002. He is the author of *The Idea of India* (Penguin, 2012).

TEJBIR SINGH has been the Editor of *Seminar* since 1987. In 1980, he won the National Award for the Best Documentary of the Year for *The Kalbelias, Nomads of Rajasthan* at the 27th National Film Festival, India. He was a Founder Member of the Ranthambhore Foundation which has been working on the fringe of the Ranthambhore Tiger Reserve in Rajasthan since 1988. He was a member of the National Committee on Management of National Parks and Sanctuaries, Ministry of Environment and Forests. He co-authored, *With Tigers in the Wild* (Vikas, 1983). From 1984-1986, he held the position of Managing Director of the Ashoka Foundation, a worldwide association of independent innovators and changemakers working for the public good.

T.N. NINAN is Chairman of Business Standard Ltd., having previously been the newspaper's editor. In a quarter-century at the helm of different publications, he has also been Editor of *The Economic Times* and of *Business World* magazine, and Executive Editor of *India Today*. He writes a widely read Saturday column, 'Weekend Ruminations' in *Business Standard*. He has been President of the Editors Guild of India and Chairman of the media committee of the Confederation of Indian Industry. He is currently a Nehru Fellow (2013-14), and has been a contributor to *Seminar* for over two decades.

3

A Question of Issues

Deep Roots

J.B. KRIPALANI

One of the main causes of political upheavals throughout history has been the widespread prevalence of corruption and nepotism among the holders of political power, whether they be kings, princes and oligarchs or politicians in a democracy and administrators in general. This is well illustrated by recent political upheavals in the erstwhile colonial countries.

The Chiang Kai-shek regime in China failed because of widespread corruption and nepotism among both politicians and administrators. The democratic regime in Egypt gave place to a military dictatorship because of political and administrative corruption. The same has been the case in Indonesia and Pakistan. The recent troubles in Burma and Ceylon (now Sri Lanka) are also due to the prevalence of corruption among the politicians and their lust for power at any cost. That is why every revolution, whether it be democratic or totalitarian, tackles the problem of corruption first, so as to gain the confidence of the people.

Under British rule, corruption in India had two distinct faces. One, which was not recognised as such, was the fundamental corruption consequent upon one nation ruling over another and exploiting it. The other was the ordinary corruption in administration.

As soon as the John Company established its rule, it systematised and sanctioned administrative corruption. Officials of the Company were paid incredibly low salaries. They were expected to supplement their income by getting or extracting compulsory levies from those who were obliged to have dealings with them. When the administration was transferred from the John Company to the Crown, the higher services manned by the British received emoluments out of all proportion to the functions they performed or the capacity of the Indian people to pay. The result was a top-heavy administration, which was condemned by the Congress year after year in its annual sessions.

Reproduced from 'Corruption', *Seminar*, April 1960. Jivatram Bhagwandas Kripalani was the President of the Indian National Congress from 1946 to 1947.

Big salaries to high officers successfully induced a certain degree of honesty. In the lower grades of the administration, however, corruption continued owing to custom and the low salaries of the employees. Yet, there was some check upon it because of the fear of the big *Sahib*. It was known that if he was not satisfied, the punishment would be swift and final, and there could be no appeal from the wrath of the British officer. He was the government.

There was some change in this pattern after the two world wars. War always provides opportunities for corruption. Total war increases these opportunities. It also undermines moral and conventional restrictions. Moreover, the amounts involved are so great that they place a heavy strain on the honesty and integrity of the average government employee and corruption spreads even to the higher services.

After World War I the British were able to clean the administration of much of the war-time corruption, but after World War II, the task became more difficult. Also, the British Government had no time to use the broom. The uncertainty about the future political set-up, and the Hindu-Muslim rioting and blood-bath that followed, afforded fresh opportunities for corruption.

When political power came to be definitely transferred it was expected that the politicians now in power, who had always denounced corruption under the British, would immediately take stringent measures, as in every revolution, to suppress this evil. It was also known that some of the leaders, especially Prime Minister Nehru, would give short shrift to all corrupt officials. Unfortunately nothing was attempted. Even the services of officers who had indulged in sadistic acts of cruelty against the nationalists, beyond the ample provision of the repressive laws of the foreign government, were retained. Occasionally, such officers were even promoted.

No revolutionary party coming to power has ever done this. One wonders what was behind all this compromise! Was it that the Congress government, harassed by the many difficult problems arising out of the transfer of power and the Partition, did not relish the idea of adding yet another problem by increasing discontent in the services? Was it that the politicians and the members of the services often came from the same strata of society, from the same caste and families? Was it that members of the services had powerful connections among the new holders of power?

Whatever the reasons, no effort was made to clean the administration of undesirable elements. Rather, the prolonged retention of war-time controls and the issue of lucrative import permits worsened the situation. The politician conveniently thought that the magic touch of the transfer of power to Indian hands had changed everything! The cruel had shed their cruelty; the dishonest had become efficient and the unpatriotic had become patriotic! This was clear from the praise lavished upon the administrative services by the political bosses even when there was no occasion for it. Is it therefore any wonder that the problem of corruption was not tackled after Independence?

It is unfortunate that the evil has increased with the years. Political corruption has been added to administrative corruption. A Persian proverb says that, 'if a king takes a grain of salt from his subjects without payment, his officers will rob the people of their entire possessions.' The result is that today nothing can be got done unless some payment is made, or there is a note of recommendation from those who can influence them. This widespread corruption has let to inefficiency in the administration and to inordinate delays in the transformation to business. The pity of it is that nothing is done to check it. Indeed, at first even its very existence was denied.

From the very beginning my voice was raised against this corruption. One of the reasons for my resignation as President of the Congress, as mentioned in my statement before the A.I.C.C., was the prevalence of corruption and an open black market. In Parliament, year after year, I have denounced this evil. Annoyed at my criticism, the prime minister in reply once said that corruption is created by those who incessantly talk of it. My answer was that we were not living in the age of Aesop's Fables where a wolf appeared because the shepherd-boy had raised the cry 'Wolf! Wolf!' Even in Aesop's Fables, the wolf did not come out of nothing, as the rabbit from the juggler's hat, but it was there in the jungle.

Under British rule, corruption in India had two distinct faces. One, which was not recognised as such, was the fundamental corruption consequent upon one nation ruling over another and exploiting it. The other was the ordinary corruption in administration.

Today, instead of any remedial measures being taken, the general impression is that the authorities, to retain their prestige, make every effort to see that corruption at the higher levels is not exposed. It is no use saying that public opinion is wrong.

After some time, owing to universal complaint, the existence of corruption was admitted, but only in the lower ranks of the services. It is at this level that the services come in contact with the people. What can one think of the efficiency of an officer if he cannot check corruption in his department.

Sometimes it appears from the prime minister's utterances that he is out to do a job as quickly as possible, the job of industrialising the country and making it modern, corruption or no corruption. He seems to be oblivious of the corroding effect of this evil. If it were merely the question of greedy officials and their clients making money, it would not matter much. But it is the moral effect on the whole community that is most dangerous. Corruption has the tendency of turning the average citizen, who is not made in the heroic mould, dishonest.

Take, for example, the case of an ailing child in the family. It is useless to ask his parents to refrain from going to the black market for medicine which cannot be purchased in the open market at the prescribed price. Similarly, it is useless to expect a merchant to refrain from indulging in bribing officials if his business is likely to suffer. Often the giver of the bribe gives it out of necessity. Sometimes he gives it to get an undue advantage. But in no case is the government employee obliged to take it. His sole motive is to make profit immorally and illegally and, in the process, to undermine the social fabric. He is a public danger and a public enemy.

The average citizen, and we all come into that category, is neither honest nor dishonest. There are a few who are congenitally honest or dishonest. We become one or the other according to social circumstances. I recently gave my own example in Parliament, and shocked the House. I am the Director of the Gandhi Ashram which produces *khadi*. The ashram has a branch in Bengal producing silk. The goods produced have to be distributed. But the railway clerks would not book them in time. When booked they would not load them in time. The goods deteriorated. The ashram had to suffer losses. My workers were harassed. These complaints were brought to me. The highest railway authority was approached, yet no relief was forthcoming. What was I to do? The ashram is a public charitable institution. It provides work for the poor. It does not do business for profit. If it suffers losses, the poor have to suffer. Had I, as the director of the institution, the moral right to make the poor suffer? I did not know. Anyhow, in desperation I asked my workers to give the necessary gratification of a few rupees and save the hundreds of rupees of the poor. The workers pointed out that the ashram was a public institution. How were they to account for this money before the auditors? I said I would certify the expenditure as being a bribe and take the legal consequence.

I related this story in Parliament. There was an electric effect in the House. The minister said that he would look into the matter. I had telephone calls from railway officers, assuring me that the matter would be attended to. I expected that after this public exposure my workers would be free from harassment. But this was a vain hope. The railway staff would neither accept the customary gratification nor give the ashram booking facilities. My workers were manhandled and abuse was showered upon me for the exposure in the House.

I again received complaints from my workers. I did not know what to do. I sent a formal letter of complaint to the minister. I also wrote to the prime minister, not in his official capacity but in his capacity as a trustee of the ashram. I pointed out to him that now, since gratification was not accepted and the goods were not booked, the only course left was to close the branch in Bengal. In that case I said there would be a loss of a couple of lakhs and some thousand spinners and weavers would be thrown out of work and lose their livelihood. It was then that some effective action was taken and we are now free from harassment. I hope permanently. However, it is not possible for average citizens to seek relief in this way.

This shows how deep corruption has gone into our political system. The pity of it is that even complaints of corruption in political and administrative circles by highly placed leaders, who were once in government, receive no adequate response from the authorities. This is what makes the situation appear hopeless. The foreign government dealt with complaints against a senior officer by sending him back home, beyond the seas. Gandhiji had his own method of dealing with corruption in high places. He would call the man, place the evidence before him and ask him to retire from public life or be exposed. In all the cases I know of, the offending politician chose to slip away quietly from public life.

Today, instead of any remedial measures being taken, the general impression is that the authorities, to retain their prestige, make every effort to see that corruption at the higher levels is not exposed. It is no use saying that public opinion is wrong. It may be wrong even in continuing Congress in power! But it is accepted. In politics and administration it is not enough that the authorities be right and correct. The public must also feel that they are so. If this does not happen there will be moral and political demoralisation, with consequences which are bound to be evil but which cannot be foretold. Will the holders of power act before it is too late?

In fact, an essential part of our character is the circular motion, the invincible zero. Never be direct, skirt the issue because you never know who you might offend and what the repercussions would be.

Our National Character

RAJ THAPAR

It is curious how terms are nourished today and sought to be wrapped up in neat little packages to be untied for ready reference. The word 'national' symbolises one such, having grown up in an age where boundaries like everything else have become completely material, physical. And over our sprawling sub-continent, one has to make a considerable effort of the mind to think of the tribals of Madhya Pradesh, the fisherwomen of the Konkan, the Pahadis of the Himalayas, the Tamils, the Nagas, the Sikhs of the Punjab, all being tied up into one single package. One wonders what they have in common. Certainly not a shared experience, environmentally or historically. Yet, when confronted with 'others' outside of the sub-continent, certain features get etched sharply.

The first hit me some years ago in Singapore at a conference of representative from all over South East Asia. The five Indians, coming from different parts of the country and not acquainted with each other, unfailingly spoke their mind, criticised their government, expressed themselves passionately on every issue. All other delegates, bar none, took the positions of their government, not out of fear alone but out of a natural propensity to conform, not to let the side down, a part maybe of the collective ethos which so dramatically demarcates us from the rest of the East. One glimpse at China's Great Wall as it meanders over rock and valley over thousands of miles reveals this enormous capacity for collective conformity.

The Indian, on the other hand, has extreme difficulty in fitting into any definite pattern outside the caste and kinship bonds. Perhaps, that is one reason why no protest movement, no revolutionary movement really grows, why splitting is the inevitable movement through the Indian psyche, even when transferred to management or political party, irrespective of what the outside reality demands. This sense of heightened individuality bubbles up unerringly despite the rigid caste and class frameworks of

Reproduced from 'Raj Thapar 1926-1987', *Seminar*, May 1987. Raj Thapar was the founder editor of Seminar Magazine from 1959 to 1987.

Indian society or, perhaps, because of them. Visually, you see it in a casual glance down any street. No two men are wearing the same length or cut of trouser, shorts, pyjamas, shirt sleeves, or pattern of tying the *dhoti*. This physical variation is reflected in the mind, in the spirit of Hinduism itself. You can worship what you like—the object becomes whatever you endow it with. The Indianness of a group of people travelling together lies not in any collective feeling but in a disparate feeling where each eats his kind of thing, has his own hours for prayer or exercise or what have you.

A friend once described his few months in jail closeted with thirty-five other political prisoners—where the whole night was interrupted by a series of aggressive affirmations of individuality. Someone did his deep breathing noisily at 3 am, another chanted something else at 4, a third wanted his tea at 4.30, a fourth had to cleanse his nose and throat with a kind of regurgitation, so essential a part of any Indian dawn, at 5. So it went on, with no one prepared to fit himself into anyone else's schedule. No wonder those in charge of delegations end up as nervous wrecks.

This inherent anarchy is reflected in a sharp critical facility where you can't bear what the other man does, so you inevitably hate your boss but hide that feeling underneath an excessive cringing, you resent your colleagues and you have contempt for those working below you. It is perhaps the Indian's way of striking a blow at his freedom, extricating himself from the suffocating family and caste restrictions. He wants to be organised no more. That is why normal western management principles when applied to our condition fall flat on their faces. Except for family business, expansion invariably leads to listlessness. The moment you realise you are a mere cog you lose interest altogether. A Japanese once explained to me that one Indian could measure up to ten Japanese with his wide ranging mind and philosophic capacity, but ten Indians could not measure up to one Japanse because together they would cancel each other out!

These fierce contradictions between the anarchic mind and the restrictive social patterns leads to the second most visible characteristic, which is the facility of an Indian to live on contradictory planes at the same moment in time. It is not a case of discrepancy in what you say and what you do. That is common the world over. It is a question of entertaining violently opposing beliefs together, the ultimate in coexistence. You can be a raving revolutionary, steeped in Marxism and ready to fling it about at the slightest provocation, and yet observe the most archaic ritual when your son takes his first morsel of solid food, you can talk about scientific advance and worship your tools by smearing them with the colour of red in remembrance of sacrificial blood, you can agree with both parties to a dispute and, in fact, that may be one reason why people drift from political party because they are never sure where they belong and could easily be in two or three places at once if their physical being could be so divided.

This ease, flexibility some call it, leads to the third most obvious characteristic—the concept of ethics has escaped us altogether because everything can be put into a relative framework. Right and wrong are for the birds. It you talk about paying your taxes or observing the law by refusing to allow your ten year old to drive a car, or telling the truth, or working during office hours, you are usually greeted with hoots of derision. This has happened to me on several occasions and I have found myself being apologetic under the gaze of people who obviously thought me plain stupid.

And, yet, this is not the complete picture, only the outline, bold as it may appear. When you begin to fill it in, you suddenly see all of this as a method of survival, the highest rate of survival at the lowest point in a way. It's the secret of our 'continuity', it's our way of coming to terms with the subjective and objective reality. Laws are neither observed, nor broken, because you might just break yourself in the process. And nothing in life is worth that. So, you circumvent the law.

In fact, an essential part of our character is the circular motion, the invincible zero. Never be direct, skirt the issue because you never know who you might offend and what the repercussions would be. Hence, the open armed eagerness with which we greeted the committee principle and the heedless way in which we have proliferated it. Ring any government office and the official will be 'not on his seat' but in a meeting where he can shed his responsibility for decision-making. Nothing controversial, of course, is said face to

The mind is forever in a state of frenzied activity, endless symposia and discussions take place, volumes are covered over with suggestions, and counter suggestions, commissions on education, police reforms, name it and it's there in some labyrinth of government, never, but never to be translated into action.

face at these meetings. So obsessed is the Indian with his own person, the self, as it were, that the slightest criticism offends, ignoring the objective issue completely. So, you go out of a meeting and release your pent up fury behind unsuspecting backs. You avoid confrontation like the plague.

All this helps to rub out whatever idea of ethic may have survived the many centuries of feverish philosophising. And, let us not forget that the idea of public ethic was a gift of the British colonisers, Rama notwithstanding. Public office and private profit have been interchangeable concepts in the minds of most people from times immemorial. As a child, how frequently I heard relatives talking to my grandmother with obvious delight at having married their daughters to government servants, or having acquired some *sarkari* status. 'He won't even need the salary now. The over and above will more than suffice.' It's not that people holding public office in other parts of the world don't stuff their pockets, but when they are exposed, they usually have to go. The number of people in India who were astonished at Nixon's ouster—after all, what did he do!—was legion. That is why exposures of people in public office, facts of corruption, nepotism, straight stealing from government funds don't make any impact other than a secret or not so secret admiration for someone who can get away with such booty.

The muffled echoes of disapproval come only from our immediate past—Gandhi and the wogs in consort to lay down the criteria for a minimum integrity. And the democratic process, in its lazy functioning has somehow freed the Indian from all of that. In fact it has been seized upon for its infinite possibilities for making money, turning politics into such a fun thing today. You can move from under one label to another with astounding speed, having stuffed your pockets adequately at every hurdle. You can get a leader announcing that he won't waste jeeps in the election campaign and next morning discover from the newspapers that he has been hopping from village to village in a helicopter (not run on batteries).

In fact, elections are the contemporary *tamasha*, complete with trapeze artists, expert tumblers and somersaulters, magicians, men and women who can turn *homo sapiens* into jelly in one second flat. India's '*leela*' of the 20th century.

The word 'leela' describes our predicament most vividly. It contains a concept which cannot be translated which is elusive and yet all-pervasive. It's a joyous happening in which everything is possible. The world is God's 'leela' and then we have Ram's leela and Krishna's leela where everything happens all at once, the right and the wrong, pleasure and pain, happiness and sorrow, the lot. Today, it is democracy's 'leela' or the politicians' 'leela'.

The voters enjoy it all, make what they can while the going is good, but they will not succumb to regimentation (famous last words!). Their normal living conceals so much violence, is so repressive, that it has to come out at some stage. The Indian cannot be fenced in for long and this is what political leadership would do well to keep in mind. A Gandhi could appear from nowhere, show a little determination to do what he said, and without the trapping of formal power, shame people into action. With what delight did they hurl their ties and hats and suits into bonfires at his command, freeing themselves from their western masters, how fervently they followed him, listened to him, walked with him.

More recently, how they voted out the Emergency in 1977, jumping over their caste and class hurdles in one unexpected, flying leap. That's just for the politicians to remember so that they don't get smug over this heightened individuality forever. Perhaps it is the rigidity of the caste and family inhibitions which makes us long to escape—from whatever it be.

The British class attitudes, when superimposed over our caste once produced a unique amalgam of super differentiation. You will never get an Indian to greet his domestic servant with a shake of the hand, with a direct communication on the human level. The hierarchies are too deeply embedded in the conscious and subconscious for anything so equalising. Most of my life I blamed it on colonialism, this touch-me-not attitude, this extraordinary arrogance but, sad to say, it is unique to this subcontinent. East of us they don't suffer from any such disease and I have never encountered it in Africa either, this tangled inferiority and superiority complex. Its most destructive manifestation is, however, in the attitude of non-caring which has been enforced and reinforced by Hinduism. There are so many little holes in the philosophy, from which you can escape retribution, so many ways in which you can translate self salvation, turning your eyes away from the horrors, convincing yourself that each is born with his or her destiny and you are not responsible, blissfully freeing yourself from any touch of guilt.

When this attitude is diverted from the human to the inanimate environment, it produces a unique, unparalleled capacity to disregard everything outside the self—almost as if the earth was created specially to receive Indian dirt. Much as everyone likes to avoid this question, to circumvent it by putting the blame on poverty, on the British who created the poverty, on the lack of this or that, we can't really absolve ourselves. It is our 'Area of Darkness' and no amount of raving against Naipaul can clean it up either. Poverty is not the cause because the boom towns of the Punjab are its most conspicuous manifestation, while the poorer, more 'backward' villages are less contaminated. It is without equal and creates problems for us which are, therefore, without equal, defeating town planners and municipal corporations alike, because no one is willing to accept this fact and then proceed from it.

As a wall is painted, it is stained with *paan* or urine, usually both happening simultaneously. Every pot hole is eagerly snatched as a possible lavatory; when public lavatories were put up in Delhi, every part was stolen so quickly that it was almost as if people couldn't bear to be deprived of the walls and the pavements. The Calcutta underground has also been seized upon with the same gleeful abandon. Of course our cities are horribly overcrowded, of course there is abysmal poverty, but why don't we do something about it. We just don't care for our environment, for our neighbour, for the things we buy, for anything or anybody except those closely related to ourselves.

As I walk to the office after having negotiated the traffic where this not-caring is so evident, I have to tread warily dodging the pavement's share of snot and spit and peels and refuse of a varied kind, only to be confronted with clouds of dust being swept ostensibly from the interior of shops even at 10.30 am, straight into one's face with a kind of childlike joy. Wherever a stone is missing in the pavement, no one replaces it because it becomes the ideal hole in the ground for dumping anything you want to. Climbing the staircase, I tune my ears to catch any sound of nose or throat cleaning so that I might avoid the spray. It is all too, too distressing. Maybe the concept of *achhut* is behind it all—for, cleaning is a task strictly reserved for the untouchable. You don't mind where you place your dirt because you will never be called upon to clean it.

It is an attitude of mind which you carry with you to work, piling up the files for posterity to clear, ordering every citizen to preserve every bill or receipt or scrap of paper forever afterwards, avoid getting anything out of the way by delaying a decision so long as humanly possible, letting machine or gadget break completely before launching on any repair and, if possible, just hurling it into the neighbour's yard. Cracked window-panes, broken knobs, tangled wires and stained floors—it's all part of the Indian condition.

When you extend this characteristic to our rules and regulations, you realise why every office is choked with outmoded procedures, like the drains, and why every new law is greeted with renewed energy to work out ways of circumventing it. Maintenance is a non-word and a non-concept in our minds. When a Japanese team came to inspect one of our power plants —in Delhi—the members were amazed that any electricity came out of it. 'We certainly couldn't make that happen,' they declared, astonished at the improvisation which, by stretching the imagination a wee bit, you might describe as 'intermediate' technology.

Recently, when a high powered (favourite hierarchical term with us) science committee was found to have been utterly useless, it was disbanded and another one created. When one of the members of the old committee found he had been invited to join the new one, hopefully, he rushed off to the first meeting only to be startled to find every single member of the previous committee sitting as usual, feeling like new people now that the label had been changed. This really is to illustrate how we avoid action at every level. The mind is forever in a state of frenzied activity, endless symposia and discussions take place, volumes are covered over with suggestions, and

The world is God's 'leela' and then we have Ram's leela and Krishna's leela where everything happens all at once, the right and the wrong, pleasure and pain, happiness and sorrow, the lot. Today, it is democracy's 'leela' or the politicians' 'leela'.

counter suggestions, commissions on education, police reforms, name it and it's there in some labyrinth of government, never, but never to be translated into action. It is enough for us that the mind has found a solution, the issue is closed forever and the situation on the ground remains as usual. Some say that all of this is the same means and ends game where the end is forgotten and the means become the end. I don't know. It certainly leads to an unending coil of harassment for the ordinary citizen, even though he is also responsible, and creates a feeling of hopelessness on one side of the coin.

On the other, it unfetters the mind, and leaves one with time, time to think, time to do the things most of the world has long forgotten to do under the pressures of industrial society like sitting and indulging in an *adda* just for the love of it, for the love of exchanging ideas without the awesome responsibility of ever having to put them into practice, time to co-relate at least within the confines of the mind. This capacity for co-relation, the philosophic attitude, exists even among the so-called unlettered, almost more so there. To recognise it as such would mean utilising it at every stage for encouraging greater participation.

The innate contempt for maintenance, for sweeping up the litter of the body and the mind, has enabled our people to give themselves up to their individual creativity, a kind of total involvement, shorn of all distraction. I remember seeing a camel in the distance outside the Jaiselmer rest house one evening. It appeared to be clothed in a richly embroidered cloth of brown. But, as it came closer, I realised that there was no cloth at all—its owner had obviously spent long winter evenings cutting its hair in intricate patterns to give that effect. This dedication is visible in every field of activity outside the sphere of management, so it's not a question of laziness or incapacity.

Our planners would do well to keep some of these characteristics in mind. The small unit which requires the minimum of management, even though Schumacher may not have had India in mind, individual responsibility, a recognition of the creative talent crying out for appreciation, might perhaps just help us to cross over to the 21st century. Only perhaps, because I continue to believe that if we could just hire people to manage the tedious processes of living today, leaving our people to their exuberant creativity spilling over on to cloth and paper and metal and wood and song and dance, we might be nearer the truth, and grasp the essentials about ourselves.

Mahashweta brought to those poor and harassed people a boundless compassion, which they instantly understood though they could neither speak her language nor she theirs. She has a strange ability to communicate with the silenced, her best speech reserved for those to whom no one has spoken.

The Adivasi Mahashweta

Ganesh N. Devy

Do I know Mahashweta Devi ? Perhaps, I do. Perhaps not.

In the early 1980s, I had launched a journal of literary translations and was keen to have a Mahashweta Devi story for it. I wrote to her, and she sent her own translation of 'Death of Jagmohan, the Elephant' and 'Seeds'. The manuscripts looked uninviting: close type in the smallest possible font size on sheets smudged with blue carbon. The stories were great, for their authentic realism and sharpness of political analysis. I knew that she had written about the kind of India that is mine.

After they were published, I sent her two money orders of ₹ 50 each as honorarium. She promptly returned the money requesting that it be used as 'donation for whatever work you are doing.' In the years that followed, I never met her at literary gatherings, not even in Calcutta where she lived. Once I was in Calcutta on a literary call. When I asked friends about the where-abouts of 'Bortika', which I thought was the name of a locality, they were quick to point out that Mahashweta did not like academics. I was clueless as to how I could get to see her.

In the mid-90s, I decided to give up academic life and enter the world of the *adivasis*. The organisation founded for this purpose was called 'bhasha' to represent the 'voice of the adivasis'. Since the work was to be in remote adivasi villages, my colleagues felt that we should institute an annual lecture on adivasis in Baroda. We decided to name it after Verrier Elwin.

Every time we started short-listing speakers for the Elwin lecture, Mahashweta Devi's name would come up first. But I had no idea how to get such a renowned person to Baroda, or even whether she would be interested to give a lecture. The Jnanapith Award and the Magsaysay Award given to her in 1996-97 only made things more difficult for me. Nevertheless, I sent her a letter of invitation. She did not respond.

Reproduced from 'Celebrating Women', *Seminar*, August 2004. Ganesh N. Devy is founder and director of the Tribal Academy at Tejgadh, Gujarat.

The utter simplicity of her bearing, the sincerity conveyed through her body language and her direct style, defeating all grammar, had completely shattered the audience.

In January 1998, I was at the India International Centre (IIC) in Delhi to meet Chandrashekhar Kambar. I ran into Dinesh Mishra who offered to introduce me to Mahashweta Devi. We went up to her room and as introduction, he said some kind words about me. She looked at me once and said that she would accept the invitation to Baroda, but gave no date. She then looked up again. I knew that my time with her was up.

In February 1998, Professor Amiya Dev invited me to Vidyasagar University, Midanapur for a seminar. I travelled to Bengal, this time with a team of ten adivasi writers and story-tellers. I was unaware till we reached the university that Mahashweta Devi was to speak at the seminar. It was the first time that I heard her. I did not follow all what she said, because she looked disturbed, speaking with pain and anger. We requested Amiya Dev to arrange a meeting with her, but since she was to leave for Calcutta the same evening, we were given only fifteen minutes. I barely managed to introduce my colleagues such as Bhagwandas Patel, the great folk-lorist and the celebrated Marathi writer, Laxman Gaikwad. She did, however, give a definite date for the Elwin lecture in Baroda.

The Elwin lecture was to be in March. Mahashweta Devi chose to speak on the 'Denotified Tribes of India'. Our practice was to combine the Elwin lecture with a major seminar. That year we had more than 50 adivasi delegates from all over India for the seminar. I had earlier fixed to take them to an island in the Narmada, some 90 km south of Baroda, the same day Mahashweta was to arrive. Since I could not receive her at the Ahmedabad airport, 115 km north of Baroda, I requested my activist friend, Ajay Dandekar and Tridip Suhrud, friend and former student, to do so and bring her to Baroda.

I returned from the island quite late. They reached Baroda even later in the night. I had asked them to dine en route, before dropping her at the guest house where she was to stay. Throughout their journey from Ahmedabad to Baroda, I kept receiving calls from them that Mahashweta seemed upset, that she was refusing to eat. So I suggested they bring her home. My wife was not in Baroda, and neither had I eaten nor did I know if there was food at home. When Ajay and Tridip arrived, they showed clear signs of some strain. I had no idea how to greet her and so I asked, 'Do you have your own teeth?' I do not think anybody had ever asked her anything so rude. My intention was to figure out if she would be able to chew the few slices of hardened bread that I was planning to offer her with some pickle and onion.

On hearing my question she burst out laughing. She laughed so hard that my neighbours, waiting behind the windows to have a glimpse of this celebrity, came out in curiosity. We had an impromptu meeting across the fencing; she spoke to each one of them with great affection. They rushed into their kitchens, cooked and brought *daal* and rice for her. She ate. We talked. I made endless cups of tea for her. She offered to stay in my simple house. When I apologised for its simplicity, she said, 'This is luxury for me. You should see my house in Calcutta.'

I asked her why she had decided to call it Bortika. She laughed again. She said, 'You have no brains, it is not the name of my house, it is the journal that I bring out.' I poured more tea for her. By now, our other colleagues whom I had packed off for the night in the two small rooms upstairs, joined us. She started telling us about herself, beginning with the famous 'non-vegetarian cow', about her father and mother, her childhood, the brief stay in Santiniketan, her very special views on Rabindranath Tagore and Bengal, and how she started work as a roving journalist, bringing to light the conditions of bonded labour and adivasis.

She spoke at length about Palamu, about her adventures collecting material on Laxmibai of Jhansi, about how she lost the Jnanapith award cheque given to her by Nelson Mandela. We all knew that she had found our gang of writer-activists a company close to her heart. She told me how, when I went to see her at the IIC, she had thought that I was a *zamindar's* son because I was wearing a clean shirt. By the time the clock struck four, our friendship was sealed. She was 73, I was 48, the youngest of my colleagues was barely 23. We knew we were all together.

Her Elwin lecture was deeply moving. She had no written script. She spoke of the civilisational graces of the adivasis, of how our society had mindlessly destroyed the culture of our great continent, and how the innocents had been brutalised. She described the context in which the infamous Criminal Tribes Act, 1871 was introduced, the process of denotification in 1952 and the plight of the nomadic communities in India ever since. The DNTs (Denotified Tribals) are human beings too, she said. She then narrated the gruesome episode of the custodial death of Budhan Sabar in Purulia in February, a day before we first met her at the Vidyasagar University.

The term 'spell-bound' is inadequate to capture the effect she had on her audience. The utter simplicity of her bearing, the sincerity conveyed through her body language and her direct style, defeating all grammar, had completely shattered the audience. Here was a no-pretence, no-rhetoric, no-nonsense person, whose compassion and clarity were an invitation for action. Perhaps Mahatma Gandhi alone, among great Indians, spoke like her.

The next morning, several of my young students and colleagues came home to meet and listen to her. Some of them brought food, which we shared. In the afternoon, I asked her if she was prepared to trek out to Tejgadh, a good 90 km from Baroda. She was more than willing to undertake the journey. That afternoon I took her to show the location of the Adivasi Academy in Tejgadh and the 12,000 year old rock painting in the Koraj hill close by.

We then trooped off to a stream meeting the Orsang river, and all of us, Mahashweta included, had a dip. She was only 73. She said, 'I have not been here before but I have seen this rock-painting a long time back. I have seen the Pithora painted in Nagin Rathwa's house a long time back. Read my "Pterodactyl".' I recognise this voice. It is beyond time. She added, 'Do you know about the Saora paintings? They no longer have figures in the same form, but the adivasi memory never forgets.' I knew that yet again Mahashweta Devi had found in Tejgadh the timeless voice and the indestructible memory that have made the adivasis what they are. This discovery was the beginning of a long journey for both of us. The next day, in Baroda, we formed the Denotified and Nomadic Tribes Rights Action Group, the DNT-RAG. The day she left Baroda, I fractured my foot.

Even before the plaster was removed, I was with Mahashweta Devi again, this time in Hyderabad, from where we travelled to Warangal. Malayalam novelist, P. Sachidanandan and literary scholar, Jaidev were with us. Mahashweta Devi spoke of her activist life; I about her literary work. We returned to Hyderabad to hold a press conference and address a gathering of activists on the DNT question. We then went to Bombay where, along with Laxman Gaikwad, we met the deputy chief minister of Maharashtra. He was keen that Mahashweta Devi address the Marathi Literary Conference.

She spoke to him about human rights violations in Bombay. I had by now observed that she spared no one, in particular snobs, ministers, insincere journalists and literary aspirants. During that meeting, I was informed that my teacher, the Kannada fiction writer Shantinath Desai had passed away the previous day. I wanted to be with his family. Mahashweta Devi declared that she would brave the overnight road journey 300 km to Kolhapur.

We travelled; she remained absorbed watching the red sky, typical of the Western Ghats, through the long hours of sunset. She also told Laxman and me how she had once decided to release an 'army' of young monkeys near Khandala. This was when she lived in Bombay with her husband, who played a prominent role in the IPTA movement and had a brush with the world of Hindi cinema. She talked of the singer Hemanta Kumar Mukherjee with the same ease as she did about Ernest Hemingway and Arthur Miller, about Madhubala as of Sadat Hasan Manto, all her great favourites.

Mahashweta, more a woman of film-songs than of the *raagas*, of laughter than long-faced pontification, is closer to that which reveals than decorates and conceals. And yet she is detached from everything, completely. You cannot please her by praise or by providing her with creature comforts. She is almost not there when one thinks she is very much there.

Soon we found ourselves together in Delhi. This time the National Human Rights Commission had responded to our letter about the DNT issue. The Commission appointed a committee to prepare a report. We visited Delhi on several

Here was a no-pretence, no-rhetoric, no-nonsense person, whose compassion and clarity were an invitation for action. Perhaps Mahatma Gandhi alone, among great Indians, spoke like her.

occasions in order to complete the report. Every trip meant meeting more people, addressing press conferences, campaigning with greater energy. We met the Election Commission, the Census authorities, the home minister, the welfare minister, former prime ministers, MPs, journalists, addressing gathering at press clubs, university hostels, colleges and institutions.

In between these trips we were in Maharashtra, making long overnight journeys to places like Ahmednagar, Yavatmal, Latur, Sholapur, Dhulia, Jalgaon and Baramati. At these places we met with the Pardhis, Wadars, Bhamtes, Bairagis and Kaikadis. We went to police stations to lodge complaints of rape, torture and humiliation, often against those whose job it was to protect people. We visited sites of old and fresh atrocities.

Mahashweta brought to those poor and harassed people a boundless compassion, which they instantly understood though they could neither speak her language nor she theirs. She has a strange ability to communicate with the silenced, her best speech reserved for those to whom no one has spoken.

Between visits to Delhi and travels in Maharashtra, she made frequent trips to Gujarat. Baroda became her second home, Tejgadh her sacred grove for communion with the adivasis. 'In Tejgadh alone,' she said, 'my bones will find rest. Ganesh, you will understand, I am tired of it all, this praise, this deification. I hate it.' In Gujarat, she was all over, in the villages of Panchamahals with the poet Kanji Patel, at the mournful ex-settlement of the DNTs in Chharanagar, Ahmedabad, in Khedbrahma to meet the singers of the Garasia-Bhil Mahabharata.

When Budhan was killed in police custody in Purulia, Mahashweta Devi had filed a case in the Calcutta High Court. The judgement ordered compensation to Budhan's widow, Shyamali. By the time this judgement was delivered by Justice Ruma Paul, Mahashweta Devi and I had already started our work at Chharanagar. We established a library there, for which she donated the amount received by her as the first Yasmin award.

The Chhara boys and girls, whose parents had been branded as thieves by the rest of the world, found in her a great pillar of support and strength. They started calling her 'Amma', mother, as thousands of adivasis in India had done. They composed a play on the life and death of Budhan and performed it before her during the first national convention of the DNTs held in Chharanagar on 31 August 1998. In the play she was depicted as a character who pleads for the dignity and rights of the DNTs in the Calcutta High Court. She cried as she watched the agony of the branded speak through the play.

Mahashweta Devi discovered for herself three places of rest in Gujarat: Tejgadh with its timeless memory and the mysterious voice of the adivasis; Chharanagar, with its intricate imagination of Indian criminality and spirituality; and Bhupen Khakhar's house with its 'forensic' approach to sentimentality. Bhupen had long been a friend, and I thought she would take to him gracefully as a friend's friend. Their first encounter was not pleasant. She scolded him for not engaging in direct social activism. Bhupen with his typical humour, said, 'Ganesh Devy is an activist. I paint.'

But soon they were friends, as profound as friendship has ever been. I knew that both belonged to a different league, akin to Gandhi and Tagore. Every time they were together she would sing for him a Suraiya or a Noorjahan number, but mostly 'Moray baal-pan-ke saathi' and Bhupen would sing for her a few Gujarati *bhajans*. Both sang with a fullness of their selves. She never failed to remind him that art is nothing if not 'forensic'. Bhupen read out his stories such as 'Phoren Soap' and 'Maganbhai's Glue'. They were happy in this togetherness, which both knew meant nothing to them because it was unreal.

When Bhupen passed away in 2003, Mahashweta Devi did not cry. She said, 'Among your friends he was the only real one, all others are superficial. He was Bhupen...'

On a Sunday morning in January 2001, we were watching the Ahmedabad news on TV; suddenly we saw the newsreader abandon his desk and run out of the studio. In another couple of seconds, our own house in Baroda started shaking violently. We all ran out of the house shouting, 'It's an earthquake.' The great quake had hit Gujarat. The next day we went through Ahmedabad. Everywhere there were collapsed and collapsing houses. She returned to Calcutta and started writing public appeals for help. For over a month she kept sending relief material.

The following year Gujarat was struck by a greater, this time man-made, tragedy. The riots in Gujarat erupted on the last day of February. By March 2, Mahashweta Devi had faxed a letter to the President asking for an inquiry by the CBI. In a week's time she was in Gujarat, when the cities were still under curfew. I will never forget the expression on her face when she spoke to the inmates of the Shah Alam relief camp. A Muslim woman who had seen 18 members of her family, relatives and neighbours killed before her eyes, was talking to Mahashweta Devi. I had to hold her as she fainted in anger and shock. She visited Gujarat twice during March and April 2002, speaking to small gatherings of peace-keepers and writers about the need for understanding, but I noticed that the idea of being in Gujarat no longer appealed to her. Her subsequent visits were mainly to spend a few quiet days with Surekha and me.

The days we spend together are very special for all three of us. When together, Mahashweta Devi becomes our mother, friend and child, in turn. She narrates stories that we are unable to read because they have yet to be translated into English. She speaks of her life and times, of experiences that she will be unable to include in the autobiography on which she has been working. She is with us as if she has always been with us, closer than a mother, sister or friend. It is difficult for me to believe that such a relationship can really exist. Yet, I know that she lives on a different plane, that Mahashweta Devi is not accessible to anyone.

Halfway through a perfectly normal breakfast, served after her medication, all of a sudden she exclaims, 'Ganesh—land, land is the root cause of it all. Give them land and everything will be "halright". Oh, this wretched "hestablishment".' As I pour another cup of black tea for her, I ask, 'Do you remember our visit to the ex-minister's farmhouse?' She then tells Surekha how she saw women's undergarments of various fashion in the toilet of the 'hhonourable ex-minister' when she was taken there by mistake by his attendants, and how 'mightily he frowned.' But even before we had finished laughing, she remarks in utmost pain, 'This woman's body is a curse!' Then she turns to me and remarks, 'You will not know, because you are not political.' The very next moment she is focusing on her cup of tea.

I have often wondered about the source of her strength, the literary influences that have shaped her powerful style of writing, the political philosophies that have gone into the making of her ideology. She confesses to having no influences, except that she mentions her uncle, the film-maker Ritwik Ghatak, with a great sense of pride. I am often amazed how someone like her, slated to be a middle-class housewife, has managed to transcend so many prisons to become what she is. What is the source of her remarkable memory, the frightening economy of her words, that great simplicity which having distributed life between the necessary and the unnecessary, shuns all that is unnecessary? Is she an adivasi taken to literature, or a writer drawn to the adivasis?

Do I know Mahashweta Devi? Perhaps, perhaps not.

There is the darker side to current trends. The focus must shift for a while, therefore, to the changing internal dynamics within media offices, with the relative decline of the editor or his equivalent, and the growing importance of the business departments.

The Changing Indian Media Scene

T.N. NINAN

Guess which are India's most valuable media companies? The chances are that you would not have thought of Adlabs and Balaji Telefilms as being among them. But they happen to be among the six media companies that are listed on the stock market, each of which has a company valuation of more than ₹ 1,000 crore. That is not the complete story, of course, because some of the largest media companies in the country are not listed—Bennett Coleman and Kasturi & Co, for instance. Still, it is interesting that among the media companies with the highest valuations, three others either did not exist in 1991 or were cottage industries then: Zee Telefilms, New Delhi Television and Television Eighteen.

Some of the largest media players are not necessarily national entities, and could be regional players. Arguably, the biggest media story of the past decade is the super-successful Sun group of southern India. And who would have thought that *Dainik Jagran* and *Dainik Bhaskar* (the leading Hindi dailies with no presence in the south, east and most of the west) would have the same stock valuation as the *Hindustan Times* (No. 2 in the English market)? But they do, at over ₹ 2,000 crore each.

And who knows, even these could be outdone by Harish Thawani of Nimbus, the advertising/ sponsorship agency that has tied up a cricket sponsorship deal for the eye-popping sum of ₹ 2,700 crore, and now thinks it is cheaper to do its own sports TV channel than sell cricket coverage to other TV operators.

In other words, check your premises before starting to debate media; it is not what you thought it was. The word does not mean just newspapers; and soon it will not mean just TV either. Nor does it mean just news. It means entertainment. And the clear line that used to be there between these two segments often gives way now to a continuum, where it is sometimes hard to decide what is which. Will an FM radio station run by Adlabs, which is debarred from broadcasting

Reproduced from 'Media Matters', *Seminar*, May 2006. T.N. Ninan is the Chairman of Business Standard Ltd., Delhi.

news under the government's bizarre formulation, not be allowed to tell you stock market prices, or cricket scores? What is news, after all? Some newspapers now refer to advertising as 'news you can use'! So ads too can be news. And newspapers find that (in comparison with an earlier age) they have to entertain more now, and educate a little less (and pander to the powerful rather than provoke them!). In short, this is not the media world of 15 years ago, when categories and rules and pecking orders and ethical choices and your place in the world were clear to everyone.

The other change is that Indian media is no more the same thing as media in India. Foreign media are here like never before (Star and Sony Entertainment are major players, and there are several international print players who have entered the Indian market); and Indian media are all over the world—NDTV and Zee, for instance, run channels across Europe and North America.

But anyone who thinks that the print media is challenged by the Johnny-come-latelies of the electronic world, had better think again—because print has fought back and by some reckonings has grown faster in the past couple of years. And there is another reason why TV cannot sit pretty, for there is the internet—as Subhash Chandra of Zee argued in some detail at FICCI's 'Frames' conference in Mumbai last month. To some extent he was echoing Rupert Murdoch, who on more than one occasion in the past year has focused on the challenges posed by the internet. Think Google News and its variants—with Google ads; think ad-erasing technologies for TV that have gained ground in Europe, like Tivo, so that you can watch time-delayed movies on TV without being disturbed by Aishwarya Rai performing over and over again for Coke; and think of customised viewing by people who don't want to follow network schedules and can soon set their own, and pick and choose. Access to news and views need not also be through TV sets or computers; it can be on 'thin devices' like mobile phones and palm tops, or through a broadband connection.

For sure, Indian TV now covers more than half the population (close to 600 million people) and therefore has among the biggest audiences in the world—one reason why the centre of world cricket has shifted to this country. So who has done the biggest sports telecast deal in history? Nimbus. Is that media? Not in the traditional sense, but it could soon be. With over 100 million TV sets, the majority of which are hooked to cable and satellite channels, the TV story is in fact the most important development of the past fifteen years. As a business, cable and satellite TV now rivals print in terms of reach (about a quarter of the population), although it is barely fifteen years old, and already carries greater political clout —quite apart from also being the pioneer with such innovations as sting journalism. But India also has 140 million phones, and 4 million are being added every month! Welcome to the world of genuine multimedia.

Even if one were to ignore the entertainment side of the business for the moment, any understanding of the media beast must begin with recognition of the fact that the news media is a two-faced animal. In one frame of reference it is the 'fourth estate', performing the public function of the free press in a democracy—and therefore blessed with the importance and recognition given to a societal 'good'. But the media, in all but the rarest of cases, is also a business, clothed as it is in a corporate entity with shareholders who expect a return on their investment.

The tension between these two objectives—of publishing (or telecasting) all the news that is fit to print (without a thought for the cost of newsprint), with no quarter given to any power (including advertisers), and at the same time of maximising profits—raises many questions: the autonomy and freedom given to the editorial function within a corporate hierarchy and pecking order; the tension between the very different goals of growing circulation and readership (which costs money) and pushing advertising (which earns it); and whether there can be virtuous circles, with strong balance sheets underwriting freedom from commercial pressures and therefore editorial independence.

These two faces of the media are usually examined without reference to each other. The general print media debate usually focuses on the editorial issues of freedom and censorship (internal, external), quality and relevance. The business media, when they look at their own sector, will focus on stock prices, growth rates, market shares, bottom lines and such. Almost no one looks at the interplay between the two, though each fundamentally influences the other and the full story cannot be told without keeping the duality in mind. (Journalists are not alone in this; political history in India is rarely studied with reference to the economic context that has often caused the birth of new political currents.)

Any holistic attempt must therefore be to understand each set of issues with reference to the other. That makes it a more complicated story, but hopefully also a more interesting one. Though one must immediately make the confession that, while several trends stare us in the face, they make no single cohesive pattern that can be immediately drawn out for the reader, all one can do is to lay out the mosaic in all its interwoven complexity.

First, even for print, there is the growth story, the rapid expansion and diversification of the Indian press, at a time when the sales of newspapers in western countries are in steady decline (in the US, by about five per cent a year). Thank India's growing population and rising literacy—both trends that should keep the country's newspapers in good nick for some time to come. Within this, there is the interesting, subsidiary trend of regional language publications coming into their own—with growth in circulation, a greater share of advertising, and (perhaps more important than both of these) growth in self-confidence. Perhaps that was inevitable at some stage, since the total readership for English publications is less than two per cent of the population, and less than a tenth of the total reach of print. And with spending power going beyond the metros, into the small towns and even villages, there is a shift of advertising and financial power as well. The stock market knows what it is doing when it values Jagran Prakashan and HT Media at about the same level.

As a natural corollary to this growth story, we have the advent of media as a sizeable and significant business—so much so that immigration forms now have media as a sub-category among the professions that you can tick. At least ten newspapers now count their daily copy sales in millions, not lakhs—three in English, as many in Hindi and the rest in regional languages. The largest publishing company (Bennett Coleman) is perhaps the most profitable among all privately held firms in India and would be worth more than a couple of billion dollars if floated on the stock exchange. Its chairperson, Indu Jain, figures in the list of twenty-three Indians listed by Forbes as dollar billionaires. This is no longer the semi-cottage industry of old; and the stakes are high.

Businesses that grow big usually cease to be wholly family-owned enterprises, and so it is that the larger Indian media companies have begun to get listed on the stock exchanges and invite public shareholding—with all the extra attention, accountability and media focus that this brings to sales trends, profits and market capitalisation. A dozen media firms are now publicly quoted, and about half these are valued at over ₹ 1,000 crore each on the stock market—including an unlikely candidate in the Deccan Chronicle. Not the stuff to set the market on fire, but a far cry from two decades ago, when the largest media company reported net profits of about ₹ 5 crore. It is a hundred times that today.

Then, there is the growing sophistication of the media market. There is the professional polish of the news channels, the production values (if not always the content) of the soaps and sitcoms, the technical wizardry of cricket coverage, and the growing range of expertise in newspaper offices (full-time defence correspondents, science reporters, agriculture editors, personal finance pages, fashion editors, food specialists, environment reporters, people who focus on gender issues, media analysts, marketing correspondents...). Those writing on these sometimes have degrees in business management or a doctorate in physics, with even the odd accountant thrown in.

The rapid growth of editions and pages has meant a sharp increase in the demand for journalists. Three things have resulted: a mushrooming of media schools of varying quality to train journalists, the preponderance of young reporters and editors in newspaper offices, and a sharp spurt in salaries for all those with some claim to ability. Though youth and energy are more in evidence than experience, perspective and (sometimes) good judgment, the pay packet for someone with 12-15 years of experience and some special quality of his or her own can hit ₹ 15-20 lakh and more. Even after adjusting for inflation, that would be more than Girilal Jain ever earned as editor of *The Times of India* (till 1988).

All these are elements of the growth story. On the business side, there is now the sophisticated computer modelling that determines media buying plans—leading to the birth of firms that do nothing other than media planning and media buying. And as printing presses of international quality have begun to get manufactured in the country, their costs have dropped dramatically, so you can now find a good printing press with colour facilities and speeds of 30,000 copies an hour in almost any major town in the country. That, plus the communications revolution, has helped newspapers start multiple editions and localise their news so as to focus on regional and district news, not just national and global—thus reaching out to new readers. In a parallel development, and as another manifestation of the communications revolution, satellite slots have become so plentiful and cheap that transponder costs are no longer a significant element of cost when launching a new channel. What you get, therefore, is media proliferation as entry-level costs have fallen.

All of these (multimedia growth, variety, size, entrepreneurship, wealth creation, technical sophistication, localisation) are positive developments, and reflect an open society with a free press that also has a rapidly growing economy and a burgeoning literate population that is hungry to read and get the news. Watch any parking lot where drivers of cars congregate, or bored guards outside affluent homes, or neo-literates in other occupations, and you will probably see a good percentage engrossed in reading the morning's newspaper. This macro-trend tends to get ignored in a media debate that usually focuses on the problem areas, perhaps because good news is still not considered news.

But of course, there is the darker side to current trends. The focus must shift for a while, therefore, to the changing internal dynamics within media offices, with the relative decline of the editor or his equivalent, and the growing importance of the business departments. This is usually attributed to specific individuals, and it is of course true that trends manifest themselves through individual personalities who are driven by their own psychological needs. But it is important to recognise the larger forces at work, linked to some of the business and technological developments already spelt out.

For, in times of stable businesses, limited competition and general status quo, editors could ignore the market and behave as kings in their offices—buoyed by the mythology (sometimes based on fact) of editors who rub shoulders with the rich and the powerful, and even with god. Once media multiplies, though, markets become contestable and circulations get threatened by new rivals. So what sells becomes as important as the editor's notion of what is important. Enter readership surveys (the editor may not know best, after all), brand managers and the rest of the marketing kerfuffle.

But even as the editor loses importance, section editors with ability gain in value—because one way to take on the competition is to upgrade quality and cater more closely to reader interests. This might mean more city coverage, or more business pages, or bigger sports pictures, or a splash on fashion, or arresting coverage of the entertainment sector. The variety is also dictated by readers' perceived desire to move away from grand national politics to either local issues (like water supply) or to the new car models being launched. It is the section editors who deliver all this, and when the 'Daily News Analysis' was launched as India's newest paper in Mumbai last year, all the section editors were hired before the editor was identified, almost as an afterthought.

Editorial quality thus becomes important, not editorial independence—and the reader usually does not care enough to know the difference. And within the newspaper world, a job offer with a 30 per cent pay hike is usually enough to make a journalist not worry too much about who actually decides what should be the news, the editor or the publisher, and to be willing to follow publisher diktat on who can or cannot be written about and how. So it's not just the reader who is indifferent, in most cases the journalist doesn't care either—in part because the gods of the media world have all too often been shown to have feet of clay.

This ties in with a parallel but reinforcing development, which is the increasing dependence on the advertiser for a newspaper's revenue,

In one frame of reference it is the 'fourth estate', performing the public function of the free press in a democracy —and therefore blessed with the importance and recognition given to a societal 'good'. But the media, in all but the rarest of cases, is also a business, clothed as it is in a corporate entity with shareholders who expect a return on their investment.

with downstream consequences. To understand how this has come about, one must go back to the time when every region or state had its own newspaper-reading pattern, not just in a particular regional language but also in the multi-region languages of English and Hindi. The Times of India ruled in Mumbai, the Hindustan Times in Delhi, the *Hindu* in Chennai, the *Deccan Herald* in Bangalore, the *Deccan Chronicle* in Hyderabad, and so on, down to the *Tribune* in Chandigarh, the *Pioneer* in Lucknow, and *Searchlight* in Patna. Enter the era of low-cost printing presses, high-speed data lines that can zap a whole newspaper page to any printing centre in minutes, and ease of transportation, and newspapers began to think beyond a city, state or region.

With the era of multi-edition newspapers and therefore multi-newspaper markets, has come greater choice and a fierce fight for the reader's attention. Along then came the vital discovery that readers may not be completely wedded to habit and to reading one newspaper, and that even a small difference in price could sometimes bring about a change of purchase decision. This has driven newspaper prices to the point where the leading newspapers fetch virtually no circulation revenue for their publishers (the little that is collected from the reader goes almost entirely to the distributor and hawker). Indian newspapers are now the cheapest in the world, though the world of completely free newspapers is still to descend on this country. Wait for the metros to become true transport pipes, though, and even that will come about in may be half a decade.

Once newspapers become virtually free, and the advertiser knows he is king (advertising usually accounts for more than 80 per cent of the revenue of almost any English newspaper, and about 50-65 per cent in the case of other languages), it is but a short step for some money-hungry publisher to give in to temptation and decide that he must keep his advertiser happy—and declare (as one publisher is said to have done to his journalists) that 'my advertiser is your reader.' Indeed, some newspapers even refer to classified ads as 'news you can use'—so advertising is now news. In through the side door, then, comes the doctoring of news so as to please the piper who is paying, and in a publishing version of Say's law in economics (bad money drives out good), bad journalism begins to drive out good. Today there is one large publisher who has openly obliterated the line that separates news from advertising by introducing a 'paid news' category that earlier was whispered about with reference to publications without a reputation to protect. If the practice gets established with other leading titles in the market, don't be surprised if others who protest today decide to follow suit tomorrow.

Advertisers determine content in more subtle ways as well. For they are interested in publications that reach more readers in the higher socioeconomic categories, with money to spend. Newspapers therefore have begun to focus editorial attention on the interests of the well-heeled, and reduced the coverage given to bread and butter issues that affect only the poor, or indeed the civic issues in the areas where the poor live. As the criticism goes, more journalists cover Lakme Fashion Week than the distress of farmers who are committing suicide week in and week out. This reflects in part the shift towards increasing the entertainment value of newspapers, in part the secession of the rich in India from the poor in Bharat (to use political short-hand), and of course the greater stress on the commercial success of publications that face more competition than at any time in the past.

Even if a publisher wants to buck these trends, he or she runs into an enormous headwind. Because the fact is that the company with the biggest newspapers, the largest sales and the fattest profits—Bennett Coleman—is usually the one that is testing the limits of what is acceptable in polite society. The equally relevant fact is (and this runs counter to the proliferation of media that one sees) that the rule of three has been seen to operate in the media industry. This rule, perhaps articulated first by Jagdish Sheth of Emory University in Atlanta, says that in most markets the leader makes a lot of money; the No. 2 makes a little money; the No. 3 probably breaks even; and everyone else loses cash.

And so it is that Bennett Coleman (which publishes the Times of India, *Economic Times*, *Navbharat Times* and *Maharashtra Times*—all market leaders in their categories) earns more profits than the rest of the publishing industry put together—and it is this financial muscle that allows it to start price wars on other publications' turf, undercut rivals and eat into their markets. The other publishers have understood what this means: if they don't make enough money to be able to invest in a fight-back, they will be history. And in a steady trickle, one and then two and then more have/will come to the conclusion that the only way to fight Bennett is to copy its tactics. Ergo, advertising rules the roost everywhere and journalists become adjuncts in a business war.

Some of the stock market listings of recent times are directly related to the increased competition and the fightback by those challenged in their markets. HT Media went to the stock market to raise money for the launch of its Mumbai edition, and a pitched battle on the Times of India's home turf. Deccan Chronicle in turn went to the market to raise the money for launching new editions in Chennai (home of The Hindu) and Bangalore (once the domain of the Deccan Herald). Others, like Dainik Jagran, have listed and simultaneously gone multimedia by launching a new TV channel. So the stock market listings are an indication that the game has got bigger, and private pockets are not deep enough to finance the battles being fought for survival and supremacy.

If in doubt that journalists are now being made adjuncts in at least some media offices, consider the meaning of the 'private treaties' that Bennett Coleman gets into—and several have been signed. These 'treaties' are basically the transfer of shares in return for advertising. Bennett has surplus cash coming out of its ears, which it invests in usually mid-rung companies that are keen to jump into the big league but without perhaps the big bucks to spend on marketing. The share purchase money is immediately taken back against the promise of guaranteed advertising in Bennett publications—to build the investee company's brand(s). Part of the deal is even said to be editorial coverage, though this remains unconfirmed.

If true, this by definition will have to be positive coverage. Even if that is not the case, the idea is that the brands have to be built up, so that the shares bought by Bennett gain in value and can be sold—with the added benefit that (unlike ad revenue) profits from long-term capital gains are tax-free! But from the editorial perspective, out goes the whole business of the press being a watchdog. Consider the likelihood of journalists writing negative stories about companies that have done a 'private treaty' with the publishing company. Logically, if not by diktat, journalists now have to write about companies in such a manner as to boost their share price.

The commercialisation of news, it must be stated in its defence, is in part a response to the growing tentacles of the public relations (PR) business. PR companies were born a little over a decade ago, and have become an essential part of the media scene. As the media has grown in reach and importance, and its power to do good and ill has become magnified, so have PR clients' needs to try and influence if not control media operations grown in importance. The methods used by PR agencies to achieve these objectives are not what you would talk about from the housetops (plain bribes are not unknown), and the enterprising publisher could well say: if the news is that important to someone, why not I make the cash and not the journalist whom I hire?

When such cynical questions get asked, retired editors are back in business before you can say Press Council, railing about the ills of contemporary journalism and how it was different in their day. But the world has changed, and the media business with it. And all the retired editors' columns and speeches will not bring back the old, clubby world of Indian newspapers, where editors ruled, the PR guys were hangdog fellows begging you to read their press release, and the marketing guys dared not step onto the editorial floor without treading very carefully.

And yet, it is also true that editors are in control in a new way, by taking on the role of publishers and responsibility for the bottom line—Shekhar Gupta at the Indian Express and Vinod Mehta at Outlook are the two obvious examples. This is a new way of acknowledging that the old diarchy of business and editorial functioning in separate silos cannot continue without damage to the enterprise. At the end of the day, one person has to call the shots. And at least some newspaper owners have found that more often than not it is the editor who has the greater commitment to the business than a marketing whizkid who may move back to selling soaps tomorrow. Putting the editor in charge also gets rid of the problem of how to maintain editorial autonomy within the office. However, the more common pattern is for the publisher (usually the principal shareholder) to take on the mantle of editor as well (or editorial director in some cases). Either way, the diarchy is no more. The question in the context of unified control is whether the wall between editorial and advertising survives, or has got porous. The logical construct must be that it is not the Chinese wall of old.

To many of the new generation, however, all of this looks and sounds like yesterday's battles in yesterday's industry. The mainstream media, especially for the young, is now television—as any readership and viewership survey establishes without difficulty. Newspapers printed on dead trees will at some stage have to adjust to these new realities and re-invent themselves, as many are struggling to do in the West. Because the natural news cycle is no longer 24 hours; it is sometimes not even hours, but minutes.

TV itself is about to undergo a major change, as the country gets ready for direct-to-home TV and a conditional access system for cable homes. The question is how many channels will decide to charge, and how many will go down the route that newspapers have taken—don't charge the viewer, be free-to-air, and hope to make mega-bucks from advertisers.

A rapidly evolving sector, with new opportunities thrown up by technology and regulation, will see new entrepreneurs making their mark, the entry of serious money into the game, and high stakes battles. In a telling comparison that speaks of the shifting balances, Prannoy Roy and Raghav Behl, through their holdings in their publicly quoted companies, may soon have more wealth to show than Shobhana Bhartia of HT Media (also a listed entity), though the first two are new entrants into the TV game and Bhartia is a third generation newspaper owner. Why, Rajdeep Sardesai and Raghav Behl, in coming together to launch IBN in partnership with CNN, have created more stock market wealth in two months than Mid-Day Multimedia has after three decades of publishing in Mumbai. Money buys talent, and so it is that the smarter journalists now get drawn to television.

But what will attract more mindspace in the coming months is the birth and steady growth (admittedly from a small base) of the internet, the rapid proliferation of websites, and the birth of a new sub-culture: interactive, democratic (no paternal editor deciding what you should read in his pages), and real-time. It isn't hard to see the internet growing as a rival force to the press and TV, and thereby to eventually redefine the news as well as the larger media business. The most likely result that one can foresee is the commoditisation of news (you can get pretty much the same news from a variety of sources), and multi-channel, multimedia accessing of news by the consumer at any time of day or night, at home or office or on the move.

So publications and TV channels and indeed any media organisation will have to go back to the drawing boards and ask the basic questions: how and why are you unique so that the reader and viewer should come to you and not to someone else? And how will you most add value to what you are doing?

At one level, the argument would remain that content is king, and the heightened competition underlines the need for more unique, high-value content. At another level, the answer could just as easily be that brand strength and distribution muscle will determine who are the winners. At a third level, the determining factor could be speed of adjustment to (and mastery of) new technologies. Since there is never one correct answer to complex questions, expect a combination of multiple responses as the Indian media grows and multiplies, fractures and consolidates.

India's claims to a significant leadership role in the world of the 21st century lie in the aspects and products of Indian society and culture that the world finds attractive. These assets may not directly persuade others to support India, but they go a long way toward enhancing India's intangible standing in the world's eyes.

21st Century Leadership

SHASHI THAROOR

As an Indian, I have become a little concerned about the proliferation of those who speak of India as a future 'world leader' or even as 'the next superpower'. The American publishers of my recent book, *The Elephant, the Tiger and the Cellphone,* even added a gratuitous subtitle suggesting that my volume was about 'the emerging 21st century power'.

Now I appreciate that this is not entirely unreasonable. Many thinkers and writers I respect have spoken of India's geo-strategic advantages, its economic dynamism, political stability, proven military capabilities, its nuclear, space and missile programmes, the entrepreneurial energy of India's people and the country's growing pool of young and skilled manpower as assuring India 'great power' status as a 'world leader' in the new century.

And yet I have a problem with that term. The notion of 'world leadership' is a curiously archaic one; the very phrase is redolent of Kipling ballads and James Bondian adventures. What makes a country a world leader? Is it population, in which case India is on course to top the charts, overtaking China as the world's most populous country by 2034? Is it military strength (India already has the world's fourth-largest army) or nuclear capacity (India's status having been made clear in 1998, and last year formally recognised in the Indo-US nuclear deal)? Is it economic development? There, India has made extraordinary strides in recent years; it is already the world's fifth-largest economy in PPP (purchasing-power parity) terms and continues to climb, though too many of our people still live destitute, amidst despair and disrepair. Or could it be a combination of all these, allied to something altogether more difficult to define—the 'soft power' of its culture?

Much of the conventional analyses of India's stature in the world relies on the all-too-familiar

---

Reproduced from 'The Republic of Ideas', *Seminar*, September 2009.
Shashi Tharoor is the elected Member of Parliament from Thiruvananthapuram.

economic assumptions. But we are famously a land of paradoxes, and amongst those paradoxes is that so many speak about India as a great power of the 21st century when we are not yet able to feed, educate and employ all our people. So it's not economic growth, military strength or population numbers that I would underscore when I think of India's potential leadership role in the world of the 21st century. Rather, if there is one attribute of independent India to which I think increasing attention should now be paid around the globe, it is the quality which India is already displaying in ample measure today—its 'soft power'.

The notion of soft power is relatively new in international discourse. The term was coined by Harvard's Joseph Nye to describe the extraordinary strengths of the United States that went well beyond American military dominance. Nye argued that 'power is the ability to alter the behaviour of others to get what you want, and there are three ways to do that: coercion (sticks), payments (carrots) and attraction (soft power). If you are able to attract others, you can economise on the sticks and carrots.'

Traditionally, power in world politics was seen in terms of military power: the side with the larger army was likely to win. But even in the past, this wasn't enough: after all, the US lost the Vietnam War, the Soviet Union was defeated in Afghanistan, and the US discovered in its first few years in Iraq the wisdom of Talleyrand's adage that the one thing you cannot do with a bayonet is to sit on it. Enter soft power—both as an alternative to hard power and as a complement to it. To quote Nye again: 'the soft power of a country rests primarily on three resources: its culture (in places where it is attractive to others), its political values (when it lives up to them at home and abroad), and its foreign policies (when they are seen as legitimate and having moral authority.)'

I would go slightly beyond this: a country's soft power, to me, emerges from the world's perceptions of what that country is all about. The associations and attitudes conjured up in the global imagination by the mere mention of a country's name is often a more accurate gauge of its soft power than a dispassionate analysis of its foreign policies. In my view, hard power is exercised; soft power is evoked.

For Nye, the United States is the archetypal exponent of soft power. The fact is that the US is the home of Boeing and Intel, Google and the I-Pod, Microsoft and MTV, Hollywood and Disneyland, McDonald's and Starbucks—in short, of most of the major products that dominate daily life around our globe. The attractiveness of these assets, and of the American lifestyle of which they are emblematic, is that they permit the US to persuade others to adopt the US' agenda, rather than relying purely on the dissuasive or coercive 'hard power' of military force.

Of course, this can cut both ways. In a world of instant mass communications enabled by the internet, countries are increasingly judged by a global public fed on an incessant diet of internet news, televised images, videos taken on the cellphones of passers-by, email gossip. The steep decline in America's image and standing after 9/11 is a direct reflection of global distaste for the instruments of American hard power—the Iraq invasion, Guantanamo, Abu Ghraib, torture, rendition, Blackwater's killings of Iraqi civilians.

But this essay is not about the US. In his book *The Paradox of American Power*, Nye took the analysis of soft power beyond the United States; other nations too, he suggested, could acquire it. In today's information era, he wrote, three types of countries are likely to gain soft power and so succeed: 'those whose dominant cultures and ideals are closer to prevailing global norms (which now emphasise liberalism, pluralism, autonomy); those with the most access to multiple channels of communication and thus more influence over issues framed; and those whose credibility is enhanced by their domestic and international performance.'

At first glance this seems to be a prescription for reaffirming the contemporary reality of US dominance, since it is clear that no country scores more highly on all three categories than the United States. But Nye himself admits this is not so: soft power has been pursued with success by other countries over the years. When France lost the war of 1870 to Prussia, one of its most important steps to rebuild the nation's shattered morale and enhance its prestige was to create the Alliance Française to promote French language and literature throughout the world.

French culture has remained a major selling-point for French diplomacy ever since. The UK has the British Council, the Swiss have Pro Helvetia, and Germany, Spain, Italy and Portugal have, respectively, Institutes named for Goethe, Cervantes, Dante Alighieri and Camoes.

Today, China has started establishing 'Confucius Institutes' to promote Chinese culture internationally, and the Beijing Olympics have been a sustained exercise in the building up of soft power by an authoritarian state. The US itself has used officially-sponsored initiatives, from the Voice of America to the Fulbright scholarships, to promote its soft power around the world. But soft power does not rely merely on governmental action: arguably, for the US, Hollywood and MTV have done more to promote the idea of America as a desirable and admirable society than any US governmental endeavour. Soft power, in other words, is created partly by governments and partly despite governments; partly by deliberate action, partly by accident.

What does this mean for India? It means acknowledging that India's claims to a significant leadership role in the world of the 21st century lie in the aspects and products of Indian society and culture that the world finds attractive. These assets may not directly persuade others to support India, but they go a long way toward enhancing India's intangible standing in the world's eyes.

The roots of India's soft power run deep. India's is a civilisation that, over millennia, has offered refuge and, more important, religious and cultural freedom, to Jews, Parsis, several varieties of Christians, and Muslims. Jews came to the south-western Indian coast centuries before Christ, with the destruction by the Babylonians of their First Temple, and they knew no persecution on Indian soil until the Portuguese arrived in the 16th century to inflict it. Christianity arrived on Indian soil with St. Thomas the Apostle ('Doubting Thomas'), who came to the Malabar coast some time before 52 A.D. and was welcomed on shore, or so oral legend has it, by a flute-playing Jewish girl. He made many converts, so there are Indians today whose ancestors were Christian well before any Europeans discovered Christianity.

In Kerala, where Islam came through traders, travellers and missionaries rather than by the sword, the Zamorin of Calicut was so impressed by the seafaring skills of this community that he issued a decree obliging each fisherman's family to bring up one son as a Muslim to man his all-Muslim navy! The India where the wail of the Muslim muezzin routinely blends with the chant of mantras at the Hindu temple, and where the tinkling of church bells accompanies the Sikh gurudwara's reading of verses from the Guru Granth Sahib, is an India that fully embraces the world. Indeed the British historian E.P. Thompson wrote that this heritage of diversity is what makes India 'perhaps the most important country for the future of the world. All the convergent influences of the world run through this society... There is not a thought that is being thought in the West or East that is not active in some Indian mind.'

That Indian mind has been shaped by remarkably diverse forces: ancient Hindu tradition, myth and scripture; the impact of Islam and Christianity; and two centuries of British colonial rule. The result is unique. Though there are some who think and speak of India as a Hindu country, Indian civilisation today is an evolved hybrid. We cannot speak of Indian culture today without *qawwali*, the poetry of Ghalib, or for that matter the game of cricket, our *de facto* national sport. When an Indian dons 'national dress' for a formal event, he wears a variant of the sherwani, which did not exist before the Muslim invasions of India. When Indian Hindus voted recently in the cynical and contrived competition to select the 'new seven wonders' of the modern world, they voted for the Taj Mahal constructed by a Mughal king, not for Angkor Wat, the most magnificent architectural product of their religion. In the breadth (and not just the depth) of its cultural heritage lies some of India's soft power.

One of the few generalisations that can safely be made about India is that nothing can be taken for granted about the country. Not even its name: for the word India comes from the river Indus, which flows in Pakistan. (That anomaly is easily explained, of course, since what is today Pakistan was hacked off the stooped shoulders of India by the departing British in 1947). Indian nationalism is therefore a rare phenomenon indeed. It is

Indian nationalism is the nationalism of an idea, the idea of an ever-ever land —emerging from an ancient civilisation, united by a shared history, sustained by pluralist democracy. Pluralism is a reality that emerges from the very nature of the country; it is a choice made inevitable by India's geography and reaffirmed by its history.

not based on language (since our Constitution recognises 23 and there are 35, according to the ethnolinguists, that are spoken by more than a million people each—not to mention 22,000 distinct dialects). It is not based on geography (the 'natural' geography of the subcontinent—framed by the mountains and the sea—has been hacked by the partition of 1947).

It is not based on ethnicity (the 'Indian' accommodates a diversity of racial types, and many Indians have more in common ethnically with foreigners than with other Indians: Indian Punjabis and Bengalis, for instance, are ethnically kin to Pakistanis and Bangladeshis, respectively, with whom they have more in common than with Poonawalas or Bangaloreans). And it is not based on religion (we are home to every faith known to mankind, with the possible exception of Shintoism, and Hinduism—a faith without a national organisation, no established church or ecclesiastical hierarchy, no Hindu Pope, no Hindu Mecca, no single sacred book, no uniform beliefs or modes of worship, not even a Hindu Sunday—exemplifies as much our diversity as it does our common cultural heritage).

Indian nationalism is the nationalism of an idea, the idea of an ever-ever land—emerging from an ancient civilisation, united by a shared history, sustained by pluralist democracy. Pluralism is a reality that emerges from the very nature of the country; it is a choice made inevitable by India's geography and reaffirmed by its history.

We are a land of rich diversities: I have observed in the past that we are all minorities in India. This land imposes no narrow conformities on its citizens: you can be many things and one thing. You can be a good Muslim, a good Keralite and a good Indian all at once. So the idea of India is of one land embracing many. It is the idea that a nation may endure differences of caste, creed, colour, culture, cuisine, conviction, costume and custom, and still rally around a democratic consensus. That consensus is around the simple principle that in a democracy you don't really need to agree—except on the ground rules of how you will disagree. Part of the reason for India being respected in the world is that it has survived all the stresses and strains that have beset it, and that led so many to predict its imminent disintegration, by maintaining consensus on how to manage without consensus.

The world of the 21st century will increasingly be a world in which the use of hard power carries with it the odium of mass global public disapproval, whereas the blossoming of soft power, which lends itself more easily to the information era, will constitute a country's principal asset. Soft power is not about conquering others, but about being yourself. Increasingly, countries are judged by the soft-power elements they project onto the global consciousness, either deliberately (through the export of cultural products, the cultivation of foreign publics or even international propaganda) or unwittingly (through the ways in which they are perceived as a result of news stories about them in the global mass media).

India produces various kinds of culture, notably including the films of Bollywood, now reaching ever-wider international audiences. The triumph of *Slumdog Millionaire* at the 2009 Oscars both reflects and reinforces this trend. Bollywood is bringing its brand of glitzy entertainment not just to the Indian diaspora in the US or UK but around the globe, to the screens of Syrians and Senegalese. A Senegalese friend told me of his illiterate mother who takes a bus to Dakar every month to watch a Bollywood film—she doesn't understand the Hindi dialogue and can't read the French subtitles, but these films are made to be understood despite such handicaps; she can still catch their spirit and understand the stories, and people like her look at India with stars in their eyes as a result.

An Indian diplomat friend in Damascus a few years ago told me that the only publicly-displayed portraits in that city that were as big as those of then-President Hafez al-Assad were of the Bollywood superstar Amitabh Bachchan. Indian art, classical music and dance have a similar effect. So does the work of Indian fashion designers, now striding across the world's catwalks. Indian cuisine, spreading around the world, raises our culture higher in people's reckoning; as the French have long known, the way to foreigners' hearts is through their palates. The proliferation of Indian restaurants around the world has been little short of astonishing. In England today, Indian curry houses employ more people than the iron and steel, coal and shipbuilding industries combined. (So the Empire can strike back.)

Globalisation has both sparked and allayed many Indians' fears that economic liberalisation will bring with it cultural imperialism of a particularly insidious kind—that *Baywatch* and burgers will supplant *bharatanatyam* dances and *bhelpuri* snacks. Instead, India's recent experience with western consumer products demonstrates that we can drink Coca-Cola without becoming coca-colonised. Indians will not become any less Indian if, in Mahatma Gandhi's metaphor, we open the doors and windows of our country and let foreign winds blow through our house—because Indians are strong enough not to be blown off their feet by these winds. Our popular culture has proved resilient enough to compete successfully with MTV and McDonald's. Besides, the strength of 'Indianness' lies in its ability to absorb foreign influences and to transform them—by a peculiarly Indian alchemy—into something that belongs naturally on the soil of India.

Indeed, from the export of Bollywood to *bhangra* dances, India has demonstrated that it is a player in globalisation, not merely a subject of it. India benefits from the future and the past—from the international appeal of its traditional practices (from ayurveda to yoga, both accelerating in popularity across the globe) and the transformed image of the country created by its thriving diaspora. Information technology has made its own contribution to India's soft power. When Americans in Silicon Valley speak of the IITs (the Indian Institutes of Technology) with the same reverence they used to accord to MIT, and the Indianness of engineers and software developers is taken as synonymous with mathematical and scientific excellence, it is India that gains in respect.

Sometimes this has unintended consequences. I met an Indian the other day, a history major like me, who told me of transiting through Schiphol airport in Amsterdam and being accosted by an anxious European crying out 'you're Indian! You're Indian! Can you help me fix my laptop?' The old stereotype of Indians was that of snake-charmers and *fakirs* lying on beds of nails; now it is that every Indian must be a software guru or a computer geek.

In the information age, Joseph Nye has argued, it is often the side which has the better story that wins. India must remain the 'land of the better story'. As a society with a free press and a thriving mass media, with a people whose creative energies are daily encouraged to express themselves in a variety of appealing ways, India has an extraordinary ability to tell stories that are more persuasive and attractive than those of its rivals. This is not about propaganda; indeed, it will not work if it is directed from above, least of all by government. But its impact, though intangible, can be huge.

To take one example: Afghanistan is clearly a crucial country for India's national security, as it is for the US's. President Obama has spoken of reinforcing American and NATO military capacity there. But the most interesting asset for India in Afghanistan doesn't come out of a military mission: it doesn't have one. It comes, instead, from one simple fact: Don't try to telephone an Afghan at 8:30 in the evening. That's when the Indian TV soap opera *Kyunki saas bhi kabhi bahu thi*, dubbed into Dari, is telecast on Tolo TV, and no one wishes to miss it. It's reportedly the most popular television show in Afghan history (at least until the onset of 'Afghan Idol' last year), considered directly responsible for a spike in the sale of generator sets and even for absences from religious functions which clash with its broadcast times. (This has provoked visceral opposition to the show from the *mullahs*, who wish to shut it down).

'*Saas*' has so thoroughly captured the public imagination in Afghanistan that, in this deeply conservative Islamic country where family problems are usually hidden behind the veil, it's an Indian TV show that has come to dominate society's discussion of family issues. I have read reports of wedding banquets being interrupted so that the guests could huddle around the television for half an hour, and even of an increase in crime at 8:30 pm because watchmen are sneaking a look at the TV rather than minding the store. One Reuters despatch recounted how robbers in Mazar-i-Sharif stripped a vehicle of its wheels and mirrors recently during the telecast time and wrote on the car, in an allusion to the show's heroine, 'Tulsi zindabad' (long live Tulsi). That's soft power, and India does not have to thank the government or charge the taxpayer for its exercise. Instead, Indians too can simply say, 'Tulsi zindabad'.

Of course, official government policy can also play a role. Pavan Varma, till recently the head of the Indian Council on Cultural Relations (ICCR), has argued that 'culturally India is a superpower' and that cultural diplomacy must be pursued for political ends. So India is highly visible at cultural shows around the world, and the ICCR is rather good at organising Festivals of India in assorted foreign cities. That's good, but I'm not a fan of propaganda, which most people tend to see for what it is. I believe the message that really gets through is that of who we are, not what we want to show.

For soft power is not just what we can deliberately and consciously exhibit or put on display; it is rather how others see what we are, whether or not we are trying to show it to the world. To take a totally different example: Politically, the sight in May 2004—after the world's largest exercise in democratic franchise (but then every Indian election is the world's largest exercise in democratic franchise!) of a leader of Roman Catholic background (Sonia Gandhi) making way for a Sikh (Manmohan Singh) to be sworn in as Prime Minister by a Muslim (President Abdul Kalam)—in a country 81% Hindu—caught the world's imagination and won its admiration. (I was travelling in the Gulf on behalf of the United Nations at the time, and the reactions of my Arab interlocutors to what had happened in India could not have been more gratifying).

So it is not just material accomplishments that enhance India's soft power. Even more important are the values and principles for which India stands. After all, Mahatma Gandhi won India its independence through the use of soft power—because non-violence and *satyagraha* were indeed classic uses of soft power before the term was even coined. India's first Prime Minister, Jawaharlal Nehru, was also a skilled exponent of soft power: he developed a role for India in the world based entirely on its civilisational history and its moral standing, making India the voice of the oppressed and the marginalised against the big power hegemons of the day. This gave the country enormous standing and prestige across the world for some years, and strengthened our own self-respect as we stood, proud and independent, on the world stage.

But the great flaw in Nehru's approach was that his soft power was unrelated to any acquisition of hard power; as the humiliation of the military defeat by China in 1962 demonstrated, soft power has crippling limitations in national security terms. Instead of Theodore Roosevelt's maxim, 'speak softly and carry a big stick', Nehru's India spoke loudly but had no stick at all. In a tough neighbourhood, the rhetoric of peace can only take you so far. Soft power becomes credible when there is hard power behind it; that is why the US has been able to make so much of its soft power.

Recent Indian history offers a somewhat mixed picture when it comes to the effective use of hard power. The 1971 war with Pakistan, leading to the emergence of Bangladesh, remains the pre-eminent example, but there are few others—the repelling of Pakistani intruders from the Kargil heights in 1999 and a swift paratroop intervention in the Maldives to reverse a coup against President Gayoom in 1996 providing rare instances of hard power success.

Against these examples are the 1962 China war, the spectacular failures of the Indian Peace-Keeping Force in Sri Lanka in 1987 (which withdrew after incurring heavy casualties in an unplanned war with the Tamil insurgents), the hijacking of an Indian Airlines aircraft to Kandahar in 1999 resulting in the craven release of detained terrorists from Indian jails, the repeated 'bleeding' of the country through terrorist incidents planned and directed from Pakistan, and innumerable unprovoked incidents on the Bangladesh border involving Indian loss of life. India is often caught in a cleft stick on such matters: it often treads softly in its anxiety not to come across as a regional bully, and in so doing it emboldens those who are prepared to test it. As a result it has been noticeably reluctant to evolve a strategic doctrine based on hard power; there is a sense in which most Indians still think that would be unseemly.

This helps explain India's growing consciousness of its soft power, though of course New Delhi knows that its soft power cannot solve its security challenges. After all, an Islamist terrorist who enjoys a Bollywood movie will still have no compunction about setting off a bomb in a Delhi market, and the US has already learned that the perpetrators of 9/11 ate their last dinner at a McDonald's. To counter the terrorist threat there is no substitute for hard power. Hard power without soft power stirs up resentments and enmities; soft power without hard power is a confession of weakness. Where soft power works is in attracting enough goodwill from ordinary people to reduce the sources of support and succour that the terrorists enjoy, and without which they cannot function.

But this means that India also needs to solve its internal problems before it can play any role of leadership in the world. We must ensure that we do enough to keep our people healthy, well-fed, and secure not just from *jihadi* terrorism but from the daily terror of poverty, hunger and ill-health. Progress is being made: India can take satisfaction from its success in carrying out three kinds of revolutions in feeding its people—the 'green revolution' in food grains, the 'white revolution' in milk production and, at least to some degree, a 'blue revolution' in the development of our fisheries. But the benefits of these revolutions have not yet reached the third of our population still living below the poverty line. We must ensure they do, or our soft power will ring hollow, at home and abroad.

At the same time, if India wants to be a source of attraction to others, it is not enough to attend to these basic needs. It must preserve the precious pluralism that is such a civilisational asset in our globalising world. Our democracy, our thriving free media, our contentious civil society forums, our energetic human rights groups, and the repeated spectacle of our remarkable general elections, have all made of India a rare example of the successful management of diversity in the developing world. It adds to India's soft power when its nongovernmental organizations actively defend human rights, promote environmentalism, fight injustice. It is a vital asset that the Indian press is free, lively, irreverent, disdainful of sacred cows.

But every time there are reports of sectarian violence or a pogrom like the savagery in Gujarat in 2002, or a nativist attack like those by a fringe group in February on women drinking at a pub in Mangalore, India suffers a huge setback to our soft power. Soft power will not come from a narrow or restricted version of Indianness, confined to the sectarian prejudices of some of the self-appointed guardians of Indian culture (*Bharatiya sanskriti*). It must instead proudly reflect the multi-religious identities of our people, our linguistic diversity, the myriad manifestations of our creative energies. India must maintain its true heritage in the eyes of the world.

And that will mean acknowledging that the central battle in contemporary Indian culture is that between those who, to borrow Walt Whitman's phrase, acknowledge that we are vast, we contain multitudes, and those who have presumptuously taken it upon themselves to define (in increasingly narrower terms) what is 'truly' Indian. Pluralist India must, by definition, tolerate plural expressions of its many identities. To allow any self-appointed arbiters of Indian culture to impose their hypocrisy and double standards on the rest of us is to permit them to define Indianness down until it ceases to be Indian. To wield soft power, India must defend, assert and promote its culture of openness against the forces of intolerance and bigotry inside and outside the country.

It helps that India is anything but the unchanging land of timeless cliché. There is an extraordinary degree of change and ferment in our democracy. Dramatic transformations are taking place that amount to little short of an ongoing revolution—in politics, economics, society and culture. Both politics and caste relations have witnessed convulsive changes: who could have imagined, for 3000 years, that a woman from the 'untouchable' community of outcastes (now called 'Dalits') would rule India's largest state, Uttar Pradesh, as Kumari Mayawati now does with a secure majority? It's still true that in many parts of India, when you cast your vote, you vote your caste. But that too has brought about profound alterations in the country, as the lower castes have taken advantage of the ballot to seize electoral power.

These changes are little short of revolutionary. But the Indian revolution is a democratic one, sustained by a larger idea of India—an India that safeguards the common space available to each identity, an India that celebrates diversity. If America is a melting-pot, then to me India

Our democracy, our thriving free media, our contentious civil society forums, our energetic human rights groups, and the repeated spectacle of our remarkable general elections, have all made of India a rare example of the successful management of diversity in the developing world.

is a *thali*, a selection of sumptuous dishes in different bowls. Each tastes different, and does not necessarily mix with the next, but they belong together on the same plate, and they complement each other in making the meal a satisfying repast.

India's civilisational ethos has been an immeasurable asset for our country. It is essential that India does not allow the spectre of religious intolerance and political opportunism to undermine the soft power which is its greatest asset in the world of the 21st century. Maintain that, and true leadership in our globalising world—the kind that has to do with principles, values and standards—will follow.

This will require the more systematic development of a soft power strategy than India currently has. So far, such strategic advantages as have accrued from India's soft power—goodwill for the country amongst African, Arab and Afghan publics, for instance—has been a largely unplanned byproduct of the normal emanations of Indian culture.

Such goodwill has not been systematically harnessed as a strategic asset by New Delhi. It is ironic that in and around the 2008 Olympics, authoritarian China showed a greater determination to use its hard-power strengths to cultivate a soft-power strategy for itself on the world stage. India will not need to try as hard, but it will need to do more than it currently does to leverage its natural soft-power into a valuable instrument of its global strategy.

I believe that the India that has entered its seventh decade as an independent country is one open to the contention of ideas and interests within it, unafraid of the prowess or the products of the outside world, wedded to the democratic pluralism that is India's greatest strength, and determined to liberate and fulfill the creative energies of its people.

Such an India truly enjoys soft power, and that may well be the most valuable way in which it can offer leadership to the 21st century world.

The Epic of the Bharatas

Romila Thapar

The *Mahabharata* calls itself *itihasam-puratanam* —thus indeed it was in times past. This is not a Rankean statement and there are no definitive claims to historicity of persons and events in the narrative. However, there is a hint that some of the narrative may have been an attempt to cull from the remembered tradition that which may have happened, even if what is culled is disordered in the retelling. The *Ramayana*, however, is most often described as a *kavya*, in fact the *adikavya*, suggesting a small distinction between the two.

There have been many commentaries in Sanskrit on the epics from the 11th to the 17th century examining their meaning and intention. An analysis of these could tell us about how the epic was perceived in periods prior to ours. One wonders for instance, whether historicity as we understand it today, was of concern to the authors and to the audience of past times. Undoubtedly among the more attractive features of the epic, although historically tantalising, are its many enigmas. Some however suggest the occasional facet of the historical past. The attempt in this essay is to point to these and indicate the problems they raise.

Epic as a genre uses narrative to represent situations from the past. It looks back nostalgically from the point in time when it is being composed and given form which is its present. The nostalgia is for a past age of heroes and the clans to which they belonged. This slowly gave way to the present where the heroes are less important in a society governed by kings and the code of castes. The nature of authority is more focused and therefore different in kingship and the determining of status and social attitudes by reference to caste gradually becomes predictable.

Given that it spans more than one kind of society, re-examining the concepts we use in interpreting the epic becomes essential. Some are inflected

---

Reproduced from 'The Enduring Epic', *Seminar*, April 2010. Romila Thapar is an Indian historian.

My thanks to Kumkum Roy, Kunal Chakrabarti, Robert and Sally Goldman for comments on an earlier draft.

Epic as a genre uses narrative to represent situations from the past. It looks back nostalgically from the point in time when it is being composed and given form which is its present. The nostalgia is for a past age of heroes and the clans to which they belonged.

by the translations we use. The context of the epic was that of clan societies and small-scale kingdoms. It is as well to remember that the term '*raja*' did not in origin mean a king, but referred simply to 'the one who shines', an appropriate title for a chief. As such it is likely to have been continued when the system changed to kingship. To translate *samrat* as 'imperial monarch' is to impose a later meaning on an earlier term. A more accurate meaning might refer to the one 'who has authority over many'. The context of the term can illumine its meaning.

Part of the transition from clan to kingdom also lay in the evolving form that was being given to *varna* and *jati*. The structure of clan societies did not require that they follow the rules of the *dharma-shastras* but a king ruling a kingdom had to uphold caste. There were of course exceptions such as Ashoka who does not mention caste in his edicts, but this was doubtless due to his heterodox thinking.

The transition is vividly etched in the different nuances of how the clans functioned. The Vrishnis in Dvaraka in western India with their eighteen *kulas*, extended families/clans, conform to a distinctive way of functioning reminiscent of oligarchies and chiefships. The Kauravas and the Pandavas battling for territory in the Doab and the western Ganga plain still observe the rules of clan ethics and codes of kin relationships but are seen to be slowly succumbing to the rules of kingship and the codes of caste, the pattern emerging in the easterly region of Magadha.

Authorship of the Mahabharata is attributed to Krishna Dvaipayana Vyasa, a brahmin of uncertain antecedents, born of the sage Parashara and a fisher woman, who is also said to have sired Dhritrashtra and Pandu. Authorship and fatherhood are coalesced and in effect Vyasa is narrating the lives of his own sons and grandsons. They in turn have no blood connection with the lineage of the Bharatas although they are constantly referred to as 'bull of the Bharatas'. The blood connection actually ended with Bhishma, unless of course his being called *pitamaha*—the paternal grandfather—is taken literally, despite his vow, but in which case the story would have been different.

Genealogies can be accurate over a few generations but are also available to those who wish to fabricate connections and latch on to a respectable ancestry. This fragment of the lineage has an equally ambiguous end since the lineage continues through Parikshit, who is stillborn but revived by Krishna. Possibly the invented connection was necessary since in the Vedic corpus the epithets used for the ancestor Puru, are not the most complimentary: his speech is said to be *mridhra-vach*, impure, and he has an *asura-rakshasa* ancestry.

The epic recitation had two beginnings a generation apart. It was first recited at the snake sacrifice of the kshatriya raja, Janamejaya (the son of Parikshit), by the brahmin Vaishampayana. A generation later it is recited at a *sattra*, a sacrificial ritual usually intended for and performed by brahmins, although the recitation this time is by the bard Ugrashravas. A brahmin recites it to the kshatriyas and a non-brahmin to the brahmins, an inversion which is curious. The epic as we know it was in origin the bard's memorisation of what he had heard from the brahmin's recital, and there is an insistence that both renderings are exactly as composed by Vyasa. One is immediately suspicious about changes and interpolations. The interleaving of brahmin and bard as authors or the likelihood of bardic origins is not unknown.

The *dasharajna*, the battle of the ten rajas, described in the *Rigveda* has been viewed by some modern scholars as the seminal event for the war at Kurukshetra. Some of the clans from the Vedic corpus such as the Bharatas, Purus, Yadus and Kuru-Pancalas reappear in the Mahabharata as lineage ancestors of the epic protagonists, but not necessarily in the same situations. Panini in the 4th century BC refers indirectly to grammatical constructions associated with words such as mahabharata, yudhishthira, arjuna and vasudeva.

Epic personalities have parallels in the Buddhist *Jataka* stories where persons with the same names occur in events that are often dissimilar to the epics. The secreting away of Krishna as a baby, his hostility as a young man to his uncle Kamsa at Mathura and the migration of his clan to Dvaraka, is part of the narrative of his clan, the Andhaka-Venhu/Vrishni. Its end came through a drunken massacre, a story repeated in the Vaishnava texts. Neither Krishna nor his clan is particularly attractive in these stories. Draupadi is depicted as a nymphomaniac who is not satisfied with five husbands and takes a hunchback lover. But as a contrast to this, stories of the descendents of Yudhishthira ruling the Kuru realm from Indraprastha and advised by the minister Vidhura-pandita, are characterised by what is called Kuru righteousness, particularly noted for its practice of virtue. Whether these variant versions were taken from the epic or contributed to the making of the epic remains a debated subject. The ideological underpinning also differs.

The stories are not identical but may go back to a common source. The boxing-in of stories as in the epic is also a technique of adding to a narrative. Subsequently when they were given an ideological gloss they served the needs of Buddhist ethics and later of Jaina versions, or the sectarian beliefs of Vaishnava Bhagavatism, each in disagreement with the other. The diversity of these initial fragments seems to be echoed in the varied regional versions and recensions of the epic, a process that continued through the centuries. This multiplicity makes it necessary sometimes to identify the version one is referring to.

The composition was doubtless in the nature of a slow accretion as is characteristic of the epic genre virtually anywhere. Nevertheless at some point it was brought together. Tradition has it that a small text, the *Jaya*, became larger, the *Bharata*, and the larger became still larger, the Mahabharata. It is, therefore, virtually impossible to calculate a date for the events and to define an 'epic period' in ancient history as was once done.

This would also be one reason for the difficulty in identifying a particular archaeological site as the archaeological equivalent of a location in the epic. Excavations have been conducted at locations that are called Hastinapur and Indraprastha. These could be ancient sites although we know that place names also travel especially with migrant populations. Distances on the ground do not always tally with the text. In today's identifications these two places were a considerable journey away from the battlefield. Equating a site with a text can raise problems of reconciling material culture with evocations of poetic licence. Will we ever find the fantasy palace of the Pandavas built by Asura Maya/*asuramaya* even if we believe it existed and dig up the whole of Indraprastha? Homer's epic met with similar problems after the extensive excavations at Troy and other sites.

The epic maintains that the war at Kurukshetra took place on the cusp of the Kaliyuga. This has been dated as equivalent to 3102 BC. Dates calculated on the basis of the genealogical lists of kshatriya lineages in the *Puranas* generally work out to between 1200-1000 BC. The archaeological evidence of a heavy silt deposit at the site of Hastinapur which has been linked to the epic reference to a flood after the war points to a date of c. 800 BC. Mention of Yavanas, Shakas, Hunas, would be interpolations in the late BCs and early centuries AD.

V.S. Sukthankar, to whom the critical edition of the epic owes much, argued that its composition ranged from 400 BC to AD 400. More recently scholars have suggested that the oral epic was put together as a text in about 150 BC and that this may have taken a century or so. Attempts have been made to correlate readings in astronomy with references to planetary configurations in the epic. These differ and would relate not to the text as a whole but to particular segments carrying the reference. Diversity in dates also makes it problematic to attribute authorship to a single author. The meaning of Vyasa is interestingly, one who edits and arranges.

To add to the complexity it has been argued that the epic had two intentions. The earliest narrative was constructed out of fragmentary stories of the heroic: tales of combats, marriages, games of dice, exile in the forest–and were probably formulaic on occasion. The same process has been noticed in the Homeric epics. Exile is a marvellous background for the bard as it can be stretched with add-ons heightening the reach of the imagination. Heroic exploits can be enlarged with every recitation, whether the hero is wandering across the 'wine-dark seas' of the Mediterranean as in the Odyssey or in the tangled forests of northern India as in the Mahabharata. Exile to the forest in India reinforced the dichotomy of *grama*, settlement, and *aranya*, forest, central to cultural perceptions.

Epic origins lay in popular compositions not in divine revelation; therefore they were not as sacred as the Vedas.

It was probably the immense popularity of the epic, both as a linear narrative of the heroic as well as in the embroidered intricacies of the stories, that led to the second intention and reformulation—its conversion into a Bhagavata text. Sukthankar argued that this was done by the Bhrigu brahmins who also 'Bhriguised' the Ramayana. Both Krishna and Rama became *avataras* of Vishnu and this changed the character of the epic. It is worth noting that on the second occasion of its recitation the bard was required to proclaim the descent of the Bhrigu lineage, perhaps to legitimise the Bhrigus and their appropriation of the epic.

The Bhrigus, were often linked to the Angiras brahmins, associated with the *Atharvaveda* and among other things, were regarded as the practitioners of sorcery and magic. Neither group was the most highly respected among learned brahmins. The Bhrigus were called *brahma-kshatra,* when they married kshatriya women. Their learning extended into knowledge and custom beyond the conventional and in addition they were said to know *niti* and *dharma*.

The question could be asked that if the Bhrigus were not pre-eminent brahmins why were they permitted to reformulate the epic. Epic origins lay in popular compositions not in divine revelation; therefore they were not as sacred as the *Vedas*. The Bhrigus may have wished to convert the epic into a Bhagavata sectarian text, if they were associated with early Bhagavatism. The didactic section was the palatable way of teaching the various brahmanical dharmas. The Mahabharata can be viewed as a civilisational text not because it reflects the propagation of a particular view of these *dharmas* but because, among other things, it speaks to the debate on social ethics, especially between the brahmanical perspective and those that question it—a debate that has continued over many centuries.

The Bhagavata religion was not identical with the Vedic even if the Mahabharata is referred to as the fifth Veda—as indeed was the itihasa-purana itself and many other bodies of knowledge. The Bhrigu brahmins may have had associations with pre-Vedic and non-Vedic ideas as has been suggested. In one *Upanishad* the Bhrigu-Angirasas are linked to the itihasa-purana. This would, up to a point, make them appropriate editors of texts pertaining to the past. Nevertheless the controversy on 'Bhriguisation' continues.

Why the Bhagavata reformulation was necessary needs an explanation. Perhaps the realisation that the Buddhist gloss on popular stories was a successful way of propagating sectarian belief may have encouraged Bhagavatas to do the same. Buddhism was subordinating the worship of clan deities to the higher ideal of the ethic of dharma as defined by the Buddha. Bhagavatism required the worship of Vishnu as the supreme deity and the *varna* dharma was its social ethic, both of which incidentally reinforced the requirements of kingship. This subsequent addition has left a heavy imprint on the Mahabharata and the epic genre of the text has tended to be subordinated. It is to this genre that I would like to give more space.

The first few books narrate the epic of the Kauravas and the Pandavas and take the story, together with whatever is tagged onto the narrative, to the point where war is imminent. The description of person and event veers towards the functioning of a clan-based society. It conforms in the main to the pattern of a segmentary system of lineages functioning as segments of an extensive network. The Puranas a little later called it the Chandravamsha, the Lunar Lineage. Identity is through being born into a clan, kinship controls behavioural relations and social functions, governance is through an assembly of the heads of families and status is relatively egalitarian within the clan.

Agro-pastoralism is the major source of income with an emphasis on cattle herding and the occasional cattle-raid, described more than once in the epic. The Vedas also refer to the Kuru-Pancala clans going out in 'the dewy season' to raid cattle. The more spectacular sacrificial rituals asserting the political authority of the patron, such as the *rajasuya* performed by Yudhishthira, are occasions for gathering-in tribute and exchanging gifts. These are largely in the form of the produce of hunting and herding, of weaving textiles, of mining gold and gems and maintaining domestic slaves—mainly women. Agricultural activity is of course a necessity but tends to be low key. Dependence on agriculture increases in the later parts of the text. Items of wealth placed as stakes in the game of dice are similar but of larger amounts. Ultimately Yudhishthira stakes the town, the territory and eventually himself.

The listing of wealth is in substantial if not exaggerated terms. Such occasions have been thought to be rituals but also gift-giving ceremonies, characteristic functions of heads of clans. On special occasions, the chief collects, consumes, distributes and if need be even destroys what remains of his wealth. The rajasuya was one such occasion with inevitable consequences. The intention is to assert status which in turn leads to a competition among clan chiefs each trying to outdo the previous one. Therefore gift-giving is not a one-way process. It assumes that the holding of these ceremonies turn by turn ensures the circulation of whatever is produced. It also prevents a chief acquiring excessive power through accumulating enormous wealth. Should this happen conflict may be unavoidable. The items brought to the *yajna*, come as gifts and tribute and not as tax.

The clans were described as kshatriyas, with status dependent not on caste but on the hierarchy among the clans. Identity came from the clan. Hence the emphases on genealogies, all of which may or may not have been taken literally, the social forms reflected in their structure also being significant. Breaks in the genealogy can be indicators of change.

That the rules of caste were not strictly observed would explain why three disparate systems of marriage are adopted over two consecutive generations in the family of Pandu. In Pandu's marriage to Madri it would seem that a bride-price was involved, even if not in material goods, making it an *asura* marriage according to the dharma-shastras. The fraternal polyandry of the five Pandavas marrying Draupadi is outside any dharma-shastra scheme and is discussed at some length in the epic before it is accepted. Draupadi questioning Yudhishthira's right to stake her in the dicing match is not the kind of statement that matches the patriarchal values advised for wifely behaviour in the social codes. The three women who command the narrative are Draupadi who poses the question of the legality of Yudhishthira's right over her, Kunti who chooses the deities she wants as surrogate husbands and Gandhari who insists on being permanently blindfolded after her marriage to a blind husband.

The third variant form was that of Arjuna's marriage to Subhadra (cross cousin) which is a *rakshasa* form according to the dharma-shastras yet the lineage continues through their stillborn grandson, Parikshit. Such flexible social practices suggest societies where alien custom could be incorporated to accommodate a new situation.

Krishna's clan, the Andhaka-Vrishni had a lower status than the Kurus. Political functioning among them lay in the *sangha*, assembly, where the senior kinsmen of the eighteen *kulas* sat to take decisions. In kingdoms, the assembly was reduced to an advisory body whose views were not binding on the king. The concentration of power required in kingship perhaps accounts in part for the hostility of the Vrishni clans towards Magadha. The kingdom of Magadha was a challenge to the *gana-sanghas*, the clans of the middle Ganga plain. Eventually the clan confederacy of Vaishali was destroyed through devious means resulting in the consolidation of kingship as a polity.

Beyond the clans was the non-caste 'Other', treated by the heroes as virtually bereft of human value, as is apparent at various points of the narrative. These were the people of the forest such as the Nishada and the Shabara, the excluded and impure *mleccha* and therefore dispensable. The episode that has been commented on is that of Ekalavya, who being a Nishada, had to give his thumb as a fee to the brahmin guru thus terminating his skill as an archer. But equally traumatic is the reference to how a Nishada woman and her five sons were left in the house of lac, which was set on fire to mislead the Kauravas about the presence of the Pandavas. As a comment on clan society this requires explanation, unless it can be argued that such episodes were introduced later when the mleccha were treated as less than human.

The war at Kurukshetra forms a substantial section of the epic. As a time-marker it touches many dimensions. It marks the end of clan societies. Krishna's comment is telling: *sarvam kshatram kshayam gatam*—it is the destruction of all the kshatriyas. It is said that the end of the war

The narrative of the epic is sequential, set in a frame of linear chronology, nevertheless there are substratum layers of structures, order, legitimation, and claims that seem extraneous to the narrative but are insightful. What is perhaps being indicated in all this is that historicity should not be sought for only in person and event for it may lie at a deeper level.

marked the end of the Dvapara age—the third of the four ages—and the start of the new and final Kaliyuga. The theory of the four *yugas* is referred to in various texts of the post-Mauryan period and was probably not in the early epic. It seems to have been a later reflection on a substantial historical change expressed literally as the coming of a new age. As with exile, war is another occasion for the bard-poet to show his skill, so the narrative extends over many *parvans*, books, of the epic. Despite references to formations of standing armies familiar from warfare in later periods, the battle was essentially heroic warfare and often single combat—thus allowing for some of the dubious manoeuvres attributed to Krishna's advice.

That the war was pushed by Draupadi's demand for revenge is an epic-heroic feature. So too was the fact that succession was contested by the absence of unchallenged primogeniture, both brothers being physically disabled. It was probably in origin a clan conflict involving those that had claims on the territory and their friends or enemies. Enlarged into a massive eighteen-day event it was said to have involved clans from all over. That this was an exaggeration is suggested by Arjuna arguing the futility of war prior to the event and Yudhishthira doing so after the event. Validating violence becomes a necessity and even the simile of the battle being a yajna, ritual of sacrifice, is used as it was in later times as well.

Although the *Bhagavad-gita* in the narrative is placed just before the start of the war, its teaching seems more appropriate to the society that emerged after the war. Arjuna, dismayed by the thought that he would have to kill his close kinsmen, questions the ethics of such an act. The killing of kinsmen seems to have been more heinous in a society where kinship was a primary identity than in a society where kin ties were subsumed in caste. Krishna speaking from the perspective of a caste society explains to Arjuna that as a kshatriya it is his *svadharma*, the social obligation of one's caste, to fight against evil even if it means killing kinsmen. Is the moral dilemma being subordinated to caste duty?

As has been pointed out in recent studies the urgency of this discourse most likely had to do with the current debate on *ahimsa* provoked by Buddhist and Jaina teaching and by the alternative ideal of kingship propagated by Ashoka. In the latter the social ethic is not dependent on caste but on the quality of human behaviour as encapsulated in *dhamma*. This may have been the context to Yudhishthira questioning the kshatriya model. Judging by inscriptional evidence, support for Buddhism and Jainism at all levels of society was extensive in the post-Mauryan period and there would doubtless have been at least ideological confrontations with the code of the dharma-shastras. Is the Shantiparvan then a polemic in the debate with the heterodoxy? Yet there is also the play on Yudhishthira being the son of the deity Dharma which would have enhanced his sensitivity to the question of ethics.

The later part of the epic, sometimes described as the didactic sections, although these were scattered briefly elsewhere as well, begins effectively after the end of the war and consists substantially of the much-quoted Shantiparvan and Anushasanaparvan. These are important in themselves but in some ways represent a discourse outside the epic. To discuss the epic largely on the basis of these sections as is sometimes done is to do it an injustice.

Yudhishthira, appalled by the violence of the war is reluctant to assume kingship and wishes to retreat to the forest. Bhishma wounded in the war and lying on his bed of arrows persuades Yudhishthira not to renounce kingship and instead to govern as an established king in a kingdom. His long peroration on various categories of dharma and even on situations where it fails is significant in these political transitions. Kingship as a political form is viewed implicitly as superior to what came before or which continued as an alternate system. The discourse by Bhishma is almost certainly a later interpolation of the time when the *gana-rajyas*, chiefships and oligarchies, had declined—but not disappeared—and in many places had been replaced by kingdoms.

The discussions on *rajadharma*—the code for kingship and administration—on punishment, on times of distress, run parallel to themes in texts such as Kautilya's *Arthashastra* and the Manu *Dharma-shastra*; not to mention the continuing memory of the Mauryan state. Kautilya's list of what constitutes a state system, assumes a kingdom ruled by a king with decision-making powers, through an administration manned by non-kinsmen, located in a capital city to which the revenue comes via taxes, and where the kingdom is identified by demarcated territory, defended by a regular standing army and where other kings are allies. These are features more familiar from the later books.

The didactic sections were in a sense looking back at the epic past, but were legitimising the coming change to kingdoms. The change was not linear and determined. It was somewhat meandering with various offshoots and in some cases earlier forms may have continued as we know that they did historically until much later. But that such a change was represented in the eventual version seems apparent. What I am suggesting is not a dichotomy between clan-society and the kingdom, nor a textbook version of each, but the difference in societies with more of one than the other.

This essay is only one passing historical perspective of the Mahabharata. Even from historians alone there are many more. And beyond them the perspectives multiply still further. The narrative of the epic is sequential, set in a frame of linear chronology, nevertheless there are substratum layers of structures, order, legitimation, and claims that seem extraneous to the narrative but are insightful. What is perhaps being indicated in all this is that historicity should not be sought for only in person and event for it may lie at a deeper level.

In the interface of the two kinds of societies that I have sketched, partially sequential and partially concurrent, there lies what might be seen as a historical tradition—the tradition of a later society remembering and reconstructing what it believes to be the earlier one, where the reconstruction becomes the perceived past. Perhaps it is because of this that the Mahabharata can call itself, itihasam puratanam.

References

Brockington, J. (1998). *The Sanskrit Epics*, Leiden.

Dandekar (ed.) (1990). *The Mahabharata Revisited*, New Delhi.

Goldman, R. (1977). *Gods, Priests and Warriors: The Bhrigus of the Mahabharata*, New York.

Hiltebeitel, A. (2002). *Rethinking the Mahabharata*, New Delhi.

Sukthankar, V.S. (1998). *On the Meaning of the Mahabharata*, Bombay, 1957/Delhi.

I recall with pride Prime Minister James Callaghan's tribute when Indira Gandhi was defeated at the polls in March 1977. Callaghan said that the ultimate mark of a true democracy is the willingness of a government defeated at the ballot box to surrender power peacefully to its opponents.

The Way Forward

FALI S. NARIMAN

A written constitution when enacted takes on a life of its own. It moves along under the guidance of its appointed functionaries who sometimes function well, but sometimes they also function badly. So, a written constitution develops its own ethos. It ultimately fulfils the destiny of the country for which it is written—if it lasts!

The Indian Constitution was barely a year old when Sir Ivor Jennings—prolific author of Westminster-type constitutions—was invited by the University of Madras to deliver a lecture on its provisions. Jennings did not think much of our document of governance. 'Too long, too detailed, too rigid', was his laconic comment.

By the 1960s, the same Ivor Jennings had been commissioned to write a new constitution—for the Island of Ceylon: the Soulbury Constitution, as it came to be known. But despite all precautions taken in its drafting, it lasted only seven years! The first lesson then about written constitutions is that they do not function on their own. A special effort has to be made by the custodians—those entrusted with their functioning—to work them.

As to how those in charge of the levers of power in India attempted this is set out in detail in Granville Austin's book published in 1999.[1] For his analysis of the working of India's Constitution in the first fifty years, Austin drew on documentary material and (what historians now call) 'personal information' painstakingly acquired through interviews with important functionaries at various levels. In the long and detailed Constitution of India 1950, Granville Austin sees three distinct strands: (i) protecting national unity and integrity, (ii) establishing the institution and spirit of democracy, and (iii) fostering social reforms. The strands are mutually dependent and inextricably

Reproduced from 'We the People', *Seminar*, November 2010. Fali Sam Nariman is senior advocate to the Supreme Court of India since 1971 and is the President of the Bar Association of India since 1991.

1. Granville Austin, *Working a Democratic Constitution: The Indian Experience*. Oxford University Press, Delhi, 1999.

intertwined in what he elegantly describes as 'a seamless web'.

It is under this seamless web of a 'lawyer's constitution' (as Jennings had sneeringly characterised it), that we have regularly held elections every five years on the basis of adult franchise: as many as 650 million people exercised their franchise in May 2004, and more than 700 million citizens voted in the subsequent general elections in April-May 2009. Despite the misgivings of constitutional historians, whenever governments in India, whether at the Centre or in the states, have been voted out, transfer of power has been according to the provisions of our written Constitution, even though occasionally it may not have been consonance with its true spirit.

I recall with pride Prime Minister James Callaghan's tribute when Indira Gandhi was defeated at the polls in March 1977. Callaghan said that the ultimate mark of a true democracy is the willingness of a government defeated at the ballot box to surrender power peacefully to its opponents. This is what had happened when the Janata Party swept the polls. And this is what happened again when those who held power since March 1977 were in turn defeated at the elections of 1980, and Indira Gandhi came back to power.

Truly then, this constitution embodying a parliamentary form of government was not only a compulsion of geography—shaken and divided by the 'earthquake' of the Partition in 1947—it was also a compelling accident of history. Because, in 1947, the British left us, somewhat in pique. Amidst the trauma of Partition, the members of India's Constituent Assembly, motivated by the urgent need to preserve the political and cultural unity of what was left of British India, valiantly rose to the occasion and forged the document that became the Constitution of India 1950.

The life of a written constitution—like the life of the law—is not logic (or draftsmanship), but experience. And 60 years of experience on this subcontinent has shown us that it is easier to draft a constitution than to work it—Pakistan and Bangladesh have drafted and crafted different written constitutions at different times, but they have been interspersed with long periods of martial law and civil and military dictatorships.

We will never be able to piece together a new constitution in this present day and age even if we tried, because innovative ideas however brilliant —howsoever beautifully expressed in consultation papers and reports of commissions—cannot give us a better constitution. There are other forces in the making of a constitution that cannot and must never be ignored - the spirit of persuasion, of accommodation and of tolerance. They bear their indelible imprint on all constitution-making and all three are at a very low ebb today.

As for me, I am proud of our Constitution. The most eloquent words in it are: We the people; they are also the opening words of the world's oldest constitution, that of the United States of America. But what about the overwhelming majority of India's now overpopulated millions, who were not born before 1950? They were not included in 'We the People'. How then are they provided for in our written Constitution? A shrewd politician gave an answer to a similar conundrum raised in connection with the USA—many years ago. She said—yes, it was a woman—a Congresswoman:

> We the people' is a very eloquent beginning. But, when that document was completed on 17th September, 1787, I was not included in that 'We the People'. I felt somehow for many years that George Washington and Alexander Hamilton just left me out by mistake.
>
> But I realize that it is through the process of interpretation and Court decision that I have been finally included in 'We the People'.
>
> Nicely put.

Well that in a nutshell describes what has been the role of our Supreme Court—by interpretation and court decision it has broadened the reach of the Constitution's provisions; it has included within the range of its beneficent provisions those who were not born when India got independence.

That is why I am proud of our judges, present and past, who have interpreted and sustained this Constitution, which was framed for only 350 million people, most of whom are not alive today. This is one of the ways in which a written constitution is made to grow into a dynamic living document. Another way is through conventions: an amendable constitution like ours has to evolve with experience. Before we think of revisions and amendments we must first establish working norms or conventions. That is how all constitutions are run.

Despite the fact that ours is the longest constitution in the world, there are significant silences in its provisions. They have been explored by enlightened constitutional functionaries from time to time—and when these silences are probed, they help to constitute precedents. Let me give one or two instances:

> Though the President is bound by the advice of his Council of Ministers regarding promulgation of ordinances, there is nothing in the Constitution preventing him from drawing attention of the Council of Ministers to the seeming impropriety of a particular ordinance being promulgated at a particular time. At a time when the Tenth Lok Sabha had, all but in name, been dissolved, the Narasimha Rao government placed two ordinances before the then President for promulgation—namely, one for shortening the period of poll campaigns from three weeks to two weeks and the other to extend reservations to Dalit Christians. The proposed ordinances embodied the provisions contained in two Bills, which the government had sought to introduce on 12 March 1996 (the last day of the Tenth Lok Sabha), but was disallowed by the Speaker (Shivraj V. Patil) because he said it could not merely be introduced and left in limbo pending a dissolution.

After the dissolution of Parliament, the ordinances were then sent to the President—they were in the same terms as the Bill that was not permitted to be introduced by the Speaker. The President, Shankar Dayal Sharma, to his credit sent the ordinances back to the government of the day with a note dated 19 March 1996 that read:

> I would like to inform you that independent of the relative intrinsic merits of the Ordinances proposed, promulgating these Ordinances would appear to be inappropriate and contrary to the canons of constitutional propriety in view of circumstances existing at this particular juncture.

His successor, President K.R. Narayanan, acting under the proviso to Article 74(1) also, returned for reconsideration the proclamation seeking to introduce President's Rule in Bihar. As was his practice, Narayanan gave elaborate reasons for his decision. And the Union government under the prime ministership of Inder Gujral wisely refrained from reaffirming its recommendation under the proviso to Article 74(1) and so 'ensured the smooth working of the Constitution.'

The opening words of the Constitution—'We the People'—tell us at the start, who this constitution is for. But in a pluralistic society like ours, in a vast subcontinent like this—in a land of a 'million mutinies' (as V.S. Naipaul has described it)—who really are the people? For me, they are all typified in that great cartoonist Laxman's 'Common Man'. Not too long ago a former President of India unveiled in Pune a eight-feet high bronze statue which was extolled as the 'worlds' tallest metal statue of a cartoon character.' It typifies—as no other single manifestation does—the quizzical doubts of the common man about whom this great document is for: every generation throws up its common man: a generation being defined as that whole body of individuals born about the same period (a generation as you know is usually computed at 30 years).

By this computation there have been two successive generations since 1950 and if we are to show the present generation (typified by the 'common man') this document of governance or tell him about it, he is bound to ask, on behalf of the common people he typifies: 'Tell me, what has it done for us? How are we better off?'

In answer, we can perhaps point to the Chapter on Fundamental Rights (part III), which owed much to the standard setting Charter of the United Nations (1945) and the almost contemporaneous Universal Declaration of Human Rights (1948). But has the Chapter on Fundamental Rights worked as truly intended? A troublesome question best left to be explored by a future constitutional historian of the stature of the late H.M. Seervai.

In his exhilarating Hamlyn Lectures, Justice Stephen Sedley[2] has reminded his readers that the rule of law of which we speak so glibly, is a necessary but not a sufficient condition of a decent society. There is more to a decent society than the rule of law (he says)—for instance: judicial enforcement of rights by courts of law do not

2. Right Honourable Lord Justice Sedley, *Freedom, Law and Justice*. The Hamlyn Lectures, Sweet & Maxwell, London, 1999.

necessarily guarantee public understanding and support for those rights; such understanding or awareness needs to be inculcated, and this is only achieved by meaningful education.

There is another reason why we cannot fashion another constitution. We are living in an age when there is an all-pervading rights culture. The experience of sixty years of working a written constitution has shown that a 'rights culture' generates greater dissatisfaction amongst persons propounding different sets of rights. For instance, to what extent should the claim based on merit and on the fundamental right of equality be ignored? How far does the Constitution, truly interpreted, direct us to go? How soon are we to atone for the oppression of centuries? Should we go on equalising downwards? And (then) for how long? These questions surface periodically.

Yet the under-representation of the underprivileged in public employment continues to remain highly disproportionate and, as Ralph Bunche, the man who was closely involved in drafting the Charter of the United Nations once said, 'Inalienable rights cannot be enjoyed posthumously.'

Amid all the controversy and vacillation one thing is certain: as long as poverty continues to stalk the land and gross disparities between the rich and poor remain, the ideal of an egalitarian society envisaged in our basic document of governance will remain a dream. Whatever the nation's *karma*, the founding fathers cannot be faulted for a lack of idealism, nor can providence. Truly, it is not in our stars but in ourselves that we are thus.

It is not because of our Constitution but despite its provisions that we have failed to achieve what were naively assumed (in 1950) to be achievable goals. We have abolished untouchability and outlawed backwardness in the Constitution of India (Article 17). But alas, most of us have not eliminated it from our hearts. We have somehow forgotten our heritage of accommodation and tolerance. It is time we remembered.

Writing in the quiet seclusion of a British prison in 1944 (during his ninth term of imprisonment for revolting against the British), Jawaharlal Nehru contemplated 'the variety and unity' of India. He wrote:

> In ancient and medieval times, the idea of the modern nation was non-existent, and feudal, religious, racial, and cultural bonds had more importance. Yet I think that at almost any time in recorded history an Indian would have felt more or less at home in any part of India, and would have felt as a stranger and alien in any other country. He would certainly have felt less of a stranger in countries which had partly adopted his culture or religion. Those, such as Christians, Jews, Parsees, or Moslems, who professed a religion of non-Indian origin or, coming to India, settled down there, became distinctively Indian in the course of a few generations. Indian converts to some of these religions never ceased to be Indians on account of a change of their faith. They were looked upon in other countries as Indians and foreigners, even though there might have been a community of faith between them.[3]

A few years after Panditji wrote his *Discovery of India*, the Human Rights Commission of the UN carried out an inquiry into the theoretical problems raised by a Universal Declaration of Human Rights. A questionnaire was circulated to various thinkers and writers of member states of UNESCO; they were asked, as individual experts, to give their views. One of the chosen experts was Mohandas Gandhi. He responded in a brief letter to Julian Huxley, the Director-General of UNESCO. The letter was written in May 1947, in a moving train (those were troubled times—the days before India's independence). This is what Gandhiji wrote:

> I learnt from my illiterate but wise mother that all rights to be deserved and preserved came from duty well done. The very right to live accrues to us only when we do the duty of citizenship of the world. From this one fundamental statement, perhaps it is easy enough to define the duties of Men and Women and correlate every right to some corresponding duty to be first performed. Every other right can be shown to be a usurpation hardly worth fighting for.

When we gave ourselves a constitution it was certainly good to provide rights enforceable

The first lesson then about written constitutions is that they do not function on their own. A special effort has to be made by the custodians—those entrusted with their functioning—to work them.

3. Nehru, Jawaharlal, *The Discovery of India*. Signet Press, Calcutta, 1946, pp. 55-57.

against the state and state agencies. But I believe that it would have made a difference to our attitudes and our national consciousness if we had stressed also the responsibilities of one citizen to another.

The subsequent inclusion in the Constitution of Part IVA ('Fundamental Duties') has not inspired much enthusiasm amongst the citizenry, possibly because this part was enacted during the period of the forced Internal Emergency of June 1975. That period of the Internal Emergency was a period when constitutional functionaries failed us—from the President downwards. And it is good to recall this once in a while.

Why did all of them—ministers, parliamentarians fail us? Was it a sense of fear? Some in high places did confess to it. I do not think this is true of persons holding key positions of power. For them, the only explanation is that they were not sufficiently imbued with the spirit of a written constitution. The constitution you see doesn't work—never works—on its own: it depends on the wisdom and statesmanship of its constitutional functionaries.

Constitutional functionaries completely failed us during that June 1975 Emergency: we could perhaps say, in retrospect and in extenuation that this was because times were 'bad'. But constitutional functionaries have failed us in other times as well, even in the good times. For instance, when the Janata government came to power in March 1977 on a tidal wave of protest against the phoney Emergency (of June 1975).

The Janata Party had always castigated the Congress Party and the Centre on the misuse of Article 356 of the Constitution (imposition of President's Rule). But gaining power at the Centre for the first time they manipulated that article to suit their political purpose.

In May 1977, a circular was issued by the Home Minister Charan Singh, a constitutional functionary in Morarji Desai's Council of Ministers. Under its terms, chief ministers of nine state assemblies were asked to recommend dissolution of their respective state legislatures even though in respect of some of them (the state assemblies of Rajasthan, Orissa and Punjab) the constitutional term of five years had not then expired (the Union Law Minister endorsed the circular of the Home Minister saying that a clear case had been made out for the dissolution of assemblies of nine Congress ruled states and there was need for holding fresh elections). All this was a pressure tactic not envisaged by either the text or the spirit of the Constitution. But it worked.

When the circular was challenged by the concerned state governments, regrettably (in retrospect), our Supreme Court endorsed approval (in May 1977) of the Home Minister's circular —in the case of state of Rajasthan vs. Union of India (by a majority 5:2) paving the way for the imposition of President's Rule under Article 356 in all the nine states, and rudely shaking the balance of the federal structure under our Constitution.

The judgement also exhibited the truth of Justice Benjamin Cardozo's oft-quoted remark that the hydraulic pressure of great events do not pass judges idly by! Because in March 1994, the Supreme Court of India did say in a larger Bench decision of nine judges (in Bommai's case) that the view taken in the state of Rajasthan case was erroneous: that the mere defeat of the ruling party at the Centre could not by itself without anything more entitle the newly elected party which assumed power at the Centre to advise the President to dissolve the assemblies of those states where the party in power was other than the one in power at the Centre. But all this was said when it was too late to have any practical effect.

Because when the Janata wave had petered out, and Indira Gandhi's Congress Party came back to power in 1980, it was the Supreme Court judgement of May 1977 (in the Rajasthan case) that was used to invoke Article 356 and to dissolve all the nine state assemblies composed at this time of a majority of Janata Party members!

President N. Sanjiva Reddy signed the Proclamation—with some hesitation. He is reported to have said: 'Given the precedent, how could I say no?' Granville Austin records in his great book, *Working a Democratic Constitution*, that Sanjiva Reddy also said: 'I told Indira that Morarji had been wrong in principle and to dissolve again was still wrong.' But even with this mental reservation, the President went along and signed the proclamation! These are but a few of the glaring instances when political expediency of the moment was made to prevail over adherence to constitutionalism and constitutional norms.

You see there is much pathos in a democracy—in fact a great deal of it. The tragedy of a free people freely participating in electing governments, and then bemoaning their fate, is often seen as the tragedy of freedom squandered. But the alternative, the alluring alternative of a would be autocracy or dictatorship, is a far greater tragedy: the tragedy of freedom denied.

I believe that we all must learn to differentiate between constitutional democracy and constitutional liberalism. The British rule in India, for instance, did not provide a 'constitution', nor any 'democracy' for the people of this vast subcontinent. But with the establishment of an even-handed justice system, it did stimulate a spirit of constitutional liberalism amongst its inhabitants. Constitutional liberalism is about government's goals rather than the procedures for selecting governments.

Democracy, and a written constitution, is simply not enough. In an age of images and symbols, elections—so essential for every representative democracy—are easy to capture on film, and be transmitted through the media to various parts of the world. In February 1999, and in May 2004 and again in May 2009, the world witnessed on television flashes of six to seven hundred million voters in India going to the polls, once again. It did help to renew one's faith in the democratic system. But we must ask ourselves this: how does one televise the rule of law? Because the rule of law is the expectation of the electorate after elections, and yet this is hardly ever reported or pictured—when it is, it only reflects a string of broken election promises.

There is little glamour in life after elections! Democracy, without constitutional liberalism, pays only lip-service to the rule of law and in its wake brings with it erosion of liberty, abuse of power, ethnic division, and strife.

We must be wary of elected governments wherever they function. And we must strive in ways that are legitimate, and with the assistance of independent and fearless judges, to keep elected governments accountable. In this 60th year of the working of our written Constitution, we must help to revive that spirit of consensus and idealism that inspired its drafting. We must help cultivate a spirit of constitutionalism amongst the people of India. As I see it, these will be the more important concerns of responsible citizens of this vast country in the next decade.

The opening words of the Constitution—'We the People'—tell us at the start, who this constitution is for. But in a pluralistic society like ours, in a vast subcontinent like this—in a land of a 'million mutinies' (as V.S. Naipaul has described it)—who really are the people? For me, they are all typified in that great cartoonist Laxman's 'Common Man'.

Today, urban rage has captured the media chronicles and defines the public discourse. But if it doesn't channelise itself into increased electoral participation and impact, it could lapse with the changing seasons.

Politicians Under Siege

BARKHA DUTT

The Indian politician may never have been this paralysed by perplexity. Abused by an agitated middle class, crippled by the absence of a decisive leadership, confused by increasing electoral fragmentation and overwhelmed by the sudden demands of social media and new technology—the old rules of the games are redundant for today's *neta*.

Accountability is the new matrix of this brave new world where, sometimes, innocence must be proven to a public inquisition before the charge of guilt can be fended off. The tectonic shift in how politicians are now viewed by the citizenry has created deep cracks in the traditional template of power. The conventional aura of invincibility around the politician has all but dissipated. Communication barriers that once kept a politician at a safe emotional distance from a volatile public—behind a teleprompter in a high-security office or on the dais talking down to the masses—are being rapidly pulled down.

In an age of hyper-information, when every beep on your phone delivers a fresh conversation, often with perfect strangers, people have come to expect their politicians to speak with them and not at them. Unsure politicians who once dismissed Twitter and Facebook as new-fangled trends best suited to teenagers are now tentatively embracing the changing idiom of their profession.

But this changing narrative has been scripted essentially by urban India. Therein is both its novelty value as well as questions around its staying power. A socioeconomic stratum long regarded as apathetic is today angry, engaged and involved enough to move out of the drawing room onto the street. It was the middle class that provided the springboard for the launch of both the recent anti-corruption crusades and the robust protests against the gang rape of a young woman in Delhi. In both cases, the political class was unnerved enough to respond, albeit belatedly; in

Reproduced from 'Politics in Our Times', *Seminar*, June 2013. Barkha Dutt is group editor with NDTV.

both cases policy was actually redrafted because of the fury of the agitators.

But both instances were also a reminder that sustaining movements is so much tougher than starting them. Arvind Kejriwal—at first the master of the media-moment—eventually had to confront the innately distracted character of the news industry and join the same political arena that he had played gladiator to from the outside. Now his success will be measured not by how many headlines he can capture but by how many votes his party can claim. Yet, if the middle class has been forced to learn that being apolitical will keep it irrelevant, its forceful, articulate antagonism to the entrenched status quo has also shaken up the system like never before.

Simultaneously, economics has had its own impact on politics. Liberalisation has seen massive migration from rural to urban areas. Villages have grown into towns; towns have expanded into cities and mofussils have become mall-strips. The middle class—once a descriptive for the highly-educated, but modest income group of professionals and bureaucrats—is today expanding exponentially to include more contemporary aspirations. Though economists remain divided over how to quantify the middle class, most conservative estimates argue that by 2015 the numbers will cross 250 million people—that's one fifth of the country's population. The 2011 Census shows that a quarter of Indian families own a motor vehicle. Rising incomes, even if modest and evolving ambitions have meant that administrative efficiency is now rewarded in a way that it wasn't previously. Incompetent governments are booted out, but it is no longer unusual for state chief ministers to buck anti-incumbency traditions and win consecutive terms if they are seen to be performers.

If the 1991 economic reforms showcased the middle class for the first time as a group of consumers, there is anticipation that the 2014 elections may underscore them as a political constituency. No surprise then that the otherwise left-of-centre-leaning Congress President warned her party that they would have to readapt to 'a younger, more aspirational, more demanding generation of voters in a "new", changing India.' And while seeking a third term as Gujarat's Chief Minister, Narendra Modi outlined a separate set of promises for what his manifesto called the 'neo-middle class'.

Up until this point politicians who, typically, befriended the wealthy and wooed the poor, treated the middle class with indifference or disdain. Their disinterest has mirrored the contempt that urbanites have usually shown for electoral politics, throwing up a classic chicken-egg riddle. Is middle class disengagement a result of the historical political obsession with either the influential or the impoverished, leaving no space for those who fall in-between? Or is political listlessness a consequence of the desultory participation of urban India when it comes to voting?

Today, urban rage has captured the media chronicles and defines the public discourse. But if it doesn't channelise itself into increased electoral participation and impact, it could lapse with the changing seasons. Though politics across the border is hardly comparable with India because of structural differences in how power is distributed, there is still an interesting lesson to draw from the amount of media attention cricketer-turned-politician Imran Khan generated and the number of seats the hoopla eventually delivered. Whether our democracy is showing any substantive changes will eventually be measured the old-fashioned way—at the hustings.

To understand whether our politics is transforming would first need us to analyse why people vote, or don't. It's a question that political scientists have grappled with for years. In their oft-quoted paper (Why the Poor Vote in India: 'If I don't vote I am dead to the State'), Amit Ahuja and Pradeep Chibber have tried to explain why those who live on the margins of national attention and have never been shown any goodwill by the state, except when elections are near, still believe enough in the system to always vote in large numbers. They argue that because of the 'capricious' nature of the Indian state, the 'poor see the act of voting as a Right. The non-poor by contrast vote either to gain some benefit or as fulfilling a civic duty.'

In other words, the poor are greater stakeholders in the system and still continue to determine the

The middle class —once a descriptive for the highly-educated, but modest income group of professionals and bureaucrats—is today expanding exponentially to include more contemporary aspirations.

outcome of elections. The non-poor, non-rich by contrast have often seceded into a parallel world with its own moral code. A sense of exclusion from the system and the absence of an identifiable political voice have created multiple resentments. For example, a number of urban citizens will argue against paying full taxes to a system they see as corrupt, impenetrable and hostile to their welfare. But today, as their demand for a better functioning, less compromised political setup finds resonance in civil-society activism and media agendas, the middle class is seeking a new contract between the state and the citizenry.

For the first time a question that has become moot to the outcome of the next elections is whether there is any leader who can appeal nationally to the growing urban base of voters while simultaneously navigating the complex caste arithmetic of individual parliamentary constituencies. Ironically, two contemporary politicians—deeply antithetical in style and ideology—have triggered middle class interest. The first was Prime Minister Manmohan Singh—initially seen as professorial, personally incorruptible, and unostentatious. In 2009, the urban classes gave him a resounding second chance especially after his assertiveness on the nuclear deal with the United States. Not many understood the details of the negotiations or the issues at stake, but middle class India, in any case culturally shaped by the West, liked the idea of a leader who stood for something even at the risk of losing his government. Besides, as an Oxbridge educated economist, in the middle class imagination Manmohan Singh was an alternative to the elite preconception of the uncouth, uneducated politician prototype.

Having lost the only popular election that he ever contested, the prime minister's main constituency was the middle class. Now it is that same class that is entirely unforgiving of him, bewildered that despite a greater political mandate than the one he got in 2004, Manmohan Singh's second term saw a sharp decline, both in his personal authority and his ability to take a stand. Besieged by multiple corruption scams, the prime minister's constantly placing an arm's length between his office and the latest scandal to stalk his government, has made him look increasingly like a man 'not in charge'. The urban perception of the UPA as being a rudderless ship that has been left adrift at sea has provided readymade material to prime ministerial aspirants from the opposition.

That is why Narendra Modi—who remains a contentious, polarising political figure—is now fashioning himself as the second middle class hope. Though the long shadow of the 2002 anti-Muslim riots continues to trail him, the Gujarat chief minister has carved out a new identity for himself as an economic enabler. By winning over the influential corporate community, while simultaneously courting those who are above the poverty line, but nowhere close to economic comfort, in other words the lower-income middle class, he has sought to move away from his original association with the politics of Hindutva and recast himself as an efficient administrator whose agenda is shaped by development.

That Modi is seen to be entirely autocratic —especially by his own party colleagues—has done nothing to diminish his appeal in the imagination of sections of the middle class who actually approve of political machismo and welcome it as a break from what they see as feeble leadership. After all, it is not uncommon for India's upper middle class to look longingly at the well-ordered social structures of China or even Singapore and lament at our own messy, vibrant democracy. A free press, civil rights, the space to abuse politicians—all the things we take for granted in our democracy—would be happily surrendered at the altar of economic efficiency by these votaries of muscular leadership.

As the Congress comes to grips with its losing influence in India's urban centres, the party is finally beginning to confront its crisis of diminishing returns in this constituency. There are whispers that Rahul Gandhi may well want to outsource the top job—if it were his for the taking—just like his mother did. And that if he looks for his Manmohan Singh, it would be politically smart to look for a personality who has resonance in the urban imagination, but is less controversial than his main challenger in the BJP is set to be.

On the other hand, this presidential style election could be the figment of a headline-hunting media that likes to centre political discourse on personalities. It is much more likely that neither of the main political parties will declare a prime ministerial candidate and complicated number crunching will determine who leads India next. One of the more significant consequences delivered by an increasingly cynical electorate is in fact the demise of the pan-India leader. It is hard to spot any single politician, from any party, who could repair the fractures across caste, religion, region and class and inspire hope. A cataclysmic turn of events could change that of course. But that would be change driven by tragedy, instead of hope.

Our abysmal indifference to what happens to the Other is what allowed the 1984 massacre of Sikhs in Delhi, and the 1992 riots in Bombay, and the cold-blooded murder of the Staines family last year. Why don't we speak up?

A Question of Issues

CHARLES CORREA

For forty years now, *Seminar* has been discussing the key issues which confront us. This represents a commitment of unique importance to our society. Stendhal, writing about Napoleon, said: 'There are no great men—there are merely great events.' Thus, for example, the extraordinary cast thrown up by the few short years of World War II—Churchill, Hitler, Roosevelt, Stalin, de Gaulle, and so forth.

Stendhal was right. But not completely. For it is not just great events—it is really the epic issues that underlie them. Hence the fundamental questions raised by our own freedom struggle—the accountability of power, democratic rights for the poorest, and so forth—gave heroic dimensions to the words and actions of our leaders: Gandhiji, Nehru, Azad, Patel, and many others. This, in a nutshell, is what is so moving about Richard Attenborough's film *Gandhi*: accountability. It was the strength of the British rule in India, but it was also their Achilles heel. Gandhiji understood this and used it to get us our freedom. The entire confrontation is encapsulated in the key scene (historically fictitious, but dramatically correct) where the diminutive prisoner in his *dhoti* enters the small courtroom, and the judge stands up. This is the moment where the audience switches from being onlooker to participant and the movie changes gears.

One of the benefits of living in the Third World is that the issues we face are so much bigger than us. In trying to deal with them, we have a chance to grow. I believe this, as much as any other factor, was decisive in the lives of Raj and Romesh Thapar, and in the journal they founded. And over the last four decades Seminar has been carrying out this mandate, brilliantly and tirelessly. It is a task that today's India needs more than ever. For, while some things in our country have become better, and some things have become worse, there is one area which has been gradually shrinking —and that is the dimensions of the issues we address.

Reproduced from 'The Idea of Seminar', *Seminar*, September 1999. Charles Correa is an architect credited with the creation of modern architecture in post-independent India.

This growing myopia is a malaise that has afflicted the West as well. This is why a century which started with Manifestos and heroic attempts to postulate a Brave New World (with Equity for the poorest, and Justice for all), is ending with the Haves in pitched battle (well, all right, in a kind of video game version of the real thing), defending their possessions, and winning, while the poor and illiterate and unemployed are likely to be left to fend for themselves. That's the New World Order, which extremely talented mercenaries are touting around the world as the End of History. Surely you and I are going to survive, possibly even triumph, but we will have become very much more tiny in the process.

What are the issues Seminar could look at in today's India? In this brief essay I will try and touch on some of them. Architects are compulsive optimists (almost pathologically so) but there are some things that fill one with dismay. For instance, in our country today, many of the essential elements of a democratic society are rapidly evaporating. In fact, we have somehow managed to reduce democracy to just the notion of voting every five years (or every year as per current practice). We seem to have completely forgotten that voting is only a means to an end. And that end, of transcending importance, is the accountability of those in power.

Our track record in this crucial matter is getting worse and worse. And perhaps, given our feudal past (and present?) it is never going to be easy. For, as someone has pointed out, essential to the principle of accountability is the notion of a single law of the land, one which applies to all. Now that runs directly counter to the caste system embodied in the laws of Manu, whereby our society is based not on a single set of rules but on a matrix of laws. This has developed a mindset where we are not really agitated about what is happening in the layers above us. Hence our basic apathy to so many political scandals—because, as far as we are concerned, they are occurring in the stratosphere. Far from holding those gods accountable to us, our response, at most, is to gossip about their misdemeanours—but not to really try and bring them to book.

On the other hand, anyone from levels below us who we perceive to be misbehaving, we stamp on with great enthusiasm—so that they do not dare to try and climb out of the box into which we've put them. This is why customs officers at our airports will cheerfully wave through passengers flying in from London and New York with bags stuffed with whiskey, chocolates and computer games, way above the official allowance, but will jump down on workers coming in from the Gulf with a few nylon saris and jewellery for their families (bought with foreign exchange they themselves have toiled desperately to earn).

The privilege we are talking about has nothing to do with achievement. The other day there was a subtle letter to a newspaper in which the writer said he would always be grateful to his father—not for the money he had left him (he was penniless), nor for his brains (he had few), nor even for his exemplary character. He was ever grateful to his father for making him a Brahmin—a gift which no power on earth could prevent him from passing on to his son. It was a wonderful letter because it conveyed in a nutshell the pathological state we are in.

One of the benefits of living in the Third World is that the issues we face are so much bigger than us. In trying to deal with them, we have a chance to grow. I believe this, as much as any other factor, was decisive in the lives of Raj and Romesh Thapar, and in the journal they founded. And over the last four decades Seminar has been carrying out this mandate, brilliantly and tirelessly.

And it seems to be a sickness which now has gone beyond Manu and infected the whole Indian subcontinent, including Pakistan and Bangladesh. Truly we three are the last sick men of Asia. All the other countries have climbed out of poverty. But not us. And as we sink lower economically, our 'privileges' become more and more important to our self-esteem. Thus, Christians in Goa or Muslims in Gujarat continue, even to this day, to remind themselves of their caste before conversion. No one, I guess, ever renounces privilege, however unfair. Yet it is precisely this that prevents us from exercising that key quality of any democratic society: holding those in power accountable. Without this, democracy can have no real meaning.

Another fundamental characteristic of democracy which is woefully absent in our country is the courage to stand up for our neighbour when his rights are being abused. Of course one understands that this will be difficult in a poor country like India, with our heritage of poverty and *zamindari* despotism. 'Show me a full stomach', said Bernard Shaw in *Major Barbara*, 'and I will show you all the petty virtues you hanker for.' Fair enough. If you and I are both poor and the *zamindar* is beating me up, you would be a fool to stand up for me; you'd only end up with a broken head as well. I understand that, so I would not expect you to intervene. But what about those of us who have full stomachs? Why don't we ever speak up? Every week we read of some village where someone drinks water from the wrong well and gets butchered. And that happens not just occasionally, it's a way of life.

That's probably as bad, or even worse, than anything the whites in South Africa ever did to the blacks. And yet it goes on all the time—together with bride burning, dowry deaths, and so forth. The standard query: 'Where were you when...' thrown at Germans today may well be asked of us a decade or less down the line. How will we respond? I was attending a reception at the Italian Embassy? Or dining at the Taj? Our abysmal indifference to what happens to the Other is what allowed the 1984 massacre of Sikhs in Delhi, and the 1992 riots in Bombay, and the cold-blooded murder of the Staines family last year. Why don't we speak up? As Martin Luther King said of the vicious events of his time, and his place: 'History will not be dismayed by the cacophony of the evil men... but by the silence of the good ones.'

And in these matters, our silence is deafening. Compare this to the UK of some decades ago when the Tory politician Enoch Powell was fulminating against Indians, advocating that they should all be sent home. Who fought and destroyed Powell? The Indians? No. It was the Conservative Party leaders themselves—many of whom probably disliked the presence of Indians as much as he did. But they didn't want to live in an England where those kinds of statements could be made. So Powell, who was one of the most powerful leaders of the Conservative Party, was isolated, never to be heard of again. Most Maharashtrians I know do not agree with the utterances of Bal Thackeray. Why do none of them come out and say so? All they have to state is: this man does not speak for me. Almost none have shown the courage to say even that little.

Why did Raj and Romesh Thapar show that courage? Why did they launch Seminar? Why did they never hesitate to speak up and be counted? Some might assume it was the confidence that comes from privilege—but this is not true. There are so many others, even more privileged, who do not ever speak up. No, I think it was because they genuinely and fiercely believed in the principles which fuelled India in that first decade of our Independence. A couple of years ago, on a visit to South Africa, I understood a bit about what those heroic years must have been like, with their whole future spread out before them. South Africa is so beautiful. So full of hope. And so fragile. Like India of the 1950s.

For us today, those moments seem long past. In the intervening decades, we have gradually gelled into quite a different kind of society. Quite mundane. Myopic. Even nasty. This is not to say that some things haven't got better, much better. The telephone system for one. Cable television for another. But that's exactly it—we seem to be much more motivated by a kind of hedonistic me-ism. And its symptoms—the runaway BMWs, the illegal speak-easies—are all around us. In fact, they are increasingly a part of the glamorous life which more and more of us crave.

Look around Mumbai or Delhi today and you will see how ugly we have become. Of course here and there you will find individuals who stand up against this tidal wave of inanity and corruption. (In Delhi, perhaps the last refuge of these other values is the India International Centre, incidentally a place which Romesh brought to life when he took over for a few years as Honorary Director in the '70s. The IIC has an extraordinary ambience—like a time warp. The women, with their handloom shawls, could be refugees from the Cottage Industries Emporium of the 1950s —and the men look like they are vice chancellors of some *mofussil* university. It's the complete opposite—thank God—of those terrible 5-star hotel lobbies in which the city abounds.)

To live simply and unostentatiously is a virtue which is fast dying out in our country. Today we find gleaming marble and polished granite everywhere. Forgotten is the noble dignity of handloom. Perhaps because, unfortunately for us, Gandhiji's enthusiasm for *khadi* was a political —and not an aesthetic—position. So it gradually faded away, as its political correctness waned.

This is quite different from what happened in Japan. At the core of their art theory is the concept of *wabi sabi*. The word wabi means humble. And the Japanese believe that if you can find beauty in a humble material like mud or sand, and I can find beauty only in granite, then your soul is much finer than mine. Sabi is also interesting. It means that as some things get older, they become more beautiful. This is why the Japanese have a special reverence for old pottery, and of course old trees. The concept of wabi sabi, which explains much of the art of Japan (including those incredible moss gardens) is, I believe, universal to mankind. And this is why the hippie revolution, that changed the world in the 1960s, had as its icon that most humble item of clothing: a pair of blue jeans. Suddenly jeans were being worn by everyone, everywhere. (It also explains why old and faded jeans commanded a very much higher premium.)

Closer to home, I remember as a young architect in the 1950s, I loved wearing khadi shirts. Not because it was politically correct, but because it looked terrific. Khadi and handloom both have a visual quality that speaks directly to our 20th century sensibilities—like *tantric* art. So you don't have to choose to be either 'modern' or to wear handloom (or to collect those sensational tantric ideograms). You can do it all in one holistic gesture.

Today we have descended into a kind of schizophrenia where people feel they have perforce to choose whether they should dress (or decorate their houses) in a way which they call 'ethnic', or in a style which they term 'modern'. This is ridiculous, because India is one of the few places left in the world where you could do both at the same time. In contrast, if a Japanese woman wears a kimono, or an Arab woman wears a *burkha*, she is signalling that she has conservative values. Not so a sari. Indira Gandhi ran the nation wearing a sari—it didn't prove she was conservative, nor did it prove (as we later found out) that she was modern. It was just something she wore everyday.

Perhaps the only hero of pre-independent India who was visual enough to understand these kinds of connections was Rabindranath Tagore. In Shantiniketan he created an extraordinary university where teachers and students sat under the trees. Not just because it was cheaper to do so, but because throughout India (and in much of the rest of Asia as well) it is the mythic image of True Enlightenment. He himself walked around dressed in a kind of maxi, of his own invention! Tagore was really incredible—a true original. Unfortunately he also proved to be one of a kind. It is sad indeed that in today's India he is all but forgotten.

In closing, I feel I must apologise for the somewhat freewheeling nature of this piece which seeks to suggest the kind of issues that, in the context of today's India, Seminar could perhaps look at. My only justification is that this really was the kind of conversation one would have had with Raj and Romesh. That is why I loved meeting them—those lunches at Connaught Place and the delicious Punjabi *khana* at the impromptu dinners at Kautilya Marg. Their's was an India of ideas. And liberal values.

The range of their enthusiasms was extraordinary—from politics and economics to cinema and theatre, to literature, art and architecture. And they shared it all so generously with their friends. This is why Seminar was so pluralistic in its themes. Some of the first pieces I ever wrote on architecture and urbanism, way before the National Commission on Urbanisation, were at their behest. Even today, there are very few journals, if any, who would publish special issues on the future of our cities, or on low-income housing, or on public transport. But Seminar did this all, and continues to do so, to the eternal credit of its present editors.

And to the credit, too, of its extraordinary founders, Raj and Romesh Thapar. Their very names remind one of the India that might have been—and which is now fast disappearing, like the Cheshire cat. Only the smile remains. And that too is gradually fading. Perhaps has already gone?

4

Remembering Raj and Romesh Thapar

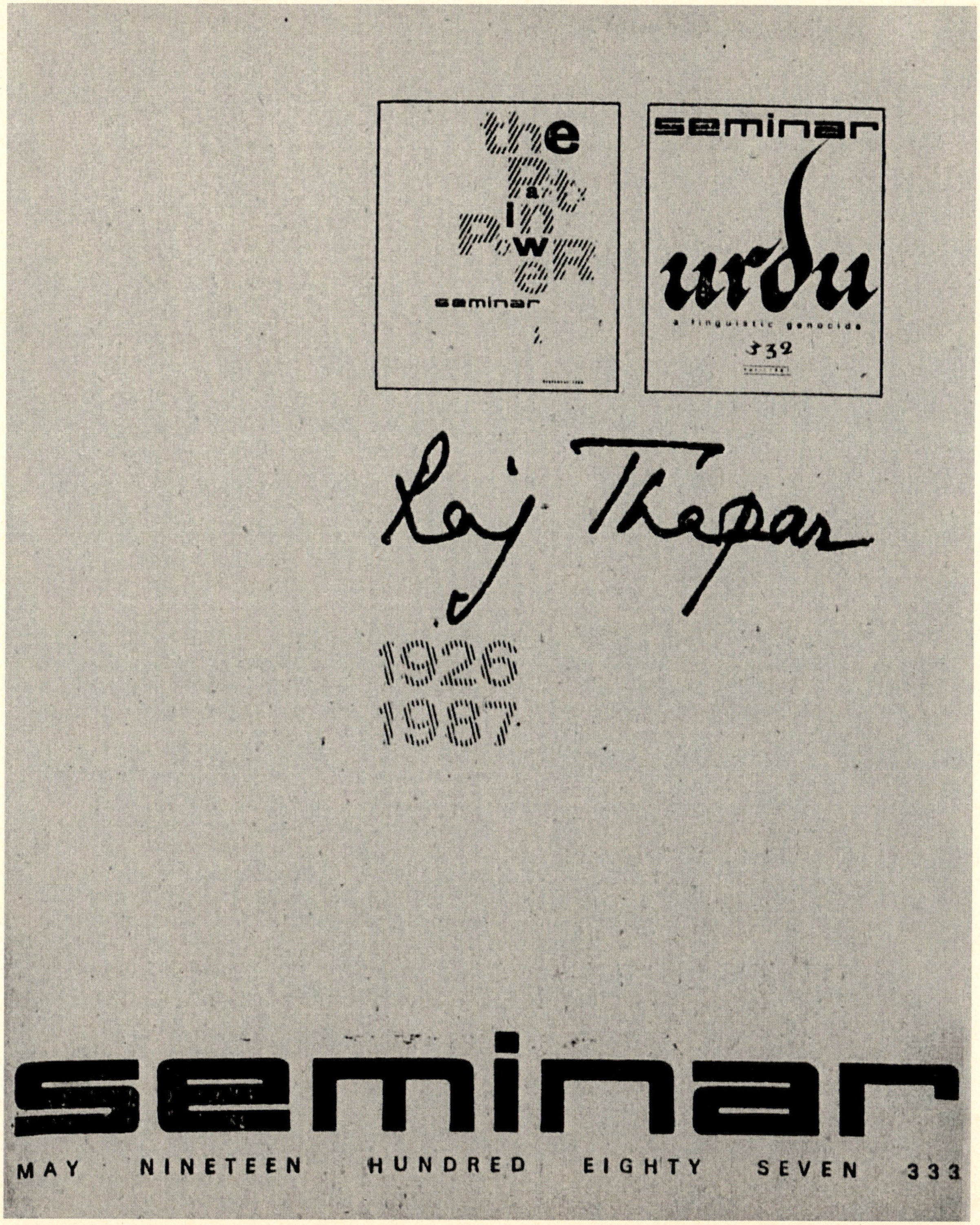
seminar
urdu
a linguistic genocide
332
Raj Thapar
1926
1987
seminar
MAY NINETEEN HUNDRED EIGHTY SEVEN 333

Raj was not an inward looking person but she had a mind that was open, free, capable of turning East or West or seeking solution in roots. This opennes and freedom gave her a contemporaneity and an authenticity.

Raj Thapar

1926-1987

Those who knew the working of *Seminar* knew that Raj was Seminar. Her involvement took in not only the planning of the themes and the deciding on participants together with Romesh, but included the more routine work of editing and proofing the articles and keeping the accounts. Over the twenty-eight years of its existence, every issue was edited and proofed by her, 332 in all, even in the last few weeks of her life.

The Seminar office was frequently converted into an actual seminar in which Raj would discuss with characteristic passion her ideas with those writing on a variety of themes. Only occasionally did she allow herself to participate in Seminar as an author.

The tributes which follow speak about her concerns which were many and reflect her insistence that every segment of life was relevant and required to be fused into an integrated perception. It was this in a sense which also gave her an insight into the young. The stories which she wrote for children were more than mere tales, for they reached out to a consciousness of many levels of existence.

To live with cancer is to live with death and no one was more aware of this than Raj. She faced the cancer with courage and this gave her the strength to accept with dignity the inevitability of death when it became inevitable. For her it was not the occasion for whimpering but rather the exploration of yet another unknown. She remains a presence among us as she was when she was with us. This issue of Seminar is very personal. It could not be otherwise...

Reproduced from, *Raj Thapar 1926-1987*, Seminar, May 1987.

Pupul Jayakar

On Friday, April the 10th, 1987, a white Easter lily came to full bloom in my garden, the sun fresh upon it. The out of season snowfall in the distant Himalayan ranges brought a breeze which cooled the April sun. A heavy blossoming on the mango tree had yielded new fruit. It was a late spring and a sprouting of life was evident.

The previous Sunday, I had visited Raj and Romesh Thapar at their home on Kautilya Marg. Ravaged by an insidious disease which had entered her body a year before, Raj was resting, but could walk out into the garden. All her mental and physical resources had been geared to fighting the disease. For life was of supreme importance. But she sensed that the fight was nearing its end.

It was easy to sit with her in silence; by now the continual reference to her illness or well-being by well-intentioned friends were exhausting her. During the time we spent together, she said, "I do not know what is taking place within my body. Strange things are happening; how long can the body bear it?" I held her two hands in mine and felt the devastating fire of the disease destroying her body.

Ashok Chatterjee came to see me unexpectedly at around 10.30 a.m. on Friday and we talked of Raj and decided to visit her together that evening. A short while after he left, I got a message that Raj had passed away. It had happened while Ashok and I were speaking of her. Silenced by death, the mind for an instant was still, then it flashed back to my first meeting with Raj in the mid-forties at the home of her father, P.C. Malhotra, who at the time was Chairman of the Income Tax Appellate Tribunal in Bombay. I, then a voracious bridge and poker player, often played cards with Raj's father at the Willingdon Sports Club. It was at one of our poker sessions at her father's home that I first saw Raj. She was an adolescent, shy, beautiful, graceful of limb.

By the mid-forties, Raj had married Romesh, a young man, vigorous of mind, passionate of spirit and for a short while, they both become ardent communists. With their temperament, disillusionment was inevitable.

I was to meet Raj again towards the end of the forties at a time when Mulkraj Anand and I jointly edited a children's magazine, *Toy Cart*. Raj took charge as Assistant Editor. The magazine was a splendid venture. The first few issues were to contain M.F. Husain's early colour drawings of a horse and bull-driven cart, Jamini Roy's toy house and rider appeared on the cover, Shivax Chawda illustrated tales for children, Von Leiden contributed a series on the history of Indian shipping, Mulk and I drew from an ancient past to recount stories for children. The yesterday and the contemporary came together in the pages of this rather splendid magazine. It lasted about two years and then faded away as advertisements were not forthcoming. Raj as Assistant Editor discovered a new world of words and the rigid demands of editing. She was earnest, diligent and had a flair for collating material. With the end of the magazine, I lost contact with her and it was many years later in the sixties that we were to meet again in Delhi. By then Raj had matured to sink deep roots in the sensitive areas of heritage and culture. Along with this, she shared Romesh's growing concerns with the distortions that were destroying the fabric of the country. The destruction of institutions, growing corruption and an erosion of values were the field of their inquiry. Of equal interest were the positive areas of development and creative thought.

The Seminar office was frequently converted into an actual seminar in which Raj would discuss with characterstic passion her ideas with those writing on a variety of themes. Only occasionally did she allow herself to participate in Seminar as an author.

Raj was not an inward looking person but she had a mind that was open, free, capable of turning East or West or seeking solution in roots. This opennes and freedom gave her a contemporaneity and an authenticity. Her passionate concerns regarding women and their place in society were visible in her words and actions. But she was not a feminist in the usual use of that word, nor did she show the fierce activism of the suffragete. Gender in a separative sense played little part in her perceptions, actions or her self-image.

Raj wore no masks. The face and mind she turned to women, or men, to the intellectual, the creative artist, the philosopher, the craftsman or the child were free of the process of becoming. She was never anything other than what she was. Perhaps in her many graces, this was what gave her uniqueness.

Soon we started seeing each other more often. Romesh Thapar's birthday fell on the New Year and over the year, I remember visiting the Thapar household and participating in the gaiety, the laughter, the conversation and goodwill. Cartoons and lampoons often self-directed, formed part of the ambience in which laughter, good humour and friendship were more potent than wine.

It was in the year 1959 that Romesh and Raj started publishing a journal called Seminar devoted to the

She practised what others only talk about. It was in this that one could see the beauty of her nature, a beauty that was even enhanced by her ignorance of the fact that she was living a spiritual life. From the certainty of her heart came the fearlessness with which she faced both the events of her life and the approach of her death.

problems of our times as related to India. Serious, probing, fearless, Seminar soon established a reputation for integrity of policy as projected by its editor who had the courage to express critical attitudes and approaches.

In 1967, a Seminar was organised by Romesh Thapar on *Design for Living*. It was a prophetic seminar concerned not only in identifiying problems that were to become vital to this country in the coming decade, but with suggesting pathways of action to counter the approaching disasters. The subject was of deep interest to me and I participated in it with much vigour. Summing up the recommendations, the final paper stressed the enormity of the pressures being generated on the outer and inner life of man, factors which had led to anxiety insecurity and growing violence. The paper went on to say:

> There is in India today a situation of existential complexity. A country with centuries of traditional memory faced with the shattering of symbol, form, function and meaning. A situation where there is want and unharnessed resources, degradation and dignity, ignorance and illumination, violence and the capacity for immense peace. A situation where there is increasing alienation of man from the happenings in the country. A growing anxiety and paralysis of will.

A refinement of perception, concern with the small and the vast, pervades the paper, which Romesh Thapar was to present to UNESCO later that year. Though Raj Thapar did not directly participate, her perceptions, enquiry, and an on-going dialogue with Romesh is reflected in much that comes through.

By the middle of 1965, Raj and Romesh became friends of India Gandhi. With the death of Pandit Jawaharlal Nehru, Indira took over the responsibility for the Ministry of Information and Broadcasting. Raj and Romesh emerged as behind the scene aides advising her on the many changes she introduced into the working of the Ministry. A new professionalism was being evolved. However, as the years passed, and Indira Gandhi became Prime Minister, there was a slow but definite shift of Romesh and Raj from the role of friends and advisers of Indira to that of her sternest critics. Their views were often reflected in Seminar. With Emergency and the ensuing censorship, Seminar ceased to publish and it was only in 1977 that it restarted publication.

Bal Bhavan, an out of school institution for children, was established by Indira Gandhi while she lived in the home of her father. She was the first Chairperson of Bal Bhavan, to be followed by Dr Karan Singh, Pupul Jayakar, and later Raj Thapar. Raj brought to her work in Bal Bhavan, an intensity, integrity and concern for excellence.

It was not what she did but what she was that made Raj unique. The doors of her home, like her mind, were open and political analysis, newspaper editors, columnists, poets, philosophers and humanists would gather under her roof and partake of her overflowing hospitality. Vigorous and free dialogue was natural in that home. What was special was that however heated the discussion and disagreement on points of view, there was never a touch of malice.

Raj and Romesh had come together in a marriage which over the years was to weave a close knit fabric of love, affection, commonality of work, an interchange and sharing of ideas sustained by spoken and silent dialogue. It was a noble relationship. Romesh with his imposing voice and personality often expressed views fiercely, even at times he appeared to attack his opponent. Raj with equal strength said what she had to say without violence, in her voice, and therefore, perhaps her views penetrated deeper into the mind of the listener.

With death, is the wholeness of the relationship broken?

As I sat by her side that Friday afternoon, her face was tender in death, like the lily that had flowered that morning in my garden, inevitably to fade away. In her passing Raj celebrated the moment.

Sri Madhava Ashish

I am not equipped to write about Raj's contributions to the many fields she worked in. Apart from meeting her at the Seminar office, I knew her as the mistress of an excellently run household, a mother and joyful grandmother, and the presiding hostess of many long evenings of conversation—well-informed, wide-ranging, stimulating and often profoundly thoughful. As often as not on these occasions, I was audience to an extraordinary range of outstanding men and women who form the intellectual spearhead of India's advance into the modern world. Romesh played the role of preceptor, analysing current affairs, vigorously propounding new views and theories, inspiring and encouraging new ventures, demanding better work and clearer thinking, and angrily demolishing cant, hypocrisy and dishonesty of any sort.

Raj would admonish Romesh to control his anger, and would smoothen ruffled feelings. But I have seen her, too, go into action against sophistical pretensions with rapier-like thrusts, so rapid and sharp, so skilful as to appear gentle, that her target collapsed before he had time to feel hurt.

What makes such people a centre of attraction? It is not just intellectual brilliance, for that by itself is fairly common; it is also apt to be diamond hard—scratching, without itself being scratched. What attracts are qualities of the heart, 'warm-hearted', 'open-hearted', are applicable but inadequate terms for Raj, for here we have the fineness of a mind that is fuelled by the passions of the heart—passions quite distinct from those that seek gain or self-aggrandisement. It was a compelling, feminine passion whose satisfaction lay outside herself.

What fired Raj was a passionate, unsentimental love for India, her people and her culture. People and culture did not mean the titivations of rootless intellectualism and stage performances. In the talk of the *sabziwallah* and of Rajasthani villagers she found a surer guide to the state of the country than in the weighty pronouncements of cabinet ministers or the editors of national newspapers. That she could communicate with both sorts of people and be loved, respected and trusted by both is but one of the signs of her greatness of soul.

There was no conventional religious flummery either in Raj's household or in her mind—a fact that has led some of my friends to question why I, the head of a conventional religious establishment, should have so close a friendship with avowed agnostics. In reality, however, Raj was a deeply religious person, her life being guided by values that derive from the inner harmony of the Spirit. She practised what others only talk about. It was in this that one could see the beauty of her nature, a beauty that was even enhanced by her ignorance of the fact that she was living a spiritual life. From the certainty of her heart came the fearlessness with which she faced both the events of her life and the approach of her death.

As I see it, Raj was inpired by a vision of human perfectibility—a vision that has many adherents. Others besides Raj have seen in India a greater potential for the realisation of such perfection than exists elsewhere.

Irrespective of whether this vision could ever be realised, it constitutes a projection of any essentially inner state of harmony onto the troubled waters of the *samsara*. To the extent that this vision wells up in the heart without a conscious perception of its origin, the failure of the samsara to conform may cause dismay and even heartbreak. The betrayal of human values that culminated in the massacre of 1984 broke Raj's heart. It shattered all that she held dear, all that was worth fighting for. The cancer that took her life away was a consequence.

If this note is confused, it is because I cannot think of Raj without thinking of Romesh. They were twin stars, each complete in itself, neither overshadowing the other, yet both circling around a common centre of gravity. Outwardly, that gravitational centre was their work on Seminar, inwardly, it was their love—a love so full that it overflowed to include all who came within their orbit. This was the secret of their attraction.

Sirius, the brightest star in the sky, has a dark companion with which it orbits around a common centre of gravity. Raj may have gone from our sight, but she will remain as Romesh's invisible companion, influencing the orbits of our lives.

It was not what she did but what she was that made Raj unique. The doors of her home, like her mind, were open...

Vigorous and free dialogue was natural in that home. What was special was that however heated the discussion and disagreement on points of view, there was never a touch of malice.

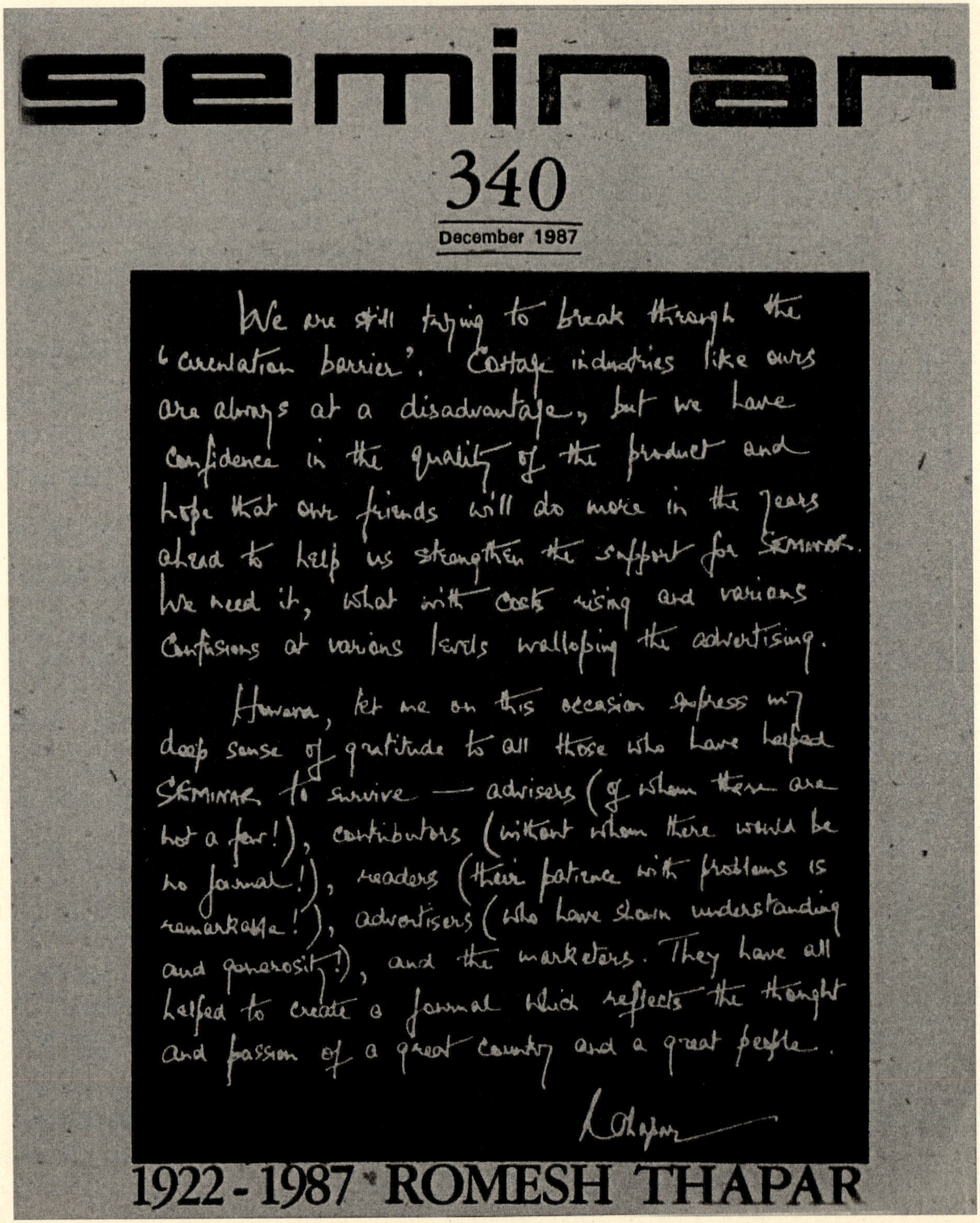

seminar

340

December 1987

We are still trying to break through the 'circulation barrier'. Cottage industries like ours are always at a disadvantage, but we have confidence in the quality of the product and hope that our friends will do more in the years ahead to help us strengthen the support for SEMINAR. We need it, what with costs rising and various confusions at various levels walloping the advertising.

However, let me on this occasion express my deep sense of gratitude to all those who have helped SEMINAR to survive — advisers (of whom there are not a few!), contributors (without whom there would be no journal!), readers (their patience with problems is remarkable!), advertisers (who have shown understanding and generosity!), and the marketers. They have all helped to create a journal which reflects the thought and passion of a great country and a great people.

1922 - 1987 ROMESH THAPAR

Romesh Thapar

1922-1987

For twenty-eight years, Seminar was edited by Romesh and Raj and attempted to capture the thinking of the crucial generation which had the responsibility of structuring an independent India. We have now moved some distance from the event of 1947. The responsiblity of structuring remains, only it has also moved to include the next generation.

In remembering Romesh Thapar we are remembering an age, a time in India, the events of which were epoch-making, the transition from colonial status to independence. Romesh was a man of that epoch and his life was in many ways a manifestation of the change. But he was also that kind of rare person who sometimes is able to step outside history and time, and demand that we reach out to nothing less than an utopia. Had he not known the many happinesses of his life—a marriage fulfilled in every way, close family relationships and intense and eager friendships over many decades, he would doubtless have emerged as a contemporary ascetic seer!

He went to no fancy schools or colleges: just the usual run of places to which anglicised Punjabis sent their sons, planning for them a job in the establishment. Bishop Cotton School in Simla, followed by Aitchison College Lahore and finally Government College Lahore from where he took his BA Honours from the Punjab University. School was always for him a miserable experience, a chore which had little meaning other than a necessity which had to be gone through. Bishop Cotton left him unmoved.

But Aitchison College was the crucible in which the man of later years was formed and the alchemist was the principal C.H. Barry, who looked upon Romesh as something of his own creation and who for Romesh remained an affectionate, paternal figure. Barry politicised the young man and made a nationalist of him but also put him through the fire of self-discipline. When in the course of an inter-university debate Romesh got carried away and referred to the activities of the then Vicereine as those of a chamber-maid when in England, Barry argued that this was unparliamentary and refused him the prize which otherwise on merits he had won. Barry encouraged him to look beyond the immediate to the concerns of a wider society, concerns which hinged on the principles now being formulated in Romesh's mind. And then there were leisure hours in college, the like of which he was never to have again. So when he was required to learn

---

Reproduced from, *Romesh Thapar 1922-1987*, Seminar, December 1987.

Romesh was a man of that epoch and his life was in many ways a manifestation of the change. But he was also that kind of rare person who sometimes is able to step outside history and time, and demand that we reach out to nothing less than an utopia.

Persian he decided to do something creative with it and finally translated into Persian a story by Fennimore Cooper, *The Deer Slayer*.

Romesh's wider view of the world was perhaps also partly inherited. His father was a distinguished officer of the Armed Forces Medical Corps, but behind this establishment exterior was his other side—a side which took him into amateur photography with such zest that whilst serving in the barren wastes and garrison forts of the North West Frontier Province in the thirties, he made one of the early silent movies, with a screenplay involving Pathan chiefs, Russion counts and British officers, all wrapped up in a story of political intrigue and romance. In later years this other side led to a more than ordinary appreciation of classical Indian art. It was this same instinct which permitted him to give way when his son Romesh rejected attractive offers of government service and decided on what his father initially thought was an absurd throwing away of talent, namely, becoming a journalist.

Romesh moved to Bombay to join *The Times of India* in 1942 and thrived on journalism, recognising it as his particular metier combining as he always did an interest in politics and happenings with the perception of one analysing each event in its broadest perspective. Bombay was for him the pulsating metropolis and he soon found himself involved in everything possible—brains trusts, broadcasting, committees of various kinds—all enlivened by his humour and his intelligent perception of the world around him. He loved the sheer pleasure of talking with friends, the teasing and the joking, the exchange of political gossip as well as the more serious concern with what was happening to the coming independence of India. His network was staggering. Spending a week with him took in an evening with Ara, the struggling impressionist painter, Sahib Singh Sokhey's talk of snake serums and classical dance, the private life of Verrier Elwin, the enthusiasm of a young naval officer. Ved Johar involved in the RIN 'mutiny', the animated questions of Indian and foreign journalists and the meetings between political leaders whom Romesh and others were helping to get together to somehow try and avert the impeding partition. Raj when she married him in 1945, feared that this vibrant world of his would overwhelm her but she soon came to enjoy their joint participation in it.

Independence in 1947 was for them the arrival of the brave new world when Indian society had a chance to move towards a new beginning. India was after all one of the earliest major colonies in the world to attain independence and its leadership in the Third World was a heady experience not only for Jawaharlal Nehru but also for those Indians who believed in the future of their country. Romesh and Raj had not the slightest doubt that something approximating their vision of utopia should at least be reached out to. This was the basis of their investment in an Indian future.

It was during this time that Romesh and Raj were drawn to marxism. Theirs was a marxism tempered by humanism and seen essentially as an ideology concerned with values, which were fundamental to their own lives. In their enthusiasm they came extremely close to the Communist Party of India (CPI) although they never joined it. It was Palme Dutt who kept advising them against it. The CPI was tied up with other matters and the values which Romesh and Raj cherished seemed to take a distant place in the routine dealings of the CPI. This was in a sense the first serious brush which their idealism had with reality. *Crossroads*, the fortnightly which Romesh had founded in 1949 and edited as an independent leftist became in some ways symbolic of this experience. Romesh had later to hand it over to the CPI with whom he had by then broken. But it was also due to a statement in Crossroads that the government attempted to ban it. Romesh took it to court and won a major case in the Supreme Court on the freedom of the press, a case which has now become a classic in Indian legal literature and which also gave him credibility in his continuting fight for fundamental freedoms.

In spite of his moving away from the CPI, the fact that he had once been close, hounded him in his search for earning a living. These were the years when communist association closed doors in his face. Speaking the commentaries for the Films Division of India kept Romesh and Raj going for a bit, until his voice was banned because of his political past. This ban was lifted at the intervention of Nehru.

Romesh and Raj had also developed another interest, that of theatre and became active in the Indian People's Theatre Association. Here possibly Raj's interest was deeper although Romesh both acted in and directed the plays. The plays which they selected were not just any theatre. They were plays which either spoke to a future dream or argued for the need to change social values. Thus J.B. Priestlcy's *They Came to a City*, carried the vision of a new society where 'men and women don't work for machines and money but machines and money work for men and women. It was almost a parallel to the *Revelations of St. John* speaking of a new city and a new world. Clifford Odet's *Waiting for Lefty* and Arthur Miller's *All My Sons* focused on another area of immanent importance, that of human relations in industrialising societies and the refusal to be conditioned by the ruthlessness of such societies.

When Zia Sarhadi persuaded Romesh that he should consider the possibility of directing films as a profession, he decided to do it the hard way and act in one first to get the feel of the business. Once again the story revolved around what were then called 'socially conscious' films, for in *Footpath* (in which he co-starred with Dilip Kumar and Meena Kumari) he plays the role of the school teacher who tries to wean away his younger brother from black marketing in medicines.

What had been important to Romesh was that he was entering films not just as a profession but rather as a person who believed that the media could be used to underline the values which he regarded as basic to any sane society, while at the same time not being oblivious of the aesthetic form of the film. This was not merely the impact of de Sica's films which were then the rage in Europe, but also the result of long conversations with close friends such as Thorold Dickinson and Roberto Rossellini. It was these earlier convictions as to what a good film should be that he carried with him when he sat on committees making awards to films in later years.

Footpath was neither a box-office hit nor regarded as a great movie. Romesh was critical of his own performance. But it had been a worthwhile experience because he came to know that the film world was not for him. Through all this experimenting with other media the written word still had primacy for him. Two pamphlets on the events of this period kept him rivetted to the political scene. *Storm Over Hyderabad* was a statement of the Telengana movement and remains a basic document commenting on the aspirations raised by the peasant struggle in Telengana attempting to combat both the oppression of the Nizam as well as the last throes of colonial rule. *Goa Crisis* centred in on the then current discussion on the supposed legality of rights overriding the wishes of a people. Romesh's break with the formal structure of the CPI did not destroy in him or in Raj a recognition of the validity of the marxist method as a way of analysing problems. This was reflected in what was probably to be his most creative book, *India in Transition*, published in 1956. It lays bare the contemporary scene and, as he was wont to do, projects a future scenario. The latter is permeated with a sense of leaving behind the ashes of a colonial experience and instead building a just society and of maximising the recently won freedom.

Perhaps as a result of their experience in politics both Romesh and Raj felt that a necessary precondition to any freedom was the exercise of choice and that this should be open to the individual and was pertinent to the entire range of human expression, be it ideas, institutions, political parties, creative art or economic planning; that it was when a range of analysis of any particlar subject was available that one would feel more confident in taking a stand. It was this conviction that led them to the founding of *Seminar* in 1959. They did not have the money to organise it on any scale. It began therefore as what they used to call a 'cottage industry'. Apart from the actual printing it was put together in their flat in Bombay with the children and visiting friends participating in writing addresses, stapling, licking stamps and posting it. It was only when they moved to Delhi that Seminar acquired an office. They little realised that when the first issue appeared it was something of a publishing event. It was decided that every subject which touches the being of an Indian must be presented in the context of a considered discussion representing a variety of views. The monthly issues of Seminar over the last twenty-eight years have sought to make such a presentation. The discussion on every subject focused on the questions of where are we at? How should we proceed? What are we aiming towards? Irrespective of whether it was the five year plans or the condition of Indian philosophy.

The idea of such a montly was uniquely their own and in fact there were some who tried to dissuade them arguing that there would not be a sufficiency of Indian intellectuals and specialists to sustain it. The 1960s however saw a burst of intellectual activity both among academics and others, departing from the given parameters of analysing India and arguing for alternative perspectives. It was a decade of changing paradigms in practically every area of thought. It is this change which Seminar captured.

Romesh and Raj moved to Delhi in 1961. It was from here that Romesh wrote his weekly column which was to become a pulse of the intelligentsia for almost three decades. 'The Capital View' in *The Economic Weekly* and later *The Economic and Political Weekly*, discussed major events emerging primarily from political activity. It was analytical and given to projecting alternatives where the assessment was critical. For Romesh the function of a political commentator was as much to enlighten and explain, if not also to entertain. Often they were angry columns when government functioning showed ineptitude and Romesh's anger moved like a swathe. The columns reflected not only major political changes and sometimes included the choicest political gossip of the week, but inevitably also his own political positions; his early conviction that Mrs. Gandhi as a politician with a modern mind could give a new direction to Indian society and his gradual disillusionment with such a leader and his final vitriolic anger at what he regarded as a betrayal of Indian society in her sole concern with personal power. Some of the subjects of Seminar were so topical, such as the issue on fascism, during the Emergency, that the government once again tried to impose censorship. Romesh and Raj refused to accept censorship and preferred to stop publication until the Emergency was lifted.

Romesh had a highly individual style of writing and a facility in creating words, sometimes skipping the rules of grammar as when he used nouns as verbs to great effect to articulate a pointedness and a pungency which was soon recognised as characteristic of his style. The columns were peppered with phrases some of which have now become the legal tender of Indian political conversation—the Syndicate, the Goons, Baba-log government. His column could be harsh and rasping at times, but it was nevertheless respected because above all it was recognised that the man behind it would never compromise on the essentials of his commitment to a just order. Even when he took a job in government it was always without a salary so that he had the option of independent action. This was not merely because he could afford to live without a salaried income, it was more a matter of temperament and conviction.

For a number of years he was a close advisor to Mrs. Gandhi and when teased about being a member of the kitchen cabinet replied that he was not in the kitchen but in the pantry. He was always willing to accept responsibility for some of her actions during that period, particularly the appointment of persons who turned out to be far from the best. He also recognised failures in actions where such actions misfired and admitted the failure of the split in the Congress, which he and some others had supported. But his closeness to power did not prevent him from noticing the tarnish which entered Mrs. Gandhi's political activities. Since he could not prevent this and rather than play along with it in order to remain close to power, he began to move away. His increasing objections led at first to a distancing from Mrs. Gandhi and eventually to open opposition. In spite of the fact that he had held government jobs, such as Chairman of the India Tourism Development Corporation or a Directorship of a nationalised bank, such jobs did not tie him to a system which he slowly perceived as being manipulated to negate the institutions which he stood for. His break with Mrs. Gandhi at this time was both an act of courage and self sacrifice.

A characteristic of democracy for him was the existence of quality institutions efficiently run. Such institutions would reduce the element of functioning on the basis of personal likes and dislikes which he saw as the hangover of a feudal past. Equally obnoxious was the resort to an over-bureaucratisation of institutions, such that initiative is destroyed in an effort to keep within the multitude of regulations and this he saw as an inheritance from the colonial past. He deplored the frequent failure of institutions in India and each time he agreed to work in one, it was with the sense of a challenge.

It was the building of an institution which interested him when he became Chairman of the India Tourism Development Corporation. Apart from this he also felt that people coming as tourists should be introduced to a new culture; that the infrastructure of tourism should help strengthen the environmental balance and not dislodge it; that it was not just the dollars that mattered but the consciousness of a policy towards tourism which tied it into development and which would not lead to the destruction of the receiving society, as it has done in many parts of the world. Romesh was eager to encourge new design and new architectural forms organic to the environment or else facilitating a process of innovation in new structures, as for example, his long discussions with Buckminster Fuller on the possible use of geodesic domes. But the rush for dollars was too powerful and tourism today has become an industry often degrading the areas where it prospers most.

Consciousness of the environment and what might almost be called an organised aesthetic in relation to one's surroundings was what motivated a project which he prepared for UNESCO and entitled appropriately, 'Design for Living'. Here again the central focus was to preserve the dignity of human living conditions and not reduce men and women to passive recipients of objects and artefacts bereft of aesthetic quality and valued only for their utility. He argued that even the simplest of objects in daily Indian life could be adapted to modern requirements and such an adaptation would be conducive to traditional design much of which was aesthetically superior to what it was being replaced by. Even more important this would blunt the edge of alienation which Indian society was experiencing with growing urbanisation and industrialisation. Alienation was to him an anathema, whether it was at the level of the suppression of individual freedom or whether at the necessity of having to wear saris made of synthetic material. Occasional Saturday afternoons were spent in picking up small objects of craftsmanship. One could be sure that birthday presents from Romesh and Raj would be something unusual and special.

The conviction that this Indian epoch had in it the roots of creativity and would release new ideas led him to insist that it was possible to locate innovative thinking and action in India. This was axiomatic to his joining as a founding member the Jawaharlal Nehru Memorial Fund and the committee giving Nehru Fellowships, searching for creative persons for whom the Fellowship would provide a break from mundane chores. His commitment to the ideas and policies of Nehru was at this time close and strong, a closeness which perhaps coloured his perception of the role of Mrs. Gandhi.

Among his political convictions was the insistence that politicials and parties must have a programme. Perhaps this insistence went back to his marxist days. He was suspicious of what might be called disc-jockey politics where popular slogans and populist speeches were used to build a quick turn over of personalities and movements and where the ultimate goal was merely a switching over of those in power The defeat of Mrs. Gandhi in 1977 was for him a vindication of his faith in the Indian people. He was anxious that the Janata Party should not become merely a replacement government. He worked therefore with a group of intellectuals and political activists to forge what came to be called *An Agenda for India*, a document which it was hoped could be the starting point of fresh programmes and policies.

The gradual disintegration of the Janata Party was therefore a deep disappointment, but nevertheless it did not make him cynical. Instead it took him in a different direction. His attempt to understand this failure led him to emphasise again the significance of greater decentralisation and the need to strengthen awareness at local levels. He argued for the creation of *mohalla* committees and urban neighbourhood communities and was passionate about the setting up of neighbourhood schools where children from various social backgrounds could be given quality education. Rural politics was also an issue where he felt that greater village representation and participation might help break the political cliques which manipulated so much of Indian rural politics.

Some of these ideas emerged from a growing interest in the thinking of Mahatma Gandhi.

The invitation to join the the Club of Rome gave him a larger arena for his ideas. It was now a battle for the dignity of the Third World as well as the future of mankind. He never gave up on his delineation of the future in which the Third World would no longer be playing a subordinate role. He recognised the areas where the Third World even without advanced economic resources or sophisticated nuclear weaponry could assert itself, could help release pressures supportive of re-establishing the authority of men and women rather than of machines and money, and was impatient when the Third World slipped repeatedly into a position of subservience. His projection of the alternative for the future of mankind was almost too close to that of a visionary demanding of men and women a sense of values which have become increasingly difficult to find. But at least his voice and that of others who thought like him was always a reminder of these values. Many of these alternatives as he saw them, both in the context of India and of the wider world are reflected in his later books, *The Indian Dimension*, *The Waste and the Want*, *An Indian Future*, *These Troubled Times*, and *A Scenario for Change*.

Closest to his heart however, remained the question of the free availability of information and the freedom to discuss it as openly as possible. Having successfully battled against press censorship, Romesh and Raj moved to the other area of their interest, the media. Romesh's last major act was to file a petition before the Supreme Court on the need for the autonomy of radio and television.

Public actions are integral to one's persona and most people judge one by these. For those of us who knew Romesh it will be the man, the very human man, that will dominate our memories of him: the large bulky man who when he walked into a room commanded attention—perhaps the rub off of belonging to a family that had commanded attention; the rugged exterior prone to deep flashes of anger, to biting satire, to expressions of contempt, to calling a fool a fool, to seeming arrogance, but hiding within all this a very soft centre. It was this centre which made him so available to friends and to strangers alike, to whomsoever walked into home and office and demanded his time, his energy and frequently his support, particularly if he felt that an injustice was being enacted or that genuine help was required.

He was quick to like and dislike and this could be instinctive. But where some dislikes were openly expressed others were shadowed over by a gut feeling that one must be tolerant of the weaknesses of people and that behind an off-putting exterior there may be qualities worth tapping. Those close to him will remember occasions when they were quietly reprimanded for being intolerant. And although he sometimes drew out the worst in those he disliked, he equally often drew out the best. The self-discipline which he acquired in his early years never left him and this was the basis as much of a well-organised office as of a person who with ease gave up cigarettes, whisky and sugar when his body demanded it.

If he will be remembered for these stern qualities he will also be remembered for his great sense of humour which often changed a dull gathering into a scintilating one. He loved entertaining and his New Year's Eve-cum-birthday party each year was a central occasion of the winter in Delhi where large bowls of his own brand of a smooth but potent punch become legendary and the party was a peaen to the sheer exhilaration of being alive. But above all it was the people who surrounded him, who had the greatest meaning in his life. There were people of all kinds and types, people whom he had touched at some level of their being and perhaps even helped change their way of looking at the world. If this is charisma then he was truly charismatic.

For twenty-eight years Seminar was edited by Romesh and Raj and attempted to capture the thinking of the crucial generation which had the responsibility of structuring an independent India. We have now moved some distance from the event of 1947. The responsiblity of structuring remains, only it has also moved to include the next generation. We hope that Seminar in the years to come will continue to reflect the thinking of all those, of all ages, who are involved in the Indian dimension.

With this issue we start the thirtieth year of the publication of SEMINAR. It continues to be our endeavour to maintain the quality which inspired the starting of this journal in September 1959. But this endeavour cannot be ours alone, as it involves everyone whose activities go into the making of this journal: people with ideas and thoughts to be discussed, people motivated by the necessity to write, a press insistent on bringing out the journal on time and advertisers who provide the wherewithall. To each go our thanks for helping us to keep going and our expectation that this goodwill remain ever present.

Thirty years makes a generation and we hope that we reflect the concerns of generational change, perhaps imperceptibly. For, the issues which initiated the founding of the journal by Raj and Romesh Thapar remain central to our lives even if they have altered in particulars. Some might say that they have become more pertinent, as, over this generation India has moved from the relatively secure moorings of national independence into the deep currents of asserting its identity as a nation. We would like to think that SEMINAR will continue to play a role in helping to define this identity.

Index

W

Y

Z